Systematic Classroom Assessment

Systematic Classroom Assessment promotes a fresh vision of assessment for student learning and achievement. Using a framework that positions assessment as both an iterative, purposeful cycle of inquiry for teachers as well as a coherent system of activities through which students engage in their own learning, this framework for classroom assessment is unique in incorporating self-regulated learning, motivation, and non-cognitive processes. Key components such as assessment for learning, feedback, emerging technologies, and specific content areas are treated in depth, and fundamental principles like reliability, validity, and fairness are approached from the classroom perspective.

Sarah M. Bonner is Associate Professor in the School of Education at Hunter College, and the Graduate Center, City University of New York, USA.

Peggy P. Chen is Associate Professor in the School of Education at Hunter College, City University of New York, USA.

Systematic Classroom Assessment

An Approach for Learning and Self-Regulation

Sarah M. Bonner and
Peggy P. Chen

NEW YORK AND LONDON

First published 2019
by Routledge
52 Vanderbilt Avenue, New York, NY 10017

and by Routledge
2 Park Square, Milton Park, Abingdon, Oxon, OX14 4RN

Routledge is an imprint of the Taylor & Francis Group, an informa business

© 2019 Taylor & Francis

The right of Sarah M. Bonner and Peggy P. Chen to be identified as authors of this work has been asserted by them in accordance with sections 77 and 78 of the Copyright, Designs and Patents Act 1988.

All rights reserved. No part of this book may be reprinted or reproduced or utilised in any form or by any electronic, mechanical, or other means, now known or hereafter invented, including photocopying and recording, or in any information storage or retrieval system, without permission in writing from the publishers.

Trademark notice: Product or corporate names may be trademarks or registered trademarks, and are used only for identification and explanation without intent to infringe.

Library of Congress Cataloging-in-Publication Data
Names: Bonner, Sarah M., author. | Chen, Peggy P., author.
Title: Systematic classroom assessment : an approach for learning and
    self-regulation / Sarah M. Bonner and Peggy P. Chen.
Description: New York, NY : Routledge, 2019. | Includes bibliographical
    references and index.
Identifiers: LCCN 2018057061 (print) | LCCN 2019005832 (ebook) |
    ISBN 9781315123127 (eBook) | ISBN 9781138565760 (hbk) |
    ISBN 9781138565777 (pbk) | ISBN 9781315123127 (ebk)
Subjects: LCSH: Educational tests and measurements. | Self-managed learning. |
    Students—Rating of. | Classroom management. | Motivation in education.
Classification: LCC LB3051 (ebook) | LCC LB3051.B625 2019 (print) |
    DDC 371.26—dc23
LC record available at https://lccn.loc.gov/2018057061

ISBN: 978-1-138-56576-0 (hbk)
ISBN: 978-1-138-56577-7 (pbk)
ISBN: 978-1-315-12312-7 (ebk)

Typeset in Galliard
by Apex CoVantage, LLC

Printed and bound by CPI Group (UK) Ltd, Croydon, CR0 4YY

Contents

Acknowledgments	vii
Introduction	1

PART I
Section I Introduction: The CA:SRL Framework   5

1 Classroom Assessment for Learning and Self-Regulation	7
2 Assessing Student Prior Knowledge, Skills, and Beliefs	20
3 Multiple Iterations of Learning and Assessment	37
4 Formally Assessing Student Learning	56
5 Reflection on Overall Performance	77

PART 2
Section 2 Introduction: Technical Quality and Technology in Assessment   95

6 Reliability: Making Sure You Can Depend on Your Data	97
7 Validity in Classroom Assessment: Purposes, Properties, and Principles	112
8 Fairness in Assessment: Classrooms and Beyond	131
9 Technology in Classroom Assessment	145

vi Contents

PART 3
Section 3 Introduction: Case Studies in the CS:SRL Framework   155

10 English Language Arts Case Study   157

11 Music Case Study   179

12 Mathematics Case Study   199

Index   221

Acknowledgments

The authors acknowledge the support of the many people who contributed to this work. Sarah M. Bonner is grateful for everything she has learned from Anthony Nitko. Peggy P. Chen is immensely grateful to both Barry Zimmerman and Dale Schunk for their knowledge and research in the field. We thank all of our students over the years, who have also been our teachers. The assistance of Katharine E. Diehl and Ching Wen Zhao was invaluable in making everything come together, from literature review to graphics and formatting. We particularly thank Katharine for helping us understand fairness in assessment, and Ching for testing out so many resources in technology for assessment. We also thank Mallory Locke, Kayla Neill, and Heather Eliason, who graciously shared their knowledge, skills, and ideas in English Language Arts, Mathematics, and Music, respectively. Nicole Lorenzetti and Emily Henry also helped with this project. Finally, Sarah M. Bonner thanks her husband, Rahul, for patiently listening and offering encouragement. Peggy P. Chen thanks her parents, Kuo-Wei and Fu-Mei, and her son, Austin, for their unwavering support throughout the process.

Introduction

The theme of this book is that classroom assessment (CA) can and should be viewed as a unified endeavor, wherein teachers and students obtain, interpret, and use information about knowledge and skills to help learning progress. Used systematically, CA processes begin prior to instruction and happen continuously as teaching proceeds. They guide student and teacher planning, instructional decisions in the moment, and interpretations of the accumulated learning of students over the course of time. In this text, we describe a system of classroom assessment that we have developed based on learning theory, our own research, and years of experience in K–12 and teacher education: the CA:SRL framework.

The CA:SRL framework includes four stages that teachers and their students typically go through as they teach a unit of instruction or cluster of concepts and skills. Stage 1 occurs before the onset of instruction for the purpose of planning and igniting student forethought. Stage 2 happens informally during and at multiple checkpoints within an instructional unit, for the purposes of monitoring students and student self-monitoring, as well as to provide an opportunity for students and teachers to make strategic adjustments for learning. Stage 3 happens at the end of a unit of instruction, in order to generate reliable and valid interpretations about what students have learned over the course of multiple lessons or clusters of learning objectives. Stage 4 happens when there is a need to combine and evaluate evidence from multiple assessments to communicate general trends in learning. While assessment at each stage has slightly different specific purposes, it is always a process for obtaining and interpreting information about learning for use.

We travel from interpretation to use by way of feedback. After teachers and students interpret assessment results, they initiate recommendations for next steps for learning, whether implicitly or explicitly. These recommendations take the form of feedback. Feedback influences actions that may promote or hinder progress. The results of those actions will be assessed again through multiple iterations. In this book, we emphasize that there are many types of feedback and that many people in the classroom generate feedback: students, peers, and teachers. When students learn to give and receive good feedback, they can use it to further their own learning and to support that of their peers. When teachers take into account not only their own interpretations of student performance, but also student feedback, their decisions about instructional adjustments are more likely to be accurate and effective. Further, teachers can use self-feedback and feedback from colleagues and students to appraise their own assessment practices and to make adjustments for continuous improvement in CA.

CA is also an important means to actively engage students in self-regulated learning (SRL). We advocate that teachers design CA tasks to provide students with opportunities to self-regulate and, when appropriate, to co-regulate learning among peers and with teacher support. By integrating SRL with CA, teachers can communicate educational values in the form of learning goals, improve motivation by helping students see their own progress, and encourage students to view peers as partners in giving and receiving feedback. Empirical studies on SRL have shown benefits for students who learn SRL strategies and have opportunities to use them (DiGiacomo & Chen, 2016; Michalsky, Mevarech, & Haibi, 2009; Zimmerman & Schunk, 2011). Many theorists have begun to consider synergies between SRL processes and some assessment practices (Andrade & Cizek, 2010; Clark, 2012), but little guidance has yet been given to teachers about how SRL and co-regulation can be continuously incorporated into the large range of assessment practices that are included in the classroom.

A Few Words About Classroom Assessment as a Specialized Field of Study

We view CA as a distinct specialization within educational assessment for three primary reasons. First, unlike most large-scale assessment, CA has blended purposes. Second, good practice in CA requires and is enriched by contextualization, interaction, and change rather than by standardization of times and conditions. Third, the potential impacts of good CA on individual learning, though they accrue very gradually, may be enormous over time.

CA: Blended, Not Opposed, Purposes

The purposes served by classroom assessment have historically tended to define arguments about their interpretation and use. The main purposes of assessment in classrooms are often described as formative and summative. You may be familiar with these terms, coined decades ago by Michael Scriven in the field of program evaluation (Scriven, 1967). They have been pervasively, sometimes simplistically, adopted in CA. Briefly, formative assessments are seen as those whose primary purpose is to guide and improve student learning and/or teacher instructional practice; hence, formative assessment is sometimes referred to as "assessment *for* learning" (A*f*L). Contemporary definitions of formative assessment stress the importance of quality feedback and the involvement of students in the assessment process in order to achieve the desired academic gains, and treat the formative purpose as the most important one in the classroom. Summative purposes of classroom assessment are characterized by a reporting function. The purpose of summative assessment is to take evidence about student achievement and report that evidence, usually in the form of grades, to one or more audiences outside the classroom. Most state, national, and international tests are considered summative. Summative assessments are not specifically intended to provide growth-oriented feedback.

In our view, the terms *formative* and *summative* are misnomers in the field, from which we should move away. They suggest a clear, but misleading, distinction between types of interpretations and the uses to which teachers put classroom assessments. When assessment results are reported at the end of instruction, they are often used to help students make good judgments about setting new goals, and to help teachers plan for the next sequence of teaching. Conversely, A*f*L may be perceived by students as purely evaluative if feedback cannot be put to use. We therefore generally avoid these terms in this text; rather, we present CA as a process that involves specific methods and actions, all of which help teachers gain, interact over, and communicate information to promote learning. The relative emphasis on gaining information, interaction, or communication may vary, but the overall goal is consistent. This is one way in which CA is different from the evaluative context where the terms *formative* and *summative* were coined. In CA, the learning purpose is never truly separated from the decision about the next instructional step.

CA: Contextualized, Interactive, and Evolving

In comparison to traditional standardized tests that yield single-occasion snapshots of individual student achievement, CA tasks often comprise evolving records of student processes as well as products. As one example, an essay assessment task in a writing class may include work completed over many days and involving many individuals and resources, with pre-writing, drafting, peer- and self-editing, feedback and responding to feedback, revision, and submission of the final product. CA in this area will typically involve multiple iterations of this type of assessment, on different topics or genres of writing, but following the same creative process. With each iteration, the group composition for peer feedback can vary, and the focus of feedback may vary as well. This is one example of how CA can capture information about multiple aspects of a content domain, multiple collaborations over learning, and repeated measures of skills and processes. We know of no large-scale assessment system that so completely covers the trajectory of a student's progress over time and draws on information from so many and such diverse sources.

CA: Impactful, Not Just Informational

Educational assessments that are designed to be administered, interpreted, or used beyond the classroom context are not usually intended to cause changes in the individuals who are assessed. This is the principle of non-reactive measurement: the fact that a person is tested should not affect the information the measurement yields (Webb, Campbell, Schwartz, & Sechrest, 1966). However, the principle of non-reactive measurement is hard to achieve in practice. People want to obtain certain "scores," even at the doctor's office. When you know your weight will be measured during an upcoming annual appointment, you may try to diet in advance. You may meditate on the way to the doctor in an effort to lower your blood pressure.

Larger-scale assessments are often one-shot matters. The assessor drops in from the sky, the test takes place, and the assessor disappears. In classrooms, assessment happens much more often. Decades ago, it was estimated that teachers spend one-third of their instructional time in some form of assessment-related activity (Stiggins, Conklin, & U.S. Office of Educational Research and Improvement, 1992). It is reasonable to expect that the amount of time both students and teachers devote to assessment has only grown in the last 25 years.

Given the human desire to show ourselves at our best, and given the frequency of formal and informal assessment in classrooms, we may be well served to think of CA as inevitably reactive. CA can leverage that reactivity for good ends. In CA, teachers can take advantage of their in-depth knowledge and long-lasting relationships with students to help students plan to be assessed, self-monitor as they perform, and reflect and use feedback after assessment to prepare for the next stage of their learning. This is reactive measurement for a good cause, and it requires a high level of scaffolding for students to attain more than superficial results. When teachers support students' SRL and are highly attuned to the quality of assessment-based interpretations and decisions, students (and teachers) can grow to react to assessment by focusing on educational objectives, setting goals, and responding to feedback with guided effort. Accumulated over time, these guided "reactions" to systematic CA have the potential for high impacts on learning.

Our Objectives

The primary objectives of the book are 1) to help teachers and other educational professionals learn to use CA systematically and iteratively rather than ad hoc and periodically; 2) to provide teachers with feasible ways to involve students in assessment so as to take full advantage of the achievement impacts associated with feedback and SRL; and 3) to communicate principles and methods for appraisal of the quality of classroom assessment practices, involving both teachers and students in the appraisal process.

The Organization of This Text

We elaborate on the four-stage CA:SRL framework in Section 1, beginning with the theoretical basis for combining classroom assessment with SRL theories (Zimmerman, 2000, 2013; Zimmerman & Schunk, 2011) and proceeding through Stages 1–4. In Section 2, we delve into technical quality in assessment from a classroom point of view, showcasing principles of reliability, validity, and fairness that teachers can put into practice. In our view, technical quality is just as foundational in CA as it is in large-scale assessment. However, the field of educational measurement has been slow to translate well-defined but often complex methods used in large-scale testing into practicable methods for the classroom context. In this section, we also devote a chapter to emerging technologies for CA, an area that is currently experiencing tremendous growth. Section 3 contains three hypothetical case studies of systematic assessment practices in different content areas: English Language Arts, music, and mathematics. In each content area, we focus on different aspects of practice, whether they be alignment to standards, use of feedback, or involvement of students in SRL. Each case study, though hypothetical, is inspired by the work of real teachers with real students.

References

Andrade, H. L., & Cizek, G. J. (2010). An integrative summary of the research literature and implications for a new theory of formative assessment. In H. L. Andrade & G. J. Cizek (Eds.), *Handbook of formative assessment*. New York, NY: Routledge.

Clark, I. (2012). Formative assessment: Assessment is for self-regulated learning. *Educational Psychology Review, 24*(2), 205–249.

DiGiacomo, G., & Chen, P. P. (2016). Enhancing self-regulatory skills through an intervention embedded in a middle school mathematics curriculum. *Psychology in the Schools, 53*(6), 601–616.

Michalsky, T., Mevarech, Z. R., & Haibi, L. (2009). Elementary school children reading scientific texts: Effects of metacognitive instruction. *Journal of Educational Research, 102*, 363–376.

Scriven, M. (1967). The methodology of evaluation. In R. E. Stake (Ed.), *Perspectives of curriculum evaluation* (Vol. 1, pp. 39–55). Chicago: Rand McNally.

Stiggins, R. J., Conklin, N. F., & U.S. Office of Educational Research and Improvement. (1992). *In teachers' hands: Investigating the practices of classroom assessment*. Albany, NY: SUNY Press.

Webb, E. J., Campbell, D. T., Schwartz, R. D., & Sechrest, L. (1966). *Unobtrusive measures: Non-reactive research in the social sciences* (Vol. 111). Chicago: Rand McNally.

Zimmerman, B. J. (2000). Attaining self-regulation: A social cognitive perspective. In M. Boekaerts, P. R. Pintrich, & M. Zeidner (Eds.), *Handbook of self-regulation research, and applications* (pp. 13–39). Orlando, FL: Academic Press.

Zimmerman, B. J. (2013). From cognitive modeling to self-regulation: A social cognitive career path. *Educational Psychologist, 48*(3), 135–147.

Zimmerman, B. J., & Schunk, D. H. (2011). Self-regulated learning and performance: An introduction and an overview. In B. J. Zimmerman & D. H. Schunk (Eds.), *Handbook of self-regulation of learning and performance* (pp. 1–12). New York, NY: Routledge.

Part I

Section I Introduction
The CA:SRL Framework

In this section, we present the four-stage framework for classroom assessment (CA) with self-regulated learning (SRL), which we name the CA:SRL Framework. We have three goals in this section: 1) to show a system of CA practices that are purpose-driven and aligned with the natural cycle of classroom planning, instruction, and assessment; 2) to explain why and how teachers can use assessment in each stage of our framework to support student learning through self-regulation; and 3) to introduce specific assessment techniques within the context of the four-stage framework. It is our intent in this book to present a cohesive model which showcases interactive processes in a CA system in order to support student self-regulated learning and emphasize assessment that promotes learning in the classroom.

In Chapter 1, we present the main theories that underlie our concept of CA:SRL, define terms, and explain how SRL processes combine with classroom assessment in the four-stage framework. We elucidate the connected processes of assessment for learning and academic self-regulated learning. We take you through these processes to help you understand ways to elicit, assess, document, and develop students' academic knowledge and self-regulation.

In Chapter 2, we focus on pre-assessment, Stage 1 in the four-stage framework. We emphasize the role of pre-assessment in identifying students' academic needs and motivation. If you misgauge students' prior knowledge, skill sets, and interest levels, you may find that your instruction falls flat and that the assessment results show a lack of learning progress. On the other hand, accurate pre-assessment results enable you to find out whether students have prerequisite skills, so you can modify your instruction as needed. Further, gathering and reflecting on information about student self-regulation prior to embarking on instruction can help you gain insight into student motivation and support your students in planning and setting goals. We showcase two methods of pre-assessment: 1) open-ended scaffolding questions, allowing a teacher to see where students stand on a learning progression; and 2) surveys or rating scales. For each assessment method, we outline a design process and provide a graphic example that shows important design features.

Chapter 3 focuses on how teachers and students engage with one another during the interactive process of assessment for learning that we identify in Stage 2. Throughout this chapter, we emphasize the use of assessment evidence as feedback to aid you and your students in monitoring and furthering learning. In this chapter, we present assessment techniques for you and your students to use to monitor learning processes. Interactive and non-interactive techniques are presented in this chapter to assess learning at various checkpoints. We describe techniques in this chapter that you can use to build systematic questioning and structured observations into your instructional practices. We focus on designing objectively scored selected responses, enhanced selected responses (i.e., interpretive exercises), and on-demand performance assessment. To continuously support learning and SRL, we describe the importance of self- and peer-assessment, and how students can self-monitor and incorporate self- and peer-feedback by using simple checklists, rubrics, and rating scales that offer them opportunities to ask themselves questions about their task performance.

Chapter 4 introduces Stage 3 of the four-stage framework, where students respond to formal classroom assessment tasks. In this chapter we present methods for designing performance assessments and essay items, as well as suggestions for designing scoring rubrics to guide judgments when evaluating student work. This section includes information on how to use analysis of item scores from relatively formal Stage 3 assessment tasks to summarize classroom results and identify trends. Most important, we conclude this chapter with information about how teacher feedback, applied skillfully, can help solidify student learning and close learning gaps.

Chapter 5 focuses on summarizing and reporting the accumulated evidence of student achievement, Stage 4 in our framework. Teachers often find that grading decisions are one of the toughest parts of their professional responsibilities. We hope that this chapter will add some clarity to your thinking about grading and reporting, as well as continuously supporting student self-assessment and reflection. At the end of the chapter, you will learn about state and national educational assessments and how their uses affect you, the teaching profession, and society.

We caution readers to be aware that although we describe different methods of assessment within different chapters and stages, you should select a method or methods of assessment, be they open-ended questions, multiple-choice items, essays or other formats, based on your learning objectives and assessment purpose. We have placed different methods within stages to illustrate some of the methodological possibilities at your disposal as you design your CA.

Chapter 1

Classroom Assessment for Learning and Self-Regulation

At the most basic level, *assessment* means any process for obtaining information. All organisms practice assessment. Even amoebas gather information. They use receptors to regulate chemotaxis—movement toward or away from certain chemicals, like sugar.

Educational assessment is distinguished within the vast universe of assessment by its purpose to promote and communicate factors related to academic achievement. Among the many forms of educational assessment, classroom assessment (CA) emphasizes the importance of promoting learning, even when learning outcomes are formally reported.

CA is characterized by certain techniques and methods. The techniques can range from highly informal, "on-the-fly" assessment to more formal assessments. Informal assessments include question/answer sessions during class, technology-based self-checking quizzes, and student conferencing. More formal CA is associated with classroom tests, projects, and performance assessment.

Teachers design or adapt specific tools for assessment that are intended to give them and their students the best possible information relevant to assessing the kind of academic learning and achievement students have studied. Throughout this book, we often refer to such assessment tools as *tasks*. Tasks are questions, the items, problems, projects, or tests that we ask students to respond to when we assess them.

Classroom assessment tasks should be designed and evaluated in terms of their usefulness for learning. Through interpreting student responses to assessment tasks, teachers learn about student strengths and needs, as well as the direction their own instruction should take; students learn about themselves in reference to their academic goals. Actions taken by teachers and students based on this evidence and sound interpretations help all students achieve their learning goals.

Assessment Informed by Theory

Assessment for Learning and Self-Regulation

In areas like education and the social sciences, researchers use *theoretical models* to explain or predict certain phenomena: how students learn, how they approach a learning assignment, how they develop from year to year. Understanding student learning includes knowing how students think and solve problems; this is termed *metacognition*. Recall that the word *cognition* means thinking. By adding *meta*, a Greek word that means "beyond," metacognition becomes a word referring to ways we think about thinking. *Metacognition* has been defined in multiple ways but was originally described as one's knowledge and understanding of his or her own cognitive processes; it was later expanded to include anything psychological, such as knowing one's and others' motives, emotions, and motor skills (Flavell, 1979, 1987). Major theorists conceptualize metacognition with similar facets, such as metacognitive knowledge, monitoring, and control (Dunlosky & Metcalfe, 2009; Nelson & Narens, 1990).

In this book we combine our focus on CA with a specific theory: the theoretical model of *self-regulated learning* (SRL). The researcher and theorist Barry Zimmerman describes SRL as a set of processes through which learners purposively manage their behaviors, cognition, emotions, and environment to successfully attain personal goals (Zimmerman, 2000). Students who are self-regulated in their learning exhibit heightened motivation and metacognitive awareness. They engage in iterative modifications of their learning strategies and actions, while incorporating self-feedback and external feedback (e.g., from teacher, peers, and parents). Such a dynamic and continuous feedback mechanism is vital to any successful SRL process, as it signals to learners that the potentially useful information they acquired during one stage of their learning progress can guide and adjust their plans and behavior for the next stage.

Recently, researchers have begun to articulate rationales and processes applicable to both CA and SRL frameworks that are grounded in cognitive, metacognitive, behavioral, and motivational principles (Clark, 2012; Panadero, Andrade, & Brookhart, 2018; Wiliam, 2007). For instance, Wiliam (2007) indicated that improvement in students' mathematics performance can be accomplished through instruction and CA by infusing support into mathematics lessons for SRL skills such as planning, monitoring, and self-reflection. The iterative nature of learning and assessment also contributes to pull the fields of CA and SRL closer together.

CA:SRL—A Four-Stage Framework for Classroom Assessment

In this text, we intentionally bring together the connected processes of CA and academic SRL to present a four-stage CA:SRL framework that adapts SRL concepts and frames them in a new way within the larger context of all the assessment activities that occur in classrooms (see Figure 1.1). We believe this framework can support teachers in a practical way to plan and design purposeful and systematic use of assessments that stimulate student learning. We present

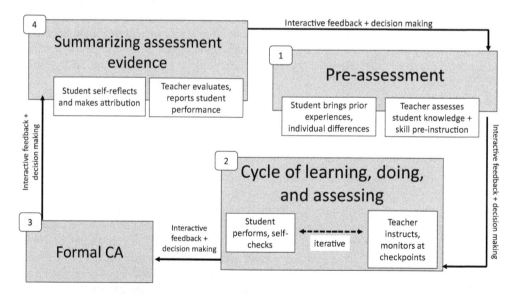

Figure 1.1 CA:SRL Four-Stage Framework

the theoretical elements of the model in this chapter; in the following chapters in section 1, we explain how to apply them when designing and administering assessments to your students.

In general, our approach to SRL follows Zimmerman's (2000) theoretical model, which describes how SRL works in three phases. Before completing a task, students examine the task and judge their own capabilities (*forethought* phase). They perform the task, maybe filling in a multiple-choice test or writing an essay (*performance* phase). Finally, they consider the outcome and reflect on ways it might be improved, how it might be graded, and so on (*self-reflection* phase). They use this process iteratively to prepare for, perform, and reflect on new tasks. With support for SRL development, students improve their SRL skills and use those skills to improve their own learning.

We mostly rely on Zimmerman's SRL model because of its focus on "intentional learning." It is unique in delineating the behaviors, cognitive and metacognitive processes, and motivational elements that learners go through as they pursue their learning goals. Having adopted an SRL model, we flesh it out with additional theory from the SRL literature and adapt it with the intent of incorporating its elements into CA.

It is important to note that the *self* in SRL always refers to the learner or student. In the four-stage CA model, we include multiple selves through the concept of co-regulation of learning (Hadwin, Jarvela, & Miller, 2018). Thus, we will also discuss the *self* as you, the classroom teacher. We advocate for an approach to assessment that is a communicative experience between you and your students, and a basis for all parties to learn and grow.

Stage I: SRL Forethought and Pre-assessment

Stage 1 in our framework comprises *pre-assessment* and SRL *forethought*. Administering an assessment task prior to instruction allows you as a teacher to see what students know and can do already. Pre-assessment also helps you learn about your students' motivation and attitudes. Information of this nature will help you decide on pacing, coverage you need to provide on pre-requisites, student misconceptions about the learning content, and student attitudes or preferences you can use as leverage points to make your instruction more effective.

Classroom pre-assessment also helps students build the metacognitive skill of forethought. Before we dive into a novel and challenging academic assignment, we analyze the task before us and assess what we believe to be our capability to complete it, as well as what strategies we may use. A pre-assessment task can ignite student forethought at the very start of an instructional cycle. Well-designed pre-assessment encourages students to mentally analyze content in upcoming learning and think of strategies they can use. Learners may engage in task analysis processes such as goal setting (e.g., prioritizing goals to reach longer-term goals successfully) and strategic planning (e.g., selecting or creating appropriate strategies to complete the target task).

Motivational beliefs are also important factors that influence learning during forethought. Motivation influences how people set goals and plan for subsequent actions. Therefore, you can also pre-assess student motivation to learn, their beliefs in their capabilities to successfully tackle problems, or how interested they are in the problem at hand and how much they value learning it. By incorporating motivational dimensions into pre-assessment, you demonstrate that you value and can take action on factors that influence learning, which helps you become a more responsive teacher and helps students develop self-awareness.

There are important benefits to students when they develop these SRL skills at the forethought phase. Learners who engage in good planning and goal-oriented strategizing are self-motivated. Learners with SRL skills are likely to have higher *self-efficacy* in comparison to others. By self-efficacy, we mean confidence that they will be able to successfully execute a task at hand. Researchers have demonstrated the importance of SRL forethought processes in influencing academic performance (Zimmerman, Moylan, Hudesman, White, & Flugman, 2011; Zimmerman, Schunk, & DiBenedetto, 2015). Research has shown self-efficacy beliefs to be one of the best predictors of students' academic performance in areas such as math, writing, performing arts, and sciences (DeBenedetto & Zimmerman, 2013; McPherson & McCormick, 2006; Pintrich & De Groot, 1990; Schunk, 2003).

Also, students who have good academic self-regulation have positive *outcome expectancies*. Outcome expectancies are personal beliefs about an anticipated action or performance. Students tend to have different reasons for engaging in a task: they may genuinely enjoy it, they may want to get an A, or they may hope to impress their teacher with their knowledge. These different reasons constitute a student's specific learning *goal orientation*. For example, this is a positive outcome expectancy about an external outcome: "If I study harder, I will earn a good grade on the reading test." A positive outcome expectancy about an internal outcome might be "If I study harder, I will feel good about myself as a reader."

When you support students in developing SRL, you are supporting them in developing positive learning strategies and motivational beliefs. Understanding motivation and goal-orientation will help you tailor instruction to build on enthusiasm and overcome social-emotional obstacles to learning.

Stage 2: SRL Performance Within the Cycle of Learning, Doing, and Assessing

Stage 2 is the *cycle of instruction and assessment for learning*, connected to the SRL *performance* phase. In the four-stage model, we break up Zimmerman's (2000) performance phase into two parts. In Stage 2, we focus on how teachers' monitoring and instruction can respond to evidence about student performance. The iterative process that is crucial to our framework for CA:SRL begins in this phase, as noted in the open line with double arrows in Figure 1.1. As a teacher, as you begin this cycle, you have some knowledge of your students' prior academic preparation or their motivational beliefs, based on your pre-assessment. As you proceed with your instruction, you continue to gather evidence about students' learning and monitor their progress and your own. There is a great deal of back-and-forth exchange of information between students and teachers, with repeated cycles of instruction, checkpoints through assessment, and continuing instruction.

During Stage 2, students are engaged in ongoing implementation of strategies to solve the target task, exercising *self-control*, and *self-monitoring* their progress. Although Zimmerman (2000) posited the importance of metacognition in the *performance* phase of his SRL model, he did not present the mechanisms of metacognition as clearly as other theorists have. Specifically, we find Nelson and Narens's (1994) depiction of the interplay between *self-monitoring* and *self-control*, from the perspective of cognition and information processing, to be clearer and more comprehensive (see also Nelson, 1996).

Nelson and Narens developed a dynamic theory of metacognition with a number of inter-related components. First, they conceptualized cognitive processes as existing in two levels: *object-level* and *meta-level*. The object-level consists of cognition (e.g., "This is a fraction divided by fraction problem"), while the meta-level consists of metacognition, or cognition of the object-level (e.g., "What does it mean to divide fractions?" "Which strategy should I use to solve this math problem?").

Second, the authors conceptualized how information flows between the two levels. The meta-level governs, regulates, and acquires information from the object-level via *monitoring*.

Monitoring signals to the individual about the state of the object-level, such as content knowledge, skills, or learning strategies. The meta-level sends information to the object-level via *controlling* or *control actions*. By exercising control, an individual can use their knowledge at the meta-level or metacognitive level to regulate or direct what to do, or not do, at the object-level or cognitive level.

Throughout the course of cognitive activity, object-level and meta-level processes simultaneously operate to deliver information (monitoring) and directives (control) between the object-level and meta-level. Like Zimmerman's SRL model, Nelson and Narens's model of metacognition is also goal-driven: the meta-level contains within it both goals and ways of regulating the object-level to accomplish the goals.

One benefit of asking students to perform multiple brief assessments is that it helps them exercise the kind of self-control described above. Students practice self-control in assessment when they draw diagrams, form imagery or mental pictures, and map concepts; manage their time; set self-consequences to motivate learning; structure the learning environment to enhance learning and complete tasks; and seek help or information (Wolters, 2003). During multiple cycles of performance, students can also gain practice though self-observation processes. Self-observation includes metacognitive monitoring as described above (i.e., covertly and mentally tracking their learning progress and performance outcomes). Self-observation can also include explicit self-recording (i.e., overtly and deliberately recording and tracking their learning progress and performance outcomes).

Designing opportunities for students to practice self-observation at the performance phase of SRL is equally desirable for teaching and assessment. All learners implicitly engage in these metacognitive processes when they perform, but highly self-regulated students are more likely to do so consciously or with better results than others. Therefore, to support student development of these crucial SRL skills, we recommend that you use tools like recording devices or checklists to aid students in monitoring their learning progress and accurately self-assessing their performance successes and gaps. The information generated during the performance phase then feeds back to the learner, who uses it to evaluate the effectiveness of their performance. We strongly suggest that you embed opportunities for students to self-assess in order to cultivate students' self-monitoring skills and their willingness to take ownership of articulating their learning and understanding.

At the same time your students are learning about their own learning, you as a teacher are learning a lot about your students, monitoring their developing knowledge and skills. While students implement their strategies to solve problems, you gauge the progress of their learning through—for example—informal questioning, homework assignments, and student self-feedback and peer-feedback sheets. It is during Stage 2 that teachers often observe students' success in meeting learning criteria and note their alternative conceptions and patterns of mistakes, which afford further teaching and learning opportunities. This information helps you as a teacher know whether your instruction is effective at helping students meet learning goals. It helps you provide feedback to students that is focused on students' specific learning needs. It helps you look back to see whether your plans for pacing and differentiation, likely drawn from pre-assessment, are working, and look forward to decide how to design formal assessment tasks that match the learning experience.

The multiple iterations emphasized in this part of our framework are a bedrock of assessment practice that is ongoing and interactive for all stakeholders in the classroom. We recognize that not all learning needs multiple iterations of instruction and assessment. As you are aware, not every topic in your content area is equally complex and difficult. If your students already have a base of knowledge about a content area (say, long division), you might only need to lead instruction and assess students on one occasion. You will be able to gather sufficient evidence for inferring, with a high certainty, your students' current knowledge and understanding. If they have no reference point or no familiarity with the content, you may need to engage in multiple iterations of teaching, assessing, and re-teaching differently. As Zimmerman (2015) indicated, tasks that people have prior knowledge of do not require the same mental attention and extensive planning to execute as do novel and complex tasks.

In sum, Stage 2 comprises ongoing successive checkpoints of learning and instruction. Students' self-observation and monitoring processes help them develop into independent learners and yield important assessment evidence for teachers. Ongoing, frequent assessment in Stage 2 incorporates continuous instructions (in-group or individualized) and information about students to help you make decisions about student learning progress and instructional effectiveness.

Stage 3: SRL Performance and Formal CA

Stage 3 refers to when students are formally assessed at the completion of a cycle of instruction. Recall that in our CA model, we have broken up Zimmerman's (2000) performance phase into two parts. In Stage 3, we emphasize the point at which students carry out a formal performance without teacher scaffolds or support. Stage 3 affords students an opportunity to demonstrate the cumulative knowledge and skill sets they have solidified by the end of an instructional period. Formal performance represents a major checkpoint for student learning and overall instructional effectiveness. The *cycle of instruction and assessment for learning* is analogous to when children first learn to ride their bikes. Many need training accessories and adults' scaffolding. After a period of instruction and learning, however, children have an opportunity to demonstrate whether they can bike without this extra support. In the context of the classroom, they are ready for formal assessment.

Because Zimmerman's SRL model was developed with the learner or *self* as its center, we needed to make sure, when we adapted it for CA purposes, that the *formal assessment of performance* in Stage 3 fits theoretically into the SRL model. We believe that distinguishing the *instruction and assessment for learning* stage from the *formal performance* stage in our framework represents a clear-cut distinction between the different grains of assessment evidence in the four-stage model. In terms of SRL, at this point, students should be independently practicing self-control and self-monitoring. You as a teacher have helped them develop these skills during Stage 2. During formal assessment, they will practice these skills on their own, without the assistance of external supports, such as their peers, their notes, or their teacher.

While we view learning and assessment as a continuous iterative process, we also know that humans need to pause and reflect. To manage learning and instruction, we have stopping points for lessons, units, and academic terms. Having periodic formal assessments provides a time for students to demonstrate what they have achieved and leads the way into the next stage, where students and teachers reflect on the learning and teaching that have taken place.

Stage 4: Summarizing Assessment Evidence

Stage 4 refers to *summarizing performance of student learning*, which we map onto *self-reflection* in SRL. By this time, you and your students have gathered evidence of learning and engaged in instruction and assessment cycles, likely multiple times. Your students have performed on a formal assessment, and you are pausing between instructional units or time periods. You and your students now do two things: summarize and evaluate. Summarizing student performance entails combining all the information provided by multiple high-quality sources. Evaluating means considering the sum of the evidence and making judgments.

Summarizing and evaluating student performance is the professional responsibility of a classroom teacher. Your evaluative summary of student achievement is most often reported as a grade, but can also be conveyed in other ways. You will use summaries of evidence to communicate about performance to many different stakeholders, including parents and school administrators, so the quality of reflection that goes into your final assessment is highly important.

The self-regulation component of this stage of our framework should not be overshadowed by the official reporting function of summation of achievement. It is in this stage that we find, according to Zimmerman's theory, the most emphasis on self-evaluation and self-reaction. *Self-evaluation* refers to the judgment one makes of one's own performance in relation to a specific standard, as well as making causal attributions for the outcomes. Affording students opportunities for self-evaluation and reflection engages them in being metacognitive and in orchestrating their learning. This can be encouraged by asking students to self-assess. Self-reflection during Stage 4 not only adds another opportunity for students to reflect on their formal performance outcomes, but also affords them a holistic view of their learning and performance outcomes.

Self-reaction refers to the learners' level of satisfaction or dissatisfaction with their performance, and their adaptive or defensive reactions to the outcomes (Zimmerman, 2000). Whether students engage in further learning and proceed to the next phase of forethought for new learning depends on these self-reactions. Some learners may experience negative self-reactions to a performance outcome; they may not willingly incorporate changes to their learning strategies, adapt other ones, or take your feedback into account during the next iteration of learning cycle.

You can help students engage fruitfully in evaluating and judging their performances by providing them with external standards or guiding them to set their own standards. Comparing their work to standards and seeing the gaps or inconsistencies between their actual performance and standards can affect students' attributions for their outcome. Students may attribute their success or failure in performance outcomes to internal sources such their own intelligence or to external sources such as their teachers. Weiner's (2010) theory of attribution has provided a way for us to understand how students' attributions for their success or failure influence their subsequent actions and learning attitudes. Similarly, knowing what sources students attribute to their performance outcomes can provide valuable information about their *mindset* of intelligence (Dweck, 2008). Children with a *growth* mindset are likely to see a less-than-stellar performance as an opportunity to improve. Children with a *fixed* mindset, on the other hand, attribute their outcomes to something that cannot be changed.

Of course, teachers also make attributions for their students' performance outcomes. The reflection and summative part of our framework is a good time for teachers and students to check the consistency of their attributions. Understanding how both you and your student make attributions for the student's performance outcome provides an opportunity for communicating and working together to best support the learner's needs for the next instructional unit or sequence of teaching, learning, and assessment.

Be mindful that at this pause in instruction, you are not only evaluating students. You also are responsible for reflecting on and evaluating your teaching craft. While you make attributions about your students' performance outcomes, you self-evaluate your instruction and adjust it to meet the instructional needs of your students. You should also take an evaluative stance toward your own assessment practices. You must consider whether your evaluations of your students are based on unbiased observations, accurate interpretations, and fair practices. Therefore, we take very seriously the quality of our interpretations and inferences that derive from information we obtain from assessment.

Interpretations and Inferences From Evidence

We ask you to think about inferences to help you remember to be aware of the mental processes you and your students use when you translate the physical evidence you have gathered from an assessment task into an interpretation of student learning or attitude. As stated earlier, we are trying to assess a *what* about students—not students as individuals, but their attributes, where they stand on a *construct*, such as motivation to learn about evolution or paragraph organization. A construct is a theoretical attribute that we want to obtain information about in assessment: knowledge of a mathematical concept, a skill in organizing writing, or a theory in science. Yes, we care about what the students can do right now. Therefore, we ask them to do something right now; we ask them to answer a question or demonstrate the behavior. However, most of the time we care not just about that behavior in the moment, but also about that behavior as a more generalized attribute. The specific behavior that the student performs in response to an individual assessment task is just a sample of the construct we are trying to assess. We don't want to know "Will my student remember to put on safety goggles before starting this lab in science?" on one occasion only. We want to know whether the student will generally put on safety goggles in the science laboratory.

Making a generalization from a single observation to a broader construct requires inference (see Pellegrino, Chudowsky, & Glaser, 2001). Inference is a mental step. It starts with interpretation of the evidence in front of us. You and your students observe their performance. The performance may be a very indirect measure of knowledge, such as circling one of several choices on a multiple-choice test. The behavior may be a more direct assessment of the skill, like an observation of the actions that the student performs as they begin to do a laboratory activity. Whichever the case, an interpretation must be made about what that performance means. Does checking the wrong answer on a multiple-choice item mean that the student did not know the correct answer, or does it mean that the question itself was confusing? Did the student put on safety goggles because she knew she was supposed to, or because she saw another student doing it? Here you make an evidence-based judgment. You should have a system for making your interpretation that applies consistently to all students. Your interpretation should not be based on bias against an individual or preference for a certain behavioral style. If you are uncertain that your interpretation of the behavior was sound, you should go back and think about the assessment task itself. Consider whether a question was confusing and hard to answer, not because the content challenged a student, but because the language in which the content was embedded posed a barrier between the learning that the student had and the action he performed. Consider whether the laboratory task was set up in a way that ensured that individual students could not simply mimic one another.

Describing what a specific behavior means in terms of the construct is one inference. Sometimes, although not always in classroom assessment, we will make another set of inferences, particularly as we move from Stage 3 of our model, the students' "final" performance for demonstrating their learning of the material they have studied, to Stage 4, the summary of the evidence or the translation of the evidence into ratings, scores, or grades. At this point we make a big inferential jump. Exactly how does the quality of the work that we have seen relate to our standards of excellence? Where does it fall on an implicit continuum ranging from a low level of achievement of the learning objective to a high level? Many sources inform our inferences at this stage: our schools' guidelines and descriptors of performance expectations, our grading scale, rubrics that we have constructed or that our schools or state have provided for evaluating student work, and, of course, our own professional and personal judgment. Again, fairness is a great concern here. The same guidelines for evaluating work according to a standard of excellence should be applied to all students (except students with special needs and English language learners), without bias against individuals or personal preferences.

The quality of your inferences based on the evidence of student behavior matters greatly in the classroom, because it is on these inferences that you provide feedback to your students about what they have learned so far and what their next goals for learning should be. The active stages of assessment that are depicted as boxes in Figure 1.1 are really only one part of a much more complex process of eliciting behavior, interpreting behavior, and feeding back interpretations that both you and your students can use to take actions to improve learning. The mental processes depicted with arrows in Figure 1.1 are just as important as the boxes.

Interactive Feedback and Decision-Making: Connections That Translate Evidence Into Action

Teaching and learning don't stop after students have been assessed and you have interpreted their work; they are continuing processes. Reflecting this, our framework is cyclical, like Zimmerman's model of SRL processes. While each stage of assessment is distinct in terms of purpose, approach, and outcome, feedback and decision-making connect each stage like "glue." They explain and guide the actions that guide classrooms from one stage to the next. You can see this labeled in Figure 1.1.

The four-stage CA:SRL framework involves multiple dimensions of feedback generated from students, peers, and teachers. Thus, we conceptualize the feedback loop in the four-stage framework to be *interactive*. Interaction in feedback is essential because we recognize that students and teachers are all active and purposeful in using feedback to move forward and take certain actions. All parties—whether they provide feedback or receive it—need to communicate about the usefulness and clarity of the feedback. Those on the providing end— usually teachers—need to ask whether students understand and can learn from feedback, because those on the receiving end—usually students—are the final arbiters of whether the feedback is useful for subsequent actions.

Feedback is particularly important in CA when students are developing self-feedback and peer-feedback skills. It is a mistake to think that feedback only comes from teachers—feedback is also self-generated and often involves peer interactions, even when such interactions are informal, such as when students compare grades or ask each other questions. To help students develop the skills to generate useful feedback, you need to provide explicit scaffolds to help them learn self- and peer-assessment skills, and communicate with them about the emerging quality of their self- and peer-assessment practices.

The interactive feedback and decision-making in the four-stage framework are strongly aligned with Zimmerman's SRL theory. Feedback in each phase of SRL is used to adjust current learning; such adjustments "feed-forward" to the next phase. In addition, research has shown that feedback is a critical component of learning that guides student learning and serves as a source of motivation (Shute, 2008). Feedback also has a regulatory function (Hattie & Timperley, 2007); as posited in Zimmerman's model, feedback generated from any given phase forms the basis of motivation, behavior, cognition, and metacognition in a subsequent phase.

Teaching, Co-regulation, and Shared Regulation

Both students and teachers have roles in each part of the four-stage CA model. We graphically depict the roles of both students and teachers to stay focused on, and explicit about, the shared experience between you and your students. SRL focuses on individuals; however, in the classroom, individuals are situated in a context. Classroom contexts are complex, with various individuals sharing and collaborating on learning instruction and assessment experience. Whenever you use the four-stage, you co-regulate with your students and *share regulation* with them.

What are the concepts of *co-regulation* and *shared regulation*? According to Hadwin et al. (2018), *co-regulation* "refers to the dynamic metacognitive processes through which self-regulation and shared regulation of cognition, behavior, motivation, and emotions are transitionally and flexibly supported and thwarted" (p. 83). They further describe *socially shared regulation* as "groups taking metacognitive control of the task together through negotiated, iterative, fine-tuning of cognitive, behavioral, motivational, and emotional conditions/states as needed" (p. 83). The four-stage CA:SRL framework incorporates the importance of having teachers give students opportunities to self-regulate by shifting regulation to individual students. Although the four-stage framework does not explicitly indicate *when* co-regulation and shared regulation occur in the model, we would like to acknowledge the importance of the ways that students, their peers, and teachers regulate their interactions. When you engage in the stages of the framework, you co-regulate with your students and share regulation with them. Our framework reflects these processes and also recognizes that teachers can provide students with opportunities to self-regulate by shifting regulation to individual students.

Our Organizing Principles

The framework we have presented here represents classroom assessment as iterative and interactive, and features both students and teachers as active agents in every stage of the system. We have demonstrated the theoretical rationales for each assessment practice within this system. Because four-stage CA is a conceptual framework for designing specific practices in individual classrooms, it must be unpacked to be meaningful and useful to practitioners.

In further chapters in this section we will delineate practices in each stage in detail and give you practical strategies for supporting student learning and self-regulation through assessment. We break down the framework in each chapter by answering three foundational questions: 1) Why do we assess? 2) What do we assess? 3) How do we assess? These questions are important for us to answer as we go through the assessment stages; they are the nuts and bolts of our approach and the organizing principles for each stage.

In some chapters, we will need to address the question "who" more than in others. The reason is simple: we do not assess people or things. We assess *constructs* or attributes. Constructs are hypothetical attributes that can be overt or covert. For example, weight is a construct that shows up mostly in the units of pounds or kilograms. Extraversion and dexterity are also constructs, which show up in certain units and scores. Academic college-readiness is a broad construct, and knowledge about the U.S. Civil War is a narrow one.

Although we do not assess people, we will remind you at appropriate points that the *unit of analysis* for assessment can vary. Assessment is not always about student attributes—it may involve attributes of teachers, schools, or larger organizations. Whether or not the unit of analysis is the student or the state, it is the construct that is the answer to the question "what?"

Because constructs are hypothetical, we define them *operationally* to make them meaningful. Researchers often operationalize constructs by asking what behaviors make the construct show up, so we can assess it. We assess the important constructs in education, such as achievement and learning. For example, the New York State (NYS) and Common Core standards are an attempt to operationalize learning in different content domains. NYS standards define what students in New York are expected to know and be able to "do" (i.e., content) at different levels of development (grades). In addition, NYS standards are available in different content domains and align with the national Common Core standards.

Even though learning is operationalized in terms of standards for various content domains, the standards are stated in general terms. We align with others in the CA field who recommend that teachers further operationalize learning standards into specific learning objectives (SLOs). SLOs are expressed in terms of behaviors that students should show to demonstrate learning or achievement. We will address SLOs in more detail in Chapter 2.

We answer the question "how?" by describing specific tools or methods you as a teacher can use to elicit evidence of learning and collecting information on what has been learned. The tools for collecting evidence can be in written and oral forms, or through physical performance (i.e., demonstrated in actions). Rather than having specific chapters devoted to writing assessment methods and item writing, we detail selected methods throughout Chapters 1, 2, and 3 that are most appropriate for eliciting various types of learning evidence. Further, we explain why certain tools or methods are pertinent to meeting the purposes of assessment, and we provide resources for you on item-writing dos and don'ts.

To answer the question "why?" we must carefully consider the rationale for conducting an assessment and making choices about assessment tools and processes. During the assessment process, every step of decision-making requires a sound rationale. Throughout the book, we will provide research evidence, learning theories, and measurement principles that support our decision-making in relation to content. In the classroom setting, your assessment-related decisions need to be guided by research and theories to ensure that your interpretations and judgments of student learning are accurate, credible, useful, and fair.

The answer to the question "when?" may be prior, during, and after an instructional period, depending on the assessment purpose. In Chapters 2–5, we will not focus extensively on timing in assessment since each chapter is focused on a single stage in our model, which is in turn associated with a timepoint in the instructional cycle.

Summary

Assessment, or any process for obtaining information, can be used in the classroom to gather relevant information about student learning and achievement. Classroom assessments can be more formal or more informal; can occur many times within any instructional unit; and can be performed, interpreted, and acted on by students and teachers alike. Broadly, CA should always promote student and teacher learning. We have presented a conceptual framework for ways in which assessment can be used to elicit student self-regulation of learning. The CA:SRL framework's four stages are each characterized by assessment approaches and student metacognitive processes; they are linked by feedback and shared decision-making between teachers and students. We will unpack each stage in the following chapters, guided by questions about why we assess, what is assessed, and how we can assess.

References

Clark, I. (2012). Formative assessment: Assessment is for self-regulated learning. *Educational Psychology Review, 24*(2), 205–249.

DiBenedetto, M. L., & Zimmerman, B. J. (2013). Construct and predictive validity of microanalytic measures of students' self-regulation of science learning. *Learning and Individual Difference, 26*, 30–41. https://doi.org/10.1016/j.lindif.2013.04.004

Dunlosky, J., & Metcalfe, J. (2009). *Metacognition.* Thousand Oaks, CA: Sage Publications, Inc.

Dweck, C. S. (2008). *Mindset: The new psychology of success.* New York, NY: Random House.

Flavell, J. H. (1979). Metacognition and cognitive monitoring. *American Psychologist, 34*, 906–911. doi:10.1037/0003-066X.34.10.906

Flavell, J. H. (1987). Speculations about the nature and development of metacognition. In F. Weinert & R. Kluwe (Eds.), *Metacognition, motivation, and understanding* (pp. 21–29). Hillsdale, NJ: Lawrence Erlbaum. doi:10.1016/S0885-2014(87)90104-3

Hadwin, A. F., Jarvela, S., & Miller, M. (2018). Self-regulation, co-regulation and shared regulation in collaborative learning environments. In D. Schunk & J. Greene (Eds.), *Handbook of self-regulation of learning and performance* (2nd ed.). New York, NY: Routledge.

Hattie, J., & Timperley, H. (2007). The power of feedback. *Review of Educational Research, 77*, 81–112.

McPherson, G. E., & McCormick, J. (2006). Self-efficacy and music performance. *Psychology of Music, 34*(3), 325–339.

Nelson, T. O. (1996). Consciousness and metacognition. *American Psychologist, 51*(2), 102–116.

Nelson, T. O., & Narens, L. (1990). Metamemory: A theoretical framework and new findings. In G. H. Bower (Ed.), *The psychology of learning and motivation* (pp. 125–173). New York, NY: Academic Press. doi:10.1016/S0079-7421(08)60053-5

Nelson, T. O., & Narens, L. (1994). Why investigate metacognition? In J. Metcalfe & A. P. Shimamura (Eds.), *Metacognition: Knowing about knowing* (pp. 1–25). Cambridge, MA: The MIT Press.

Panadero, E., Andrade, H., & Brookhart, S. (2018). Fusing self-regulated learning and formative assessment: A roadmap of where we are, how we got here, and where we are going. *The Australian Educational Researcher, 45*, 13–31.

Pellegrino, J. W., Chudowsky, N., & Glaser, R. (Eds.). (2001). The nature of assessment and reasoning from evidence. In *Knowing what students know: The science & design of educational assessment* (pp. 37–56). Retrieved June 15, 2009, from http://books.nap.edu/openbook.php?record_id=10019&page=37

Pintrich, P. R., & De Groot, E. V. (1990). Motivational and self-regulated learning components of classroom academic performance. *Journal of Educational Psychology, 82*, 33–40.

Schunk, D. (2003). Self-efficacy for reading and writing: Influence of modeling, goal setting, and self-evaluation. *Reading and Writing Quarterly, 19*, 159–172.

Shute, V. J. (2008). Focus on formative feedback. *Review of Educational Research, 78*, 153–189.

Weiner, B. (2010). The development of an attribution-based theory of motivation: A history of ideas. *Educational Psychologist, 45*(1), 28–36. doi:10.1080/00461520903433596

Wiliam, D. (2007). Keep learning on track: Classroom assessment and the regulation of learning. In F. K. Lester, Jr. (Ed.), *Second handbook of research on mathematics teaching and learning* (pp. 1053–1098). Charlotte, NC: Information Age Publishing.

Wolters, C. A. (2003). Regulation of motivation: Evaluating an underemphasized aspect of self-regulated learning. *Educational Psychologist, 38*, 189–205.

Zimmerman, B. J. (2000). Attaining self-regulation: A social cognitive perspective. In M. Boekaerts, P. R. Pintrich, & M. Zeidner (Eds.), *Handbook of self-regulation research, and applications* (pp. 13–39). Orlando, FL: Academic Press.

Zimmerman, B. J., Moylan, A., Hudesman, J., White, N., & Flugman, B. (2011). Enhancing self-reflection and mathematics achievement of at-risk urban technical college students. *Psychological Test and Assessment Modeling, 53,* 108–127.

Zimmerman, B. J., Schunk, D. H., DiBenedetto, M. K. (2015). A personal agency view of self-regulated learning: The role of goal setting. In F. Guay, H. Marsh, D. McInerney, & R. G. Craven (Eds.), *Self-concept, motivation, and identity: Underpinning success with research and practices* (pp. 83–114). Charlotte, NC: Information Age Publishing.

Chapter 2

Assessing Student Prior Knowledge, Skills, and Beliefs

In this chapter, we take you through the why, what, and how of the pre-assessment and fore-thought phase. We will demonstrate how to examine state or national learning standards, and how to break down the learning standards into manageable and assessable learning outcomes to be aligned with instruction and assessment. We then suggest some simple types of tasks to assess prior knowledge of content. We also suggest that you may on occasion think it important to assess student characteristics in the affective domain, such as interests, attitudes, and beliefs. We therefore provide brief guidelines for writing items in rating scales. Remember that whether you are measuring content knowledge or attitude, the most important thing is the relevance of your questions to the learning outcomes you have in mind. Focusing on the learning outcomes from the beginning helps you ignite student mental processes at the brink of the learning journey, helping them to see that new content is only a step away, not a foreign territory.

Whom We Pre-assess and When

When students first enter your classroom, you have limited information about their academic preparation or their motivation for the content area. If you are teaching ninth-grade algebra, you know that your students probably passed eighth-grade math. However, you may not know how academically prepared they are, how motivated they are to learn mathematics, or their attitudes about math. Even if your school gives you access to students' academic data and you know how well they did in their prior math classes and eighth-grade state math results, you need more information about your students to be able to plan your academic year or even the first unit of math in your ninth-grade math class. Gathering information about students to make decisions before the start of instruction is what we call pre-assessment. In pre-assessment, "before" is the answer to "when." In this stage we involve student self-regulation through *forethought* (see highlighted area from our model in Figure 2.1). Pre-assessment is like conducting a litmus test to check where your students are in their preparation before your instruction.

Why We Pre-assess

Stage 1 pre-assessment is important to both you and your students. You, the teacher, can use the information you gather during this stage to gauge what lessons and instructional strategies will be most appropriate for upcoming instruction. This is the time to find out whether your students have the pre-requisite skills and knowledge for the unit that you are to teach. Your task is to determine the topics and related subtopics and skills. For example, if your unit of instruction is on "linear functions," you analyze the subtopics of "linear functions" and

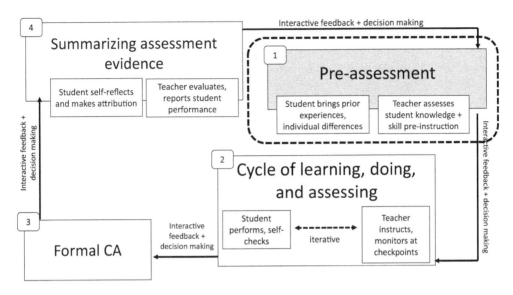

Figure 2.1 CA:SRL Four-Stage Framework: SRL Forethought and Pre-assessment

select the important pre-requisite knowledge and skills that you would like to include in the pre-assessment.

While you contemplate instruction and assessment, your planning should center on the learners' prior exposure to that content, with a focus on eliciting any misconceptions or alternative conceptions they have. Misconceptions or alternative conceptions are common. Such valuable information should then be incorporated into your instructional planning. For instance, empirical research studies about interventions in the domain of science have shown mostly positive results in altering student misconceptions in their scientific understanding of lunar phases (Chastenay, 2016; Hobson, 2008), the solar system (Karsli & Patan, 2016), and force and motion (Eryilmaz, 2002). In math, many studies that included interventions have generally shown a positive impact on altering students' misconceptions of concepts such as decimals (Durkin & Rittle-Johnson, 2012), fractions (Heemsoth & Heinze, 2016), and algebra concepts (Zielinski, 2017). During pre-assessment, it is therefore important to elicit any prior concepts—particularly misconceptions—that are likely to affect the instruction of the unit and influence student learning.

Pre-assessment should also include unearthing your students' motivation for learning. It is important to learn about your students' motivational beliefs because these may influence how they allocate their efforts, set goals, plan for study time, and seek or don't seek help if needed. If you know your students' prior attitudes and beliefs as well as their pre-requisite skills, you can plan lessons to improve motivation, such as explicitly teaching the real-world value of upcoming learning topics. You can build confidence by scaffolding difficult projects into more easily attainable steps. We therefore suggest that you gather information during the pre-assessment stage on students' beliefs about their capability to solve problems in the topic area they are preparing to study, and how much they value and are interested in the topic.

Pre-assessment is also important for students because of its relationship to SRL. As we know from the theory of self-regulated learning, all people analyze novel and challenging academic assignments before diving into them. We self-assess what we believe to be our capability for completing or mastering the task, and we think about what strategies we may use and how to use them. Such thought processes and planning are what we mean by forethought. Through forethought, students develop SRL skills. An important construct associated with SRL is *self-efficacy*. Self-efficacy refers to a learner's beliefs about their capability to complete or master an undertaking and bring it to a desirable outcome (Bandura, 1997). During forethought, students assess their self-efficacy, as well as other skills that support their later achievement, such as interest in learning tasks, value for learning, and orientation toward academic learning goals. During forethought, students can also engage in purposeful goal setting, sequencing smaller goals that will lead to successful completion of the main goal, which is discussed in detail below.

Although we've described many ways that good pre-assessment benefits teaching and learning in the classroom, it is also important to point out that pre-assessment should be relatively brief. Like a movie trailer, it's not the main feature. We suggest that pre-assessment be done in some depth at the beginning of the academic year, but more briefly—and at a greater level of specificity—during transitions to new instructional units, especially when you know little about students' prior knowledge of the topic they will be studying.

What We Pre-assess

Stage 1 pre-assessment needs to start somewhere. To identify students' prior skill sets and knowledge, begin with the current unit and design backward to identify the pre-requisite knowledge and skill sets. Although we are not examining curriculum, CA is tied to what is taught in the class, which should be aligned with what is required by the school. In public schools, good assessment starts with the appropriate state learning standards, or in other cases, with standards set by your professional organizations. The Common Core State Standards (CCSS, 2018) have been adopted or adapted by many states, so we will be using them as a reference. The Common Core standards were developed in the United States over a period of many years by content experts and researchers on learning. For instance, the CCSS in mathematics draw on a general consensus about how high school mathematics curriculum is shaped by concepts students learned in pre-K through grade 8, with a conceptual progression starting from understanding Number and Operations in Fractions (introduced in upper elementary grades 3–5), to Ratios and Proportional Relationships (introduced in grades 6–7), to Expression of Equations (introduced in grade 8), which then funnels into high school algebra. Concepts in algebra are further connected to geometry, probability, and modeling. Mathematical concepts learned in high school are also extended to concepts in other content areas, such as chemistry and physics, and to college and career readiness.

If you have access to curriculum packages that include instructional and assessment materials (including pre-assessment), we encourage you to examine any pre-assessment carefully and only adapt it, partially or entirely, as you believe it appropriate. You also need to consider the larger context of your school's norms and expectations, and whether students have Individualized Education Programs (IEPs).

Looking at Learning Standards

State and national standards and curricula help you guide and plan, but only you can translate the general learning standards of your state into more specific learning goals that are appropriate for your students. Your interpretations of CCSS and your adaptation of them for the grade levels that you are teaching are a good beginning for developing a pre-assessment. Let us look

> **Middle School: Space Systems**
>
> MS-ESS1-1. Develop and use a model of the Earth-sun-moon system to describe the cyclical patterns of lunar phases, eclipses of the sun and moon, and seasons.
> MS-ESS1-2. Develop and use a model to describe the role of gravity in the motions within galaxies and the solar system.
> MS-ESS1-3. Analyze and interpret data to determine scale properties of objects in the solar system.
>
> **Grade 5: Space Systems (Stars and Solar System)**
>
> 5-PS2-1. Support an argument that the gravitational force exerted by Earth on objects is directed downward.
> 5-ESS1-1. Support an argument that differences in the apparent brightness of the sun, as compared to other stars, are due to their relative distances from Earth.
> 5-ESS1-2. Represent data in graphical displays to reveal patterns of daily changes in the length and direction of shadows, day and night, and the seasonal appearance of some stars in the night sky.

Figure 2.2 Comparison of New York State Standards* in Science for Middle School and Grade 5

* *New York State P–12 Science Learning Standards. New State Education Department, 2016.*

at Figure 2.2, on the topic of space systems for middle school grades. We begin by consulting the New York State P–12 Science Learning Standards. The state learning standards are defined in broad strokes and therefore serve as a reference for developing your classroom instruction and assessment. For detailed information and a thorough understanding of the learning standards for your content area and your state, we encourage you to understand and interpret how the multiple dimensions of the learning standards work together.

The three standards listed are provided to New York State science educators. In this example, for comparison purposes, we included fifth-grade learning standards on the same topic (of space systems). By examining the subtopics of space systems in both middle school and fifth-grade standards, we notice overlapping subtopics, such as gravity, Earth, sun, and seasons. The apparent differences are related to the depth and practices of some of the subtopics. As a content expert and a professional, you use your judgment to determine which learning standards and performance expectations students should be able to demonstrate at the end of your instruction.

If you look at multiple grade levels on a topic (here we continue to use the space system as the content area), you can see what core ideas the disciplinary experts deem critical for the grade levels. Based on the fifth-grade standards, you can see that the subtopics in 5-ESS1–1 are related to MS-ESS1–1 (i.e., a systematic relationship between sun, Earth, and moon) and that 5-ESS1–2 is related to MS-ESS1–2 (i.e., analyzing, interpreting, and displaying data). To develop a pre-assessment for a middle school science class on a unit on space systems, you need to know whether your students have a certain understanding of the solar system and are able to interpret data.

Breaking Down Standards

Going further, to design a good pre-assessment, you need to get into the nitty-gritty details of identifying student learning gaps—the possibly missing links between what they already know

24   Section I Chapter 2

and what they have yet to learn. The rationale for taking a general learning standard and breaking it down into a *specific learning objective* (SLO) is that it allows us to think about what learning steps are needed to achieve or get closer to the general goal. The SLOs are stated in terms of students' learning outcomes; you develop the appropriate assessment tools to elicit them. Once we have listed the SLOs, we can identify the pre-requisite skills and knowledge so that pre-assessment questions can be targeted to elicit that specific knowledge and those skill sets.

Pre-assessment is not intended to gather information on every topic that students have learned or encountered prior to entering your class. Rather, the *what* of pre-assessment involves being selective about which pre-requisite concepts and skill sets are most relevant for eliciting the information you need to obtain a basic grasp of your students' exposure to those concepts and skills. To identify students' prior skills sets and knowledge, begin with the current unit and design backward to identify the pre-requisite knowledge and skill sets. Instead of describing exactly what you should pre-assess for your class, we are taking you through the "thinking process" of pre-assessment.

To describe this process, we take another example, this time in algebra. Specifically, we break down a standard (i.e., general learning goal) into more detailed specific learning objectives (or SLOs) using high school algebra on the topic of interpreting functions. According to NYS learning standards for mathematics in P–12, the standards for algebra I (Figure 2.3) are shared with those for an earlier grade (NY-8.F.5) and a later course: algebra II (AII-F.IF.4b). Different content areas map out learning standards differently, as we show here in Examples 1

Standards
AI-F.IF.4. For a function that models a relationship between two quantities:

i. Interpret key features of graphs and tables in terms of the quantities; and
ii. Sketch graphs showing key features, when given a verbal description of the relationship.

Algebra I key features include: intercepts, zeros; intervals where the function is increasing, decreasing, positive, or negative; maxima, minima; and symmetries.

Based on this, we write Specific Learning Objectives (SLOs):

1. Given a set of terms, students will be able to recall their definitions.
2. Given function graphs, students will be able to identify specific key features (intercepts, zeros, maxima, minima, symmetries).
3. Given sets of graphs, students will be able to describe the increasing and decreasing functions.
4. Given a set of key features, students will be able to construct a graph that satisfies the given key features.
5. Given a set of function graphs, students will be able to categorize by key features into function families.
6. Given a set of function graphs from the same function family, students will be able to identify shared key features.
7. Given various function graphs, students will be able to provide real-life examples illustrated in the graphs.

New York State Next Generation Mathematics Learning Standards, New York State Education Department, 2017, used with permission.

Figure 2.3 General Goals and Specific Learning Objectives for Algebra-Interpreting Functions at the High-School Level

and 2. However, an intent of P–12 learning standards is to show the progression of conceptual knowledge and skills/practice that would be linked between grade levels. Thus, if you know that the standards are shared with other grade levels, you can expect that your students have been provided with a progressive understanding of the topics. Previously introduced standards provide you with another source document that you can use to target pre-assessment knowledge and skills.

You can think of the SLOs in Figure 2.3 as the smaller learning outcomes that would lead to the larger learning outcomes list of the state's learning standards. These SLOs are not an exhaustive list, and they vary in complexity. For example, SLO 1 requires students to demonstrate "recall" of definitions of the key features of functions. Compared to SLO 4, which requires students to "construct" a graph with all the key features in it, SLO 1 does not require considerable mental processing or steps. Using your knowledge of your students' prior academic preparation or performance from the previous unit, you can write SLOs with varying complexities of learning outcomes. Always, ask yourself what your students should be able to do at the end of the instructional period.

Writing a Specific Learning Objective

We encourage you to include the following three elements in writing each SLO: *condition*, *performance*, and *audience*. For this, we adapt three of Mager's (1997) four elements of writing SLOs. Mager advocated for a fourth element, *criterion*, in writing objectives. The main reason we do not include criterion in writing SLOs is that most learning outcomes take time to develop and, for the purpose of CA, we would like you and your students to work toward narrowing the learning gap and continuing to develop students' knowledge and skills. Of course, under some circumstances, you may want to set a mastery level in your SLOs—a 100% criterion—that you deem necessary as a learning outcome. For example, if you include an SLO in a science unit that students should be able to set up equipment (e.g., "students should be able to use a Bunsen burner in science lab"), you would want to make sure, for safety reasons, that all the students are able to do so with 100% accuracy or at a mastery level. In Figure 2.4, we provide examples for writing SLOs that include the three elements of condition, audience, and performance. We have renamed *performance* as *behavior* so you can remember these guidelines as ABCs.

Please note that based on the pre-assessment evidence, you may need to modify your SLOs to reflect additional learning outcomes that should be included. You may discard any SLOs that are no longer appropriate for the unit. In addition, when writing SLOs, the *condition* should *not* be stated in terms of an assessment format such as "given three multiple-choice questions." That would restrict students to showing you their learning only in a very narrow manner. Assessment formats (e.g., multiple-choice questions, short answers, or matching exercises) are tests or tools that we use to collect information; they should not be the conditions in which students demonstrate their learning. A tool can be appropriate to show learning outcomes—for example, "using a calculator or protractor" to demonstrate math knowledge and skills, "using a hammer and saw" in shop to demonstrate knowledge of how to operate equipment, or "using a musical instrument" to make different melodic patterns in music learning—but tools are distinct from conditions.

The last point about writing SLOs is to state them in terms of students' learning outcomes rather than your instructional intentions; ask yourself what evidence of learning students should exhibit after the instructional period. We too often see SLOs that are written in terms of teachers' instructional approaches or the learning activities that teachers plan to implement.

26   Section I Chapter 2

Audience: Students/learners are the audience for a learning objective.

Ask: What is my students' prior learning experience?

Behavior: A measurable behavior or performance that indicates attainment at the end of instruction.

Ask: What should my learners be able to do?

Condition: A specific context that stimulates desired behavior and under which it will be observed.

Ask: Under what conditions would I like my students to be able to do/perform the behavior?

Example: Writing a language other than English (e.g., Spanish) for high school intermediate level

---

SLO 1: Given a short story written in Spanish (*condition*), intermediate-level students (*audience*) will be able to select (*behavior/performance*) evidence to show the actions the main character employs to resolve her dilemma.

SLO 2: Given a paragraph written in Spanish (*condition*), intermediate-level students (*audience*) will be able to conjugate (*behavior/performance*) the verbs in it.

Figure 2.4 ABCs of Writing SLOs

The following example of an SLO demonstrates what *not* to do: "In class, students will debate a current political issue." In this example, students engage in learning through the instructional activity of a debate. But the intended learning outcome of this activity is not stated.

Analyzing SLOs

Webb (2002) conceptualized four Depth of Knowledge (DOK) levels, based on Bloom's Cognitive Process Dimension (for updated Bloom's Taxonomy, refer to Krathwohl, 2002). DOK levels can be used to guide and focus teachers on different thinking processes learners will be expected to use when they engage in an assessment task. Although performance or behavior verbs are used in the DOK framework, depth of knowledge should not be determined solely by these types of verbs. The DOK levels are essentially a guide to distinguish the complexity of various mental processes and learning outcomes, from the simpler cognitive process at Level 1 to more complex ones at Level 4 (see Figure 2.5). Once the DOK levels of the learning outcomes have been determined, you can draft SLOs to reflect these DOK levels.

The concept of *learning progressions* is another way to think about relationships among specific learning objectives. Learning progressions describe developmental sequences of typical progress in understanding or being skilled in a domain (Heritage, 2008; Hess, 2008). The learning progression of adding single digits (e.g., $3+4$), starts with children using "count all," then "count on," and finally "recall." At the initial stage of learning, children use manipulatives or objects for addition (cubes, chips, or their fingers). When they encounter the need to add single digits that are larger numbers (e.g., $8+9$), children can build on their prior learning and move to using more complex strategies, such as making a ten ($8+9=10+7=17$) or doubling ($8+9=8+8+1=17$) (NRC, 2001). This is an example of

DOK Levels	Descriptions of Thinking
Level 1: Recall and Reproduction	Students recall information that they have remembered, such as specific facts, definitions, a set of simple procedures, or steps of performance.
Level 2: Skills and Concepts	Students engage in more complex cognitive processes, such as making comparisons, summarizing, explaining a cause/effect situation, and making predictions with well-defined problems and contexts.
Level 3: Strategic Thinking	Students engage in abstract reasoning, using evidence to justify their positions or responses, and making arguments. The cognitive processes are more elaborated, requiring students to plan, analyze, and use evidence and multiple methods to arrive at solutions.
Level 4: Extended Thinking	Students carry out very complex cognitive demands. They research and make connections among ideas within as well as across disciplines, before devising a plan (among multiple alternatives) to solve a problem. Under such cognitive demands, the scope of the problem or context can be ill-defined.

Figure 2.5 Webb's (2002) Four Depth of Knowledge Levels

learning progression for single-digit addition from using objects and counting methods to understanding "base ten" and "doubles" concepts. As you may be aware, many of the state learning standards (e.g., ELA, math, sciences) are designed to show progression of learning and performance expectations.

How to Design Pre-assessments

Although many pre-assessment tools are available, we focus in this chapter on two methods for pre-assessment. First, open-ended scaffolding tasks that have both low-entry questions and high-ceiling questions allow a teacher to see where students stand on a learning progression. Low-entry questions require only short responses and definitive answers, while high-ceiling ones require learners to provide explanations, and have a range of acceptable answers. Open-ended questions can provide you with a glimpse into students' thinking processes, approaches to problem-solving, and writing skills. You will need to construct these items in a well-structured way so that they can elicit particular aspects of students' thinking processes. It is best to use the open-ended format to detect misconceptions, subprocesses where students stumble, or incomplete knowledge that students may have.

Second, surveys or rating scales can be used to gather information about students' motivation, attitudes, interests, and values about specific content, or even toward learning in general. For each assessment method, we outline a design process and provide a graphic example that shows important design features, along with our commentary. First, we suggest that you create pre-assessment tools that include a range of questions, from those that are low-entry to those that are high-ceiling. To assess students' affects or beliefs, we advocate using surveys and questionnaires.

Open-Ended Questions

Open-ended questions are also known as constructed-type or supply-type questions. These questions require students to generate their own responses and can be presented in formats such as fill-in-the-blank, short answers, and essays. The format types of open-ended questions suggest a range or gradient of the extensiveness of responses elicited by the questions (see Figure 2.6). For example, a fill-in-the-blank item elicits a word, a short phrase, or a number. A short-answer item can elicit responses that are a single word, short phrases, a couple of sentences, or a simple math solution. An essay question elicits responses that are more extensive, which gives you another way to assess students' writing skills. We will examine writing essay questions closely in Chapter 4 when we discuss Stage 4 in the CA:SRL framework: formal assessment.

It is important to think about the extensiveness of the short-answer items that you would like to incorporate in the pre-assessment. The decision should be guided by the types of knowledge and skills required and the mental processing involved, so that you can write appropriate questions to measure the various complexities of learning outcomes. You can think about the responses elicited by the open-ended questions as being on a continuum, from those for which a single-word response is a definitive answer to open-ended questions that require extensive writing and do have not definitive answers. To obtain simple kinds of knowledge (i.e., knowing basic terms and simple steps), we suggest that you use fill-in-the-blank or short-answer questions.

In Figure 2.7, you can see examples of open-ended items in different formats. The *direct-question* format is easier to comprehend than the *completion* format, because it is stated in the form of a question, which is naturally easier to interpret than the completion format, which breaks the flow of a sentence. Therefore, we recommend that you use the direct-question format with younger students, students with special language processing needs, and English or multilingual language learners (ELLs/MLLs). The examples included here all have definitive correct answers and measure learning outcomes at lower DOK levels to see whether students have foundational knowledge. We considered that all the questions measure cognitive processes at DOK level I (recall and reproduce), except question 5, which we consider to be at DOK level II (simple application or two steps of mental processes) and involves simple

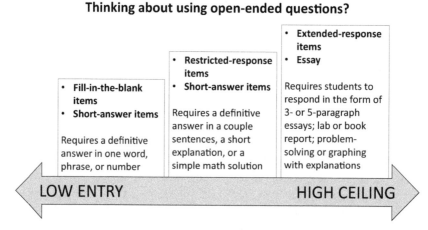

Figure 2.6 Thinking About Using Open-Ended Questions?

Assessing Prior Learning and Beliefs 29

Fill-in-the-blank (science)

1. Directions: For each element, please fill in the symbol associated with it.

Element	**Symbol**
Barium	_____
Calcium	_____
Potassium	_____
Zinc	_____

Direct-question format (social studies)

2. Directions: Please answer the question.
   a) What are the five branches of the U.S. Armed Forces?

Direct-question format (mathematics)

3. Directions: Please answer the question.
   a) How many millimeters make up 1 centimeter?

Fill-in-the-blank (music)

4. Directions: For items *a* and *b*, please write in the correct answer.
   a) The music note (♪) is called a(n) _____ note.
   b) This is a note (♪) you would play for _____ of a beat.

Fill-in-the-blank (mathematics)

5. Directions: Please fill in the blank.
   a) $4 + 6^3 =$ _____

Figure 2.7 Low-Entry Assessment Methods

arithmetic and the order of operations. You may wonder whether, for pre-assessment purposes, question 5 should be written differently so that students can show the steps they used in solving the question. This takes us back to the point we made earlier about using questions for pre-assessment that are low-entry as well as high-ceiling. The rationale for using questions that are low-entry is to provide you with a snapshot of students' foundational knowledge and skills with "guessing free" and relatively easy-to-score responses.

The flexibility of open-ended questions permits you to develop items that can elicit more complex learning outcomes. For pre-assessment, you may like to know how well students can write for informative or explanatory purposes on a given topic; such types of writing cut across grade levels (upper elementary and middle school). You may want to know the extent to which students can write clearly and convey their ideas in a logical manner before you begin the unit on developing students' use of evidence, precision of language, and depth of written vocabulary. For the pre-assessment, you may use open-ended questions that provide students with opportunities to show their knowledge of writing and their writing skills in more structured ways. We can write items similar to those of several items in Figure 2.7 to afford students ways to be explicit about their mental processes, as we demonstrate in Figure 2.8.

The purpose of using open-ended questions that show an increasing demand on mental processes is to demonstrate the question formats' flexibility. The questions in Figure 2.8 measure

Social Studies

1. Directions: Please answer to the best of your current knowledge.
   a. How is the function of the Army different from that of the Marine Corps?

Mathematics

2. Directions: Please answer to the best of your current knowledge.
   a. Comparing 5 millimeters to 1 centimeter, explain which is larger.

Music

3. Directions: For items *a* and *b*, please explain your answer or show the steps of your work.
   a. For 4/4 time, how are a quarter note and an eighth note different?
   b. For 4/4 time, what do a quarter note and an eighth note look like?

Mathematics

4. Directions: Please answer the question and show the steps of your work.
   a. How would you solve $4 + 6^3$?

Figure 2.8 Measuring More Complex Thinking

more complex cognitive processes than those in Figure 2.7, although they address similar content. Questions 1a, 2a, and 3a involve making comparisons and providing explanations. Question 4a asks students to show how. The music-related questions measure not only students' recognition of the names of the music notes, but also their ability to draw representations of the notations and compare them.

It is important to note that we also modify the directions for how to answer questions when we modify questions to measure more complex mental processes involved in a topic. Students should be made aware that the focus of the answers is not just to provide a simple response, but to "show their work" or their thinking process. It is never appropriate or professional to conduct any assessment without clear directions. Even though students have countless encounters with "fill in the bubble" or "circle the correct answer" before they get to your class, it is good assessment practice to make explicit your directions and expectations. Assessment for learning should be high quality at every step of the process. To summarize this section in relation to designing short-answer questions for pre-assessment, Figure 2.9 provides a list of guidelines.

Rating Scales

Another pre-assessment tool that may be valuable to you is survey methods, particularly rating scales. The rationale for the introduction of survey methods is to familiarize you with another data collection tool. This tool is useful for gathering students' motivational or attitudinal information. Surveys are often used to collect data about people's perspectives of a phenomenon, attitudes or opinions about an issue/event, or frequency of certain behaviors. In this stage of pre-assessment, which aligns with Zimmerman's (2000) SRL phase of *forethought*, we focus on gaining information about students' self-perceptions about learning before beginning formal instruction.

> • Structure the item so that the correct response is a single or definitive phrase.
> • Place blanks in the fill-in-the-blank item in the margin for direct questions or near the end of ones that are incomplete statements.
> • For incomplete statements, use only one or at most two blanks.
> • Make sure the blanks for all the items are equal in length, so that the length of the blank does not provide a clue for the length of the response sought.
> • For numeric answers, indicate the degree of precision you expect and the units (e.g., feet and inches) in which they are to be expressed.

Figure 2.9 Guidelines for Writing Short-Answer Items

Most of the construct that we attempt to measure in CA is students' learning that ties to the contents of curricula. However, students' beliefs, attitudes, and behaviors influence their academic choices and performance (Wigfield & Cambria, 2010; Lin-Siegler, Ahn, Chen, Fang, & Luna-Lucero, 2016). From the perspective of cognitive theorists, students' *self-efficacy* has been shown to consistently influence their academic performance outcomes across various content areas, such as math, reading, writing, sciences, and sports (McPherson & McCormick, 2006; Moritz, Feltz, Fahrbach, & Mack, 2000; Parajes, Britner, & Valiante, 2000; Pajares & Valiante, 2006; Pintrich & De Groot, 1990; Schunk, 2003; Usher & Parajes, 2009). Self-efficacy refers to a learner's beliefs about their capability to complete or master an undertaking and bring it to a desirable outcome (Bandura, 1997). When encountering a novel learning situation, highly self-regulated learners not only analyze the target task, but also assess their capability to complete it. Students who are less self-regulated and poorly performing students are less likely to think about the capabilities, skill sets, and strategies required to complete the task.

We suggest that you can promote students' awareness of their capabilities and knowledge/ skills by surveying them on their self-efficacy beliefs. Self-efficacy can be operationalized as one's beliefs about their capabilities in terms of "confidence of can dos." (Bandura, 1997). To measure self-efficacy, we suggest that you take the SLOs and modify them into question format. The rating should then correspond to the qualitative descriptions of each numeric quantity.

Figure 2.10 presents a sample rating scale of self-efficacy based on SLO 2 in Figure 2.3 (content: math; topic: functions). Bandura (2006) provided a set of guidelines for designing measures of self-efficacy that use a scale from 0–100. For research purposes, we would adhere to the guideline of using 0–100 categories on the rating scale. For pre-assessment purposes, however, we suggest using considerably fewer categories on the rating scale: from four to seven (Spector, 1992). When a rating scale contains too few points (such as two or three), the data differentials are insufficient. On the other hand, a rating scale that contains too many points (eight or more), makes it difficult to come up with qualitative descriptors for each point on the scale. After all, it is necessary to make sure that the points on a rating scale have clear and unambiguous labels. At times, it is necessary to provide a middle category (i.e., neutral) on the rating scale, if you suspect that students may be "on the fence" about their beliefs, views, or interests toward a situation or experience, or prior exposure to it.

When drafting survey questions, you want to make sure that the questions are measuring the construct you want them to, and not another construct. Questions must have the same meaning to all respondents. To ensure that the survey questions are clearly interpreted by

32   Section I Chapter 2

your students, we suggest that you pilot your survey questions before using them. The other option is to adapt good quality or published survey questions. Why re-invent the wheel? If you are going to adapt existing survey questions, be a critical and conscientious consumer. Survey questions can be written in both open-ended and closed-ended format. For CA purposes, we do not suggest using open-ended questions to measure students' attitudes, frequency of behaviors, or beliefs. Our reasons for this are that open-ended questions elicit a variety of responses that require extensive time to analyze, while pre-assessment should be purposeful and brief. For pre-assessment, we suggest that you draft closed-ended questions with corresponding rating scales. Try to write both positive and negative questions that measure the same construct. A caution about using negative questions: Negatively stated questions add complexity that students need to interpret when the accompanying rating scale contains descriptions that are polar opposites of each other (e.g., agree/disagree; completely/not at all). A "double-negative" interpretation is harder to process for younger students. Figure 2.11 shows some guidelines for drafting survey questions.

SLO 2: Given function graphs, students will be able to identify specific key features (intercepts, zeros, maxima, minima, symmetries).

Directions: For each question, circle one number that represents your confidence level.

Questions	Rating Scale			
	1 not at all	**2** not so much	**3** somewhat	**4** highly
On a function graph, I am ___ confident that I can identify the intercepts.	1	2	3	4
On a function graph, I am ___ confident that I can identify the maxima point.	1	2	3	4
On a function graph, I am ___ confident that I can identify if the graph is symmetrical.	1	2	3	4

Figure 2.10 Pre-assessment of Student Self-Efficacy

- Do not use jargon. Use words that are easily understood by all of your students. For example, **avoid** "How high is your self-efficacy?" Instead, ask "On a scale of 0–100% confidence, how confident are you that you can . . .?"
- Present one clear idea in each question. For example, **avoid** "How important is it for you to set study goals, keep track of your homework grades, and ask for help from your teachers, if needed?" Separate a question like this into three separate questions.
- Be specific: present the idea explicitly in the question. For example, **avoid** "How do you study at home?" Instead, ask about a specific behavior, for instance, "How often do you refer to your textbook when you study at home?"
- Do not use a personal leading question. Present the question as neutrally as possible. For example, **avoid** "To what extent do you like my social studies class?" Ask instead, "How much do you enjoy learning social studies?"

Figure 2.11 Guidelines for Drafting Survey Questions

Checklists

Checklists are easy to construct and a good method for recording whether a behavior/skill is present or absent. Unlike rating scales, checklists do not record variations or degrees of a construct or behavior. For pre-assessment, checklists are useful for gathering information about students' prior exposure to learning, particularly if the content is presented in a developmental progression of skills. Teachers can do a quick check on whether students have pre-requisite skills, or students can fill in the checklists to provide self- and pre-assessment. Checklists are also useful if the target behavior or performance can be broken down into a sequence or smaller sub-behaviors. Since checklists are easier than rating scales to use and interpret the results, we show you a checklist for the teacher to record students' behaviors, as well as one for students to self-assess their prior skills (see Figure 2.12). Please note that you should use a checklist if and only if the quality of the behavior is not an important factor to document. Do not use checklists like rating scales, as if they had multiple levels of variation. We have observed

Purpose (Teacher Form): To assess whether each student can do the basic five positions (ballet). **Directions**: Check YES or NO to indicate whether the skill has been demonstrated.		
Name of the student:		
The student can do . . .	*YES*	*NO*
1st position		
2nd position		
3rd position		
4th position		
5th position		
Purpose (Student Form): For the student to self-assess whether they can do the basic five positions (ballet). **Directions**: Check YES or NO to indicate whether you think you have demonstrated the skill.		
My name is:		
I can do . . .	*YES*	*NO*
1st position		
2nd position		
3rd position		
4th position		
5th position		

Figure 2.12 Checklists for Measuring Desired Behaviors

countless times when teachers render "check pluses/minuses" on students' homework assignments to indicate degrees of quality. If variation of quality is important to note, you can modify the checklists into rating scales or other scoring systems, which would provide various degrees of quality.

We also advocate the use of checklists to help students set goals. Goal setting (Zimmerman, 2000) is an important process in the forethought phase of SRL, which requires learners to take a complicated task and divide it into small chunks of tasks. Goal setting refers to intentional identified learning outcomes and standards that serve as a comparison for one's subsequent actions. Research has shown that students who are self-regulated are likely to set useful goals – goals that are specific, moderately challenging, and proximal – when they first encounter a target task or learning situation (Zimmerman, 2002). By setting goals, students apply a set of standards they can compare to their current performance. Engaging in the comparison process throughout learning serves as one of the monitoring processes. Further, the setting of goals directs and guides students' attention and effort in the subsequent phase of the SRL cycle:

SLO: Without using their notes, students will be able to deliver an oral presentation in Spanish.					
My name:					
Sub-goals	Descriptions	YES	Date of Completion	NO	Planned Date of Completion
1.	Have I identified a topic?				
2.	Has the topic been approved by the teacher?				
3.	Have I drafted an outline in Spanish?				
4.	Does the outline include all the components specified by the teacher?				
5.	Have I written the introduction?				
6.	Have I included at least 3 examples?				
7.	Have I included details for each example?				
8.	Have I included a summary section?				
9.	Is the summary linked to the purpose stated in the introduction?				
10.	Have I check the grammar and vocabulary for accuracy?				
11.	Have I timed myself to make sure the presentation is within the timeframe?				
12.	Have I practiced the presentation at least 3 times?				

Figure 2.13 Support for Student Goal Setting at DOK Level 4

performance. Although self-set goals are more powerful and effective in sustaining students' commitment than are externally imposed goals, many students do not have the know-how to set specific, moderately challenging, and proximal goals. Therefore, we suggest that you give students the option to self-set learning goals. Students with special needs may need your particular assistance in setting appropriate and challenging goals. You can model how to set goals for the students who need your support. When you provide options for students to either set their own goals or have you assist in goal-setting, you practice shared regulation of learning and assessment.

In pre-assessment, goal setting requires us to think about how to articulate a complex SLO or learning outcome (at DOK level 3 or 4) into a coherent set of sub-goals, and to design appropriate assessment tools which will be used to measure the SLO. It is helpful, at this juncture, to think about the developmental sequences of typical progress in understanding the main concept in the unit. To help students initially set effective learning goals, you can show students what process goals are (focusing on using strategies to attain the goal). You can switch to an outcome goal (focusing on completion or the end-product of the goal) when the task becomes more familiar or automatic to students. Figure 2.13 shows an example of goal setting accompanied by a checklist, which could be used at multiple checkpoints during the learning and assessment cycle.

External Resources for Pre-assessment Design

If you have access to pre-assessment materials developed by publishers or given to you by your schools, we suggest that you examine them and adapt the items carefully. We advocate that you evaluate the materials by identifying the learning goals and SLOs that are appropriate for your classrooms, gauging the quality of the pre-made assessment questions, and making changes as needed. If you are designing your own pre-assessments, we suggest that you consult the professional standards of your content area, check with your local school curriculum guides, and then think about how to design the pre-assessment in a way that really works to gather information about your students.

References

Bandura, A. (1997). *Self-efficacy: The exercise of control*. New York, NY: W. H. Freeman and Company.

Bandura, A. (2006). Guide for constructing self-efficacy scales. *Self-Efficacy Beliefs of Adolescents*, 5, 307–337.

Chastenay, P. (2016). From geocentrism to allocentrism: Teaching the phases of the moon in a digital full-dome planetarium. *Research in Science Education*, 46, 43–77.

Durkin, K., & Rittle-Johnson, B. (2012). The effectiveness of using incorrect examples to support learning about decimal magnitude. *Learning and instruction*, 22, 206–214.

Eryilmaz, A. (2002). Effects of conceptual assignments and conceptual change discussions on students' misconceptions and achievement regarding force and motion. *Journal of Research in Science Teaching*, 39(10), 1001–1015.

Heemsoth, T., & Heinze, A. (2016). Secondary school students learning from reflections on the rationale behind self-made errors: A field experiment. *The Journal of Experimental Education*, 84(1), 98–118.

Heritage, M. (2008). *Learning progressions: Supporting instruction and formative assessment*. Paper prepared for the Formative Assessment for Teachers and Students, Washington, DC: State Collaborative on Assessment and Student Standards of the Council of Chief State School Officers.

Hess, K. (2008). *Developing and using learning progressions as a schema for measuring progress*. [online] Retrieved from www.nciea.org/publications/CCSSO2_KH08.pdf

Hobson, S. M. (2008). *Young elementary students' conceptual understandings of lunar phases before and after an inquiry-based and technology-enhanced instructional intervention.* (Doctoral dissertation). Retrieved from https://etd.ohiolink.edu/rws_etd/document/get/osu1227588332/inline

Karsli, F., & Patan, K. K. (2016). Effects of the context-based approach on students' conceptual understanding: "The umbra, the solar eclipse and the lunar eclipse." *Journal of Baltic Science Education, 15*(2), 246–260.

Krathwohl, D. R. (2002). A revision of bloom's taxonomy: An overview. *Theory into Practice, 41*(4), 212–218.

Lin-Siegler, X., Ahn, J. N., Chen, J., Fang, F. A., & Luna-Lucero, M. (2016). Even Einstein struggled: Effects of learning about great scientists' struggles on high school students' motivation to learn science. *Journal of Educational Psychology, 108*, 314–328.

Mager, R. F. (1997). *Preparing instructional objectives* (3rd ed.). Atlanta, GA: The Center for Effective Performance, Inc.

McPherson, G. E., & McCormick, J. (2006). Self-efficacy and music performance. *Psychology of Music, 34*(3), 325–339.

Moritz, S. E., Feltz, D. L., Fahrbach, K. R., & Mack, D. E. (2000). The relation of self-efficacy measures to sport performance: A meta-analytic review. *Research Quarterly for Exercise and Sport, 71*(3), 280–294.

National Research Council. (2001). Knowing what students know: The science and design of educational assessment. In J. Pellegrino, N. Chudowsky, & R. Glaser (Eds.), *Committee on the foundations of assessment.* Washington, DC: National Academy Press.

Parajes, F., Britner, S. L., & Valiante, G. (2000). Relation between achievement goals and self-beliefs of middle school students in writing and science. *Contemporary Educational Psychology, 25*(4), 406–422.

Pajares, F., & Valiante, G. (2006). Self-efficacy beliefs and motivation in writing development. In C. A. MacArthur, S. Graham, & J. Fitzgeral (Eds.), *Handbook of wiring research.* (pp. 158–170). New York, NY: The Guilford Press.

Pintrich, P. R., & De Groot, E. V. (1990). Motivational and self-regulated learning components of classroom academic performance. *Journal of Educational Psychology, 82*, 33–40.

Schunk, D. (2003). Self-efficacy for reading and writing: Influence of modeling, goal setting, and self-evaluation. *Reading and Writing Quarterly, 19*, 159–172.

Spector, P. E. (1992). *Summated rating scale construction: An introduction.* Newbury Park, CA: Sage Publications.

Usher, E. L., & Parajes, F. (2009). Sources of self-efficacy in mathematics: A validation study. *Contemporary Educational Psychology, 34*, 89–101.

Webb, N. (2002, March 28). *Depth-of-knowledge levels for four content areas.* unpublished paper. Retrieved from http://ossucurr.pbworks.com/w/file/fetch/49691156/Norm%20web%20dok%20by%20subject%20area.pdf

Wigfield, A., & Cambria, J. (2010). Students' achievement values, goal orientations, and interest: Definitions, development, and relations to achievement outcomes. *Developmental Review, 30*, 1–35.

Zielinski, S. F. (2017). *From no to yes: The impact of an intervention on the persistence of algebraic misconceptions among secondary school algebra students.* (Doctoral dissertation). Retrieved from https://search.proquest.com/docview/2003245602?pq-origsite=gscholar

Zimmerman, B. J. (2000). Attaining self-regulation: A social cognitive perspective. In M. Boekaerts, P. R. Pintrich, & M. Zeidner (Eds.), *Handbook of self-regulation research, and application.* Orlando, FL: Academic Press.

Zimmerman, B. J. (2002). Becoming a self-regulated learner: An overview. *Theory into Practice, 41*(2), 65–70.

Chapter 3

Multiple Iterations of Learning and Assessment

Once you have set your instructional pace and made appropriate decisions for differentiation, addressing misconceptions and so on, you begin a series of back-and-forth teacher-student interactions, where you and your students engage in learning activities and short bursts of assessment. This is Stage 2, which takes place on an ongoing basis throughout the bulk of your instruction and students' engagement in learning. You can see this iterative process of feedback and decision-making illustrated with the double-headed arrow within this stage, as shown in Figure 3.1.

While assessments are frequent in Stage 2, they are relatively informal. The assessment evidence elicited and collected during this stage should not be used evaluatively (see Chapter 5). Small snapshots of student progress where the information can be quickly turned around to guide your teaching are often more useful for decision-making while instruction is ongoing than are lengthy tests or projects. You glean a large amount of information about your students' learning progress at this stage through multiple iterations and multiple short bursts of individualized or group assessments.

In Stage 2, we incorporate metacognitive processes involved in the *performance* phase of Zimmerman's SRL model, which guides the CA:SRL framework. In the SRL model, performance includes many subprocesses that happen simultaneously. During performance, learners who are highly self-regulated use self-control strategies and engage in self-monitoring to make headway in their learning and ascertain what strategies are effective. In your assessments, you can encourage students to use SRL learning strategies such as drawing diagrams, forming imagery or mental pictures, and making concept maps. You can set short deadlines that help them to manage their completion time or provide guidelines for when these tasks should be completed, how to complete them, and from whom to seek help. You can provide students with self-recording devices such as charts, checklists, and journals so that they monitor their learning progress.

Zimmerman's theory of SRL contains concepts of self-control and self-monitoring at the performance phase. Although Zimmerman emphasized the importance of monitoring one's performance progress and use of learning strategies in his SRL model, we consider that the concept of metacognitive awareness could be better articulated. Hence, as we mentioned in Chapter 1, we develop our articulation of this phase of SRL using Nelson and Naren's (1994) theory of metacognition, because it includes both control and monitoring processes that regulate the flow of information between cognitive and metacognitive levels.

Stage 2 is interactive, with a focus on students' individual learning, learning among peers, and learning with you. The interactive nature of Stage 2 is particularly emphasized in current literature on assessment *for* learning (AfL), in terms of promoting both student self-assessment and peer assessment (Black, 2013). Having students reflect continuously on their work and periodically review their records propels them to self-correct their performance and adjust

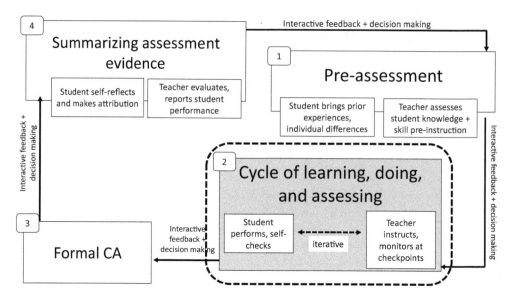

Figure 3.1 Four-stage CA:SRL Framework: SRL Performance Within the Cycle of Learning, Doing, and Assessing

their use of learning strategies or seek assistance. The back-and-forth between learning and assessment in Stage 2 ensures that students are moving closer to meeting their learning targets. In other words, student learning during Stage 2 involves modifying, growing, and building on their current content knowledge and skills. The *why* of Stage 2 focuses on iteration, or the continuous identification of students' learning strengths and learning gaps, and is both intentional and purposeful.

Through peer assessment and self-assessment processes, learners engage in monitoring their learning and articulating content knowledge and skills through explanations to their peers. Explanation has been linked to learning gains (King, 1998). The quality of the dialogue between learners contributes to these differences in learning. Research has documented that when dyads of students engage in dialogue to actively construct and generate new knowledge by self-explanation, notetaking, or drawing diagrams, such quality dialogue promotes learning (Chi & Menekse, 2015).

Student self-assessment and peer assessment have also been linked to learning through *feedback*. Feedback refers to the information provided by oneself (internal) or communicated to learners by others (external) about their performance or understanding (Hattie & Timperley, 2007). Feedback, internal and external, plays an integral role in Zimmerman's SRL model. Feedback is inseparable from the learning process and is a key catalyst of the regulatory process by connecting how learners and their environments communicate (Bangert-Drowns, Kulik, Kulik, & Morgan, 1991). Research has shown that feedback has a positive effect on student achievement (Bangert-Drowns et al., 1991; Hattie & Timperley, 2007), especially if it informs them how to complete a task or achieve a goal (Kluger & DeNisi, 1996). Thinking about feedback in terms of *process* versus *outcome* feedback can be helpful (Butler & Winne, 1995). *Process* feedback focuses on how learners attempt to complete a task and focuses on the methods and strategies they use to do so. *Outcome* feedback, on the other hand, focuses on how well learners perform, which provides little guidance on how they can change or improve their current performance.

Learning to provide feedback to peers is a way to negotiate conceptual understanding between students. By prompting students to give feedback to their peers, we give them opportunity to co-regulate learning, unearth one another's content knowledge errors, and make suggestions for improvement. Gan and Hattie (2014) found that secondary students who learned to provide feedback to their peers pointed out content knowledge errors and made suggestions for improvement more frequently than did students who were not taught to give feedback. There is also evidence that when students negotiate conceptual understanding through providing feedback to their peers, they better identify their own learning gaps.

Why We Iterate Assessment

You can provide more individualized, differentiated, and better targeted instruction if you continually re-assess and re-appraise student learning as you proceed in your teaching. Stage 1 pre-assessment data guided your initial instructional decisions, but should not determine how or what you teach throughout a whole unit or topic of study. Your pre-assessment provided only a basis on which to build. As you proceed with your teaching plans, you should continually question and re-examine whether students are "getting" the new concepts, skills, and knowledge they need to meet your SLOs. You as a teacher need frequent checkpoints for assessment throughout instruction to re-evaluate whether your lessons within a teaching unit or segment appropriately challenge students, and whether they have acquired effective strategies to meet the larger goals. Challenging intellectual endeavors require students to engage in multiple learning opportunities to get closer to desired outcomes. When students first encounter such challenges, you as a teacher should provide appropriate scaffolds along the way toward achievement that are informed by your constant learning about student needs.

Frequent informal assessment during instruction also allows you to gather multiple pieces of evidence from many sources about student learning. As we said in Chapter 1, your interpretations about student achievement are inferences. Making inferences in Stage 2 requires taking mental steps. These steps involve making inductive generalizations from any single observation to a broader construct. Your interpretations about learning start from the evidence students give you when they perform an assessment task—when they answer an oral question, complete a worksheet, or play a song in music class. The more evidence you obtain about student learning, the more complete your view of their learning will be.

Having collected multiple pieces of evidence, you can check for the *reliability* or consistency of your assessment results and interpretations. Because students are also making inferences about their learning in the four-stage framework, you can add students as a source of information to the evidence you compile. Mentally combining all these streams of evidence, you can make more accurate interpretations of your students' learning, which improves the *validity* or credibility of your inferences about that learning. When you identify consistent trends in your interpretations and can confirm their accuracy, you can be more confident that the decisions you make based on your interpretations are sound. The qualities of reliability and validity of assessment are presented in Chapters 6 and 7.

The quality of your inferences is crucial, because the actions you take based on them lead students into their next experiences. Observing discrepancies between what you expect students to be able to perform and the evidence of their performance triggers metacognitive awareness in your students and shows them that something needs to be done. Moreover, if consistent discrepancies are observed in a student's recordings, they signal that the student needs assistance and you need to intervene. As part of the class norm, you can encourage students to seek peer or teacher assistance when they note discrepancies between their performance outcomes and learning goals—or, if they are able to meet or succeed their goals, you and your students can together set more challenging goals.

Continual Assessment Improves Learning

While students learn through your instruction, they benefit from becoming self-aware of the new learning they are acquiring. They strategize solutions to newly encountered challenges as they meet them and recognize their growth. Student self-awareness in Stage 2 can build from their ideas and forethought in Stage 1. As learning proceeds, you can have your students refer back to their initial self-assessment to evaluate whether they have resolved misconceptions or to re-assess their confidence in meeting the SLOs. They can incorporate new personal objectives that reflect important elements they self-identify during their learning progression.

In Stage 2, students can reap even more strongly the benefits of setting their own goals and clarifying their understanding of the learning objectives and criteria. These benefits increase as instruction proceeds, because the students are constantly gaining more information about themselves in relation to the criteria and can therefore set increasingly accurate goals for themselves. While you have formed an overall hypothesis about the learning progression you expect for students in general (Stage 1), each student as an individual has a slightly unique learning progression, along which you can provide them checkpoints for self-reflection. Learning progressions are like a path through a forest. You want all your students to travel all the way through, so you lay out the clearest, most expeditious path through the forest that you can through your overall instructional planning. Some students will wander, tarry, or take shortcuts, because that is the way they as individuals travel. This is true for all individuals, including those with special learning needs.

Although our examples mostly focus on general education students, your classrooms have students with diverse needs who require differentiated instruction, assessment, and feedback. In the math case study (Chapter 12), the classroom includes students with Individualized Education Programs (IEPs) and English Language Learners (ELLs). There you will see that teachers can administer different complexities of assessment tasks, all measuring the same SLOs, so that all the students have opportunities to be assessed on key concepts in algebra. In addition, the teachers use interactive assessment methods to work with students with IEPs, incorporating more support for students to follow directions and use graphics. Research informs us that connecting graphics/images with verbal explanations and integrating abstract concepts with concrete representations are effective practices that positively impact learning for all students (Pashler et al., 2007).

When you provide checkpoints for students to monitor progress and refine personal goals along the path, you allow them to self-differentiate while maintaining common major objectives. Always remember that while you as a teacher have identified standards and set expectations for students' progress, it is the students themselves who embark on the learning journey. To be successful in their journey, they must begin to take control of their way by monitoring their own performance. To do this, you can help them by giving them ways and times to systematically record their progress and to compare this information to the learning goals you have set. When students actively record their performance and check it against their goals and criteria, they can better see the gap between their actual performance and the desired goals.

Therefore, Stage 2 is an excellent time to incorporate student self- and peer assessment into your classroom practice. When students self-assess their performance and give themselves feedback, they engage in the SRL metacognitive processes of self-monitoring and self-control. Self-assessment activates students' metacognitive awareness and deliberately shifts the learning responsibilities to them. Having students engage in self-assessment helps to ensure that students will internalize their learning and maintain motivation.

Peer assessment and peer feedback also develop a support system among students in the classroom. By learning to give feedback to others, students gain practice in assessing their own work in reference to learning criteria and develop the skills and metacognitive awareness for their own learning. They learn to share regulation and act as resources for one another, which is important for building a classroom community. Moreover, help-seeking is a part of self-regulation. It should be the culture of your classroom to establish continual assessment for learning as a class norm, including seeking help and resources. Students should see that providing feedback to others is as important as receiving feedback, and that they can use it to further their own understanding. Self-regulation is part of individual learning, but shared regulation develops a classroom community with common goals and common values about continuous learning and assessment.

However, self- and peer assessment are skills that must be learned. Self- and peer assessment should be supported by assessment scaffolds during Stage 2. You can help students give themselves and their peers feedback for learning by explicitly teaching them the specific learning goals addressed by assessment tasks and the criteria for success. You can teach them the elements of quality feedback (covered later in this chapter) so that they attune their feedback to task goals instead of superficial judgments. As they practice giving and reflecting on feedback, you co-regulate their responses to feedback, supporting and enhancing self- and peer feedback to develop it into useful information to further learning.

If students who receive self- or peer-feedback do not know how to interpret and use the feedback to move forward with their task, the feedback is superfluous. It can even interfere with learning if students make maladaptive attributions about their work based on the feedback. You should therefore take time during self- or peer assessment to co-regulate their response to their own performance and make appropriate attributions. Self- or peer assessment should be not be done without interactions with you, at least at the start of Stage 2. When your students record and reflect on their own and one another's learning progress, you intentionally look to see how they perceive their learning; you check students' own records and their perceptions against your assessment of their learning progress. If there is any discrepancy, you can use that information as a starting point for discussion with your student to further diagnose their learning needs, strengths, and/or gaps. Self- or peer assessment about how close students are to meeting their learning objectives and desired outcomes informs you and your students about what they need to work on.

What We Assess in This Stage

Instruction in Stage 2 builds from your pre-assessment in Stage 1, which was in turn largely defined by the learning standards and your specific learning objectives for your students. Stage 2 begins when you and your students jointly examine their pre-assessment information and the goals that were set in Stage 1. If Stage 1 pre-assessment results indicate that students have the pre-requisite skills, you can proceed to implement your instruction or modify SLOs to include more challenging ones at higher DOK levels. If the information you obtain indicates that students still need to work on pre-requisite skills or knowledge, make sure that those skills and this knowledge are reinforced during the early stage of instruction in the new content. The first and foremost consideration in deciding what to assess is the SLO and its alignment to the overall standards and expectations for learning. A corollary of this primary consideration is to assess the key ideas and skills related to each SLO. Your time with your students in the classroom is precious. The emphases of your instruction should match the importance of the learning objectives relevant to standards and the curriculum, as well as the primary learning needs of your students.

How to Engage in Iterative Assessment

A Continuum of Methods

To assess learning during Stage 2 instruction, we describe techniques in this chapter that you can use to build systematic questioning and structured observations into your instructional practices. We focus on designing non-interactive selected-response items, both simple and in the form of interpretive exercises, and interactive methods. To continuously support learning and SRL, we describe techniques of self- and peer assessment and show how students can self-monitor and incorporate self- and peer feedback by using simple self-ratings and guided questions about their own perspectives on their task performance. We emphasize the use of assessment evidence as feedback to aid you and your students in monitoring and furthering learning.

You can think about assessment methods as *non-interactive* or *interactive*. Non-interactive assessment methods are tasks and processes that involve only individual learners in providing evidence about learning. When students answer questions by themselves, during quizzes or independent seatwork, they do not interact with their teachers or peers until they have completed the assignment or certain parts of the assignment. Non-interactive assessment tools are those that students respond to on their own. Interactive methods are those that students respond to with others' input, whether teachers or peers. Interactive methods can range from short performances to problem-solving interviews. The core concept underlying these methods is the interaction, or the rapid back-and-forth between multiple individuals in the assessment process.

Although we define each type of method separately, we ask you to think about assessment methods on a continuum of interactivity, rather than in one bucket or another (see Figure 3.2). You can modify almost any non-interactive assessment method to interject dyadic

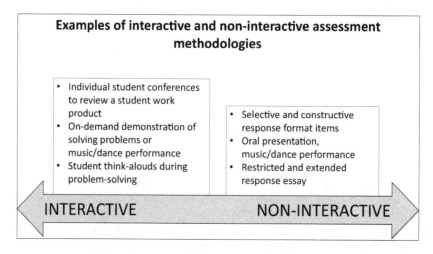

Figure 3.2 Types of Interactive and Non-Interactive Assessments

communication between you and your students or to include an opportunity for peer assessment. The rationale for thinking of the assessment methods used during Stage 2 as being on an interactive and non-interactive continuum is to help you understand that different methods are most suited for different purposes, especially for the different types of information you want to obtain. When choosing a method along this continuum, what should first drive your decisions is alignment with the SLOs that you drafted at the beginning of the unit. For each stage along a learning progression toward meeting an objective, you should choose the type of method that most directly gives you actionable information to help you teach and help your students learn. Each different method has its own advantages and disadvantages. Over the course of time with your students you should expose them to many different methods of assessment. Multiple methods will allow you to look at their thinking and knowledge from different angles and through different lenses.

We will begin with examples and guidance on using non-interactive methods, which may be more familiar to you from your own experiences in K–12 education. Then we'll discuss interactive methods and suggest ways to blend methods to attain the best combination of student SRL and information. In addition to the interactive/non-interactive assessment methods of Stage 2, we will provide examples of self- and peer feedback techniques that you can use as tools for students to monitor their own learning.

Non-interactive Selected-Response Methods

A common type of non-interactive method with which you are undoubtedly familiar is the selected-response method, which includes multiple-choice (M-C) items. When you develop a set of selected-response items as an assessment task to measure SLOs, you should strategically create questions that are highly aligned with the content you and your students have worked on in class. In particular, you should use questions that relate to important content, where your check on student understanding is needed to inform your next instructional steps. The content often should relate to concepts where your prior observations, including information you gathered in Stage 1, showed patterns of misconceptions you have tried to address. Selected-response items can give you rapid information about whether students are set to move forward. We advocate that you draft your own M-C items or modify others to which you have access, because published items may not measure the particular concepts and misconceptions you are concerned about.

There are several selected-response methods, such as true/false, matching exercises, and M-C items. These assessment tools are considered selected-response because students are asked to "select" or "pick" what they recognize or deduce to be the correct or best answer among the choices. In this chapter, we only focus on M-C item writing for its versatility and familiarity to you and your students. M-C items can be used to assess learning at the first level of the DOK framework (recall and reproduction) and at the second DOK level (application of skills and concepts). M-C items that refer to evidence students must interpret or analyze can assess DOK level 3 (strategic thinking and reasoning). For most SLOs that measure complex cognitive processes (DOK level 3) or for any DOK level 4 SLO (extended thinking, making various connections), supply-type items or performance-based tools are more appropriate to collect students' evidence of learning. Complex cognitive processes that require performance-based assessment or extensive supply-type items will be discussed in the next chapter (Chapter 4).

When constructing M-C items, you need to create the following components: (1) directions, (2) the stem, and (3) the choices. We will take you through each component and provide examples.

The directions for M-C items should state clearly how students are supposed to indicate their choice for the correct or best answer, such as by circling the letter. For more formal assessments of upper-grade-level students (Stage 3, Chapter 4), you should indicate in the directions how points are allocated. This is particularly useful when a test consists of multiple sections with different formats of assessment. Such information can be used by students to evaluate how much time they may spend on the M-C item section, as compared to other types of items on the test.

The *stem* and *choices* together compose one M-C item (see Figure 3.3). The stem in an M-C item precedes the list of choices that a student can select. The stem can be stated either as a direct question (example 1) or as an incomplete statement (example 2).

For younger students and English and multilingual language learners (ELL/MLLs), direct question stems are easier to process than are incomplete statement stems. Each stem should be written with one clear and definitive concept in it. A way to check the clarity of a stem is to hide the choices and see whether you can understand what the stem is asking you to do (i.e., without looking at the options). All stems should be stated in a concise manner, without extra words or fluff (see example 3). Extra verbiage, such as the language "They believe that joining the program will motivate them to lose weight and eat healthier" in example 3 is not relevant to solving the problem. Fluff in stems merely makes the item more difficult to comprehend and takes time from the test-takers (especially ELLs), when it is not a learning objective that the given M-C question intends to measure. The stem of an M-C item can be elaborative if it

---

Example 1: Direct question stem

Which of the following is a mammal?
a) Bird
b) Bat*
c) Frog
d) Fish

Example 2: Incomplete statement stem

Granite cools below the surface of the earth, and it is a(n)
a) Igneous extrusive rock
b) Igneous intrusive rock*
c) Sedimentary rock
d) Metamorphic rock

Example 3: Fluffy stem

There are 10 pre-service teachers (3 men and 7 women) in a school of education who recently registered for the college-sponsored weight-loss program. They believe that joining the program will motivate them to lose weight and eat healthier. At the beginning of the program, each was weighed, and the 10 had a mean weight of 139.4 pounds. The mean weight of the 3 men in this group was 180 pounds. What was the mean weight of the 7 women at the beginning of the program?
a) 115.0 pounds
b) 122.0 pounds*
c) 140.0 pounds
d) 159.7 pounds

Figure 3.3 Structures of Multiple-Choice Items

Note: * represents Answer Key

intends to measure a learning objective that requires students to identify, analyze, or interpret information, evidence, or data, but it should not include unnecessary verbiage for students to sift through.

Items with stems that include extensive information and are followed by a set of questions that are related to the same stem are called *interpretive exercises* (see Figure 3.4). Here, we

---

Example 4: Table 1 presents the quiz scores from Ms. Boyle's chemistry class. The maximum score for each quiz is 10 points. The maximum score of the final exam is 100 points.

Directions: Based on the data in Table 1, please answer questions 1, 2, and 3 by circling ONE correct answer per question.

Table 1. Ms. Boyle's Class Test Scores

Student name	Quiz 1	Quiz 2	Quiz 3	Final Exam
Adam	7	6	9	82
Bob	5	6	7	60
Cole	5	5	8	90
Dave	7	6	9	82
Eric	10	4	10	90
Fran	8	6	10	74
Gigi	7	6	9	70
Hanna	5	5	9	90
Iris	9	10	10	90
Jane	7	6	9	72

1. Based on the data in Table 1, which of the three quizzes was hardest for the students?
   a. Quiz 1
   b. Quiz 2
   c. Quiz 3

2. Looking at the final exam scores, what are the mean and the mode for this class?
   a. 78; 82
   b. 80; 90
   c. 82; 74

3. Based on the final exam mean and median, what can you conclude about the distribution?
   a. It is a slightly positively skewed distribution.
   b. It is a slightly negatively skewed distribution.
   c. It is a normal distribution.

Answer key: 1 = b; 2 = b; 3 = b

Figure 3.4 Interpretive Exercises

show you three M-C questions that are related to the same data. With the same data set in Figure 3.4, you could use a set of short-answer questions instead of the M-C items to measure the same learning objective, if you need more evidence of your students' problem-solving processes. Interpretive exercises are excellent ways to measure DOK level 2 (application of skills and concepts).

Please note that DOK is about the complexity of thinking, not the difficulty of an item or question. For example, the following question measures students' recall of vocabulary: "What is the definition of *deceptive*?" Recall is not considered a complex thinking process, and is at a DOK level 1. We can come up with a question that is more difficult but still measures students' recall and is still at DOK level 1: "What is the definition of *guileful*?" More individuals know the definition of *deceptive* than *guileful*, even though both questions measure the same learning objective and address DOK at level 1. The difficulty of an item refers to how many students answer a specific question correctly.

You may wonder how we can then draft questions with various difficulty levels that measure the same SOL or learning objective. To make M-C questions more difficult and yet measure the same SLO, you can vary the options students have to choose from when they respond. This leads us to the discussion of M-C choices.

The *choices* in M-C items are also called *alternatives* or *options*. The correct answer or the best choice in an M-C item is called the *key*, and the remaining choices are called *distractors*, *decoys*, or *foils*. For M-C items, we recommend providing three to five choices. The quality of choices should drive your decision whether to have three, four, or five choices for an item. The more choices that an M-C item contains, the smaller the chances that test-takers can guess the correct answer if all the choices are of high quality.

That said, it is a difficult task to create many plausible choices in an M-C item, and each choice should be plausible; otherwise, the choice is similar to fluff and is wasting space and test-taker time. We suggest that you use three good-quality choices for an M-C item, rather than including poor-quality choices just to make M-C items uniformly contain four or five choices. During your own schooling, you may have answered M-C items for which some options were obviously inaccurate, nonsensical (like "Mickey Mouse"), or comical. Teachers may use nonsensical choices to try to reduce students' testing anxiety or simply to have a uniform number of options for all questions. We hope that you will not include options in M-C items for any purpose other than identifying misconceptions. Since assessment tools are useful in helping us gather student evidence of learning, poorly designed items hinder the assessment process, and compromise the interpretation of evidence. Why waste test-takers' time and increase their cognitive load (i.e., exertion of working memory) by making them read completely implausible choices during any assessment? The distractors of M-C items should be made up of frequently occurring misconceptions so that you can spot them in student learning.

Returning to our earlier discussion on developing items with varying levels of difficulty: modifying choices will make one M-C item more difficult than another, even when measuring the same SOLs at the same DOK level. Examples 1 and 2 in Figure 3.5 show two M-C items that measure the same SLO at DOK level 1. Which example (1 or 2) is more difficult to answer? By changing the choices, the second M-C item is more difficult because the options are barely different in their degree of correctness. The third M-C item, however, is likely to be an easy item, because the state name New Mexico provides a clue that this is a border state. This clue would allow even those students who cannot recall the border states without such clueing to answer correctly.

For an SLO that involves less complex cognitive processes and is fundamental to other SLOs, we suggest that you have several items to measure it or ask similar questions at different levels of difficulty on several nearby occasions. This is a rule of thumb so that you

Multiple Cycles of Learning and Assessment 47

SLO: Students will be able to identify geographic locations of all the states in the U.S. in relation to neighboring countries, without using any references.

DOK Level: I

Example I

Which of these states borders Mexico?
   a. Illinois
   b. Oregon
   c. New York
   d. Texas

Example 2

Which of these states borders Mexico?
   a. Arizona
   b. Florida
   c. Louisiana
   d. Mississippi

Example 3 (easy item due to clueing)

Which of these states borders Mexico?
   a. Alaska
   b. Florida
   c. Hawaii
   d. New Mexico

Figure 3.5 Relative Difficulties of Multiple-Choice Items

will have evidence from multiple items, with varying degrees of difficulty, each targeting the same SLO.

The guidelines that follow should help you in the challenging work of writing high-quality M-C items (see Figure 3.6).

The art and science of creating M-C items has been honed for many years, and we have not created these guidelines, but adapted them from the work of others (see Haladyna, Downing, & Rodriguez, 2002). As with any assessment tool, the first guideline is to make sure that an M-C item is written to measure a learning objective and aligns with an SLO. Again, the stem should be meaningful by itself and should present a definitive problem or question. Avoid using a negatively stated stem, except when you think that significant learning objectives require it. If a negatively stated stem is used, make sure to underline, highlight, or bold the word or words (e.g., **not**, <u>except</u>, or "non-example") to draw attention for your students. Further, avoid negatively stated choices. Double negatives in an M-C item cause confusion for test-takers and add difficulty to interpreting the question.

As for the choices, most importantly, all distractors should be plausible. They should be the most common misconceptions of the specific concept being assessed. Again, having three quality options is enough. Each M-C item should contain only one correct or clearly best answer. Make sure that all the alternatives are grammatically consistent with the stem of the item. As for using options such as "none of the above" or "all of the above," we do *not* advocate using

48   Section I Chapter 3

- Measure a single learning outcome per item, and align to an SLO.
- Contain one central idea in the stem.
- Use positive rather than negative wording in the stem.
- Check the consistency of grammar and the homogeneity of the choices.
- Make sure there is only one correct or clearly best answer.
- Include plausible distractors.
- Avoid using "all of the above" as an option.
- Use cautiously the "none of the above" option.
- Avoid verbal association between the stem and the answer.
- Avoid trick M-C items.
- Use simple vocabulary, unless measuring vocabulary use is the SLO.
- Format M-C items and options vertically rather than horizontally.
- Within a set of M-C items, arrange items in ascending difficulty.
- Vary the positions of the correct answers.

Figure 3.6 Guidelines for Writing Multiple-Choice Items

"all of the above." The reason for this is that if someone recognizes two of the options to be *correct*, they can select "all of the above" as the key, even though they may not know why the remaining options are also correct. Questions that require students to derive their own answer, without using the process of elimination, may include a "none of the above" option (see Figure 3.7 for an example). We further caution you to attend to possible verbal associations between the stem and the key or answer. In other words, make sure that the stem does not contain clues that link to the key or answer. When M-C questions are poorly written, it is difficult to know whether students have selected the right answer because they have the knowledge or because clues embedded in the item reveal the answer.

M-C items have many advantages as an assessment tool. They each have a single correct answer, so they can be objectively scored using a key. They can be used to detect and measure a wide range of learning objectives, from simply knowing facts and recall procedures to interpreting evidence and reasoning. Further, quality M-C items can indicate students' misconceptions and common mistakes, and do not require students to write out and elaborate on their answers, which can minimize the opportunities for less knowledgeable students to "bluff." Finally, M-C items are helpful for the Stage 2 process, because the distractors that students select, if carefully chosen, may provide you with insight into the reasons that students are having difficulties and the misconceptions they hold.

As with any assessment tool, M-C has certain limitations. M-C items do not require students to express their own ideas or supply their solutions. Poorly written M-C items can end up measuring trivial knowledge. Finally, because each M-C item contains one option that is the key, more thoughtful and academically advanced students may think the key is too simplistic for the answer and choose something else; in other words, students can over-analyze options because the options in M-C items are stated in short sentences, phrases, or words, without elaborated explanations. To check whether M-C options function as intended, we recommend that you conduct item analysis to check the difficulty level and discrimination index. We discuss the concepts and process of checking the difficulty levels of M-C items and the discrimination index in Chapter 4. Some publishers include item difficulty in their M-C items, so you can use the difficulty levels as a guide for selecting the appropriate items for your own classroom use. If you are adapting M-C items written by other teachers or even by professionals, you should

---

Example 1

If $x = (1, 2, \text{and } 3)$, what is $\sum(9 + x)^2 = ?$
   a. 41
   b. 225
   c. 365
   d. 1,089
   e. None of the above

Example 2

If $x = (1, 2, \text{and } 3)$, what is $\sum(9 + x^2) = ?$
   a. 41
   b. 225
   c. 365
   d. 1,089
   e. None of the above

Figure 3.7 Use of "None of the Above" as a Key or Plausible Distractor

evaluate them using the same guidelines as you would your own and make sure they strongly relate to your own SLOs and the misconceptions your own students may hold.

Interactive Methods

Interactive assessment probes into students' thought processes, which we may not be able to observe via other forms of assessment. For example, you can use a structured one-on-one interview to ask students to describe the thinking behind the statements they made on open-ended response to a question about a process or concept. We say this is a structured interview because the student has their work in front of them, and you are purposefully using questioning to gather evidence related to the SLO you were assessing with the task. During the interview, you can first observe what the student does, verbally and/or non-verbally, so you can verify whether their thinking processes are conceptually and procedurally appropriate. You can ask the student to explain the reasoning behind the way they answered the question.

A strong advantage of interactive assessment over any other type is that through use of this method you can identify and address learning challenges as they occur. Then, you can demonstrate, encourage, and adjust the behaviors that students are expected to perform. If a student demonstrates a misconception, you have an on-the-spot teaching opportunity to give them prompts. What is a prompt? Prompting may begin with a simple reminder of the context in which the material was previously learned. If further support is needed, you can then provide scaffolding prompts, followed by example prompts (see Figure 3.8). Prompts can be stated as questions or direct statements. We suggest that you state prompts in question form when possible and focus on the learning goals of the task, uses of learning strategies, and self-regulation.

Several iterations of interactive assessment, with immediate instructional responses, promote learning matched to student's individual needs (i.e., differentiation). Such individualized interactions also build student-teacher relationships. Further, interactive methods promote SRL by giving students opportunities to see and hear their own thinking, cognitive processes, and problem-solving strategies. Problem-solving in the moment raises student self-awareness.

50   Section I Chapter 3

Recap prompts

These questions or statements serve as a bridge between what students did or did not learn before, and where they get stuck while solving problems or answering questions.
- "Remember the rules about computing the circumference."
- "How would you add details to ...?"
- "Do you remember when you worked on a similar question in the homework?"
- "Can you recall the sequence of events we discussed in class regarding the impetus of event ...?"

Scaffolding prompts

These questions and statements serve to provide more support than just reminders by posing questions that target key elements or highlight the connects of the tasks.
- "Think about how this ... and that ... are similar or different."
- "Can you find ...? Then can you now do ...?"
- "Can you find the key words that suggest multiplication? Which numbers needed to be multiplied?"

Example prompts

These questions and statements serve to demonstrate and model the work that students need to do. Students can use one of the teacher's examples or create their own examples with their teacher's help.
- "I will show you how to do ... to get you started. What step do you think is next?"
- "Why don't you use phrases from ... to describe your characters? Try to say it this way ..."
- "Let's draw a structure of.... Then you can add detail with ... to the structure."

Figure 3.8 Question and Statement Prompts

However, interactive assessments are a time-consuming process, mostly because the number of students we can work with interactively and pay attention to is inherently small compared to the number we can effectively address through non-interactive assessment methods.

Refer back to Figure 3.2, which lists examples of interactive assessment tools that you can use with your students. For example, you may use a simple, quick interactive performance assessment in a music class for the following SLO: "Having heard a basic rhythm pattern, students will be able to perform the pattern themselves." You can show students a pattern through clapping (c c c x c c c x c c x c c x) and have them repeat what they heard by clapping the pattern. You will know immediately whether students can repeat and show you the rhythm pattern. A similar task in a language class for non-native speakers would be to have students individually come to your table and engage in a quick conversation in the language of instruction. In a unit of study in science, you might set up a station in the classroom where each student weighs an object on a triple beam balance while you observe them and ask them questions about their process.

For more in-depth interactive assessment, we suggest that you sample students or small groups, making sure that you have a chance to interactively assess each individual at some point over the course of the unit. A think-aloud interview is a very useful method for interactive assessment. With this method, you ask a student to "think aloud" while they solve a problem, for instance, $218 + 888 = x$. First, you simply observe how they use various strategies to solve the problem. They may verbally tell you or show you on paper how they approach solving this problem. If, during this interactive assessment episode, you notice that the student can arrive at the right answer but does not provide any explanations, the method allows you to probe and ask students to show you in their own words or on paper—using graphics or both—to provide explanations. Asking for verbal elaboration helps you see whether students have generalized concepts underlying the procedures they follow. Their graphics help you see how they organize knowledge. When a student runs into a wall, you may give them prompts as shown in Figure 3.8. However, before you give prompts, give students time to think and share their thoughts with you, instead of being too quick to provide prompts, cues, or hints, or in any way re-teach or show them how to answer the question.

Self- and Peer Assessment

Self-assessment and peer assessment processes in the classroom can be effective learning and assessment tools that provide feedback to support students' monitoring of their learning progress in Stage 2. Self-assessment functions as a self-monitoring and self-controlling mechanism for students' learning and performance progress, with an emphasis on the "self." Figure 3.9 presents general guidelines and suggestions for implementing self-assessment in this stage.

Note that students can participate in setting criteria on which to self-assess. This is an important and perhaps unique advantage of self-assessment. The learning goals and criteria for self-assessment purposes can be flexible. More advanced students may be ready to set their own criteria more independently, while others may adapt pre-determined learning goals and criteria. At some point, students who have become highly self-regulated may even be ready to set their own learning goals and define how and when they will show evidence of their achievement. Individualized learning goals or criteria are expected to vary among students, according to their individual challenges.

For students:	For teachers:
• Review your work *without* making any judgments. • Define the criteria by which you are going to assess your own work. Consult with your teacher, if you're unsure whether the criteria are appropriately stated or challenging enough for you. • Compare your work against the rubric or criteria without making a judgment. • Keep a record of your progress by using a checklist, journal book, graph, etc. • Review your performance progress periodically with your teacher. • Reflect on your records and think about what is next for your learning.	• Be selective about the explicit aspect(s) of students' learning that they should self-assess. • Co-define the criteria with the students; students can compare these criteria against their work. If students self-define their learning criteria, make sure you have a copy of those criteria. • Teach students explicitly how to apply and use the rubric and criteria. • Make sure students record their performance and periodically reflect on self-assessment data. • Provide enough time for revision after self-assessment. • Remind students that self-assessment is not self-evaluation, and that judgment is inappropriate during this stage. • Do not count self-assessment data toward students' grades.

Figure 3.9 Guidelines for Implementing Self-Assessment

52   Section I Chapter 3

Regarding self-assessment, many students may accurately self-assess in comparison to criteria but not be aware of the next steps they will need to make further progress, and thus not be able to give high-quality self-assessment. They may also make attributions about their own performance that impede further learning; for instance, they may attribute lack of progress to low intelligence. If you ask students to consider how or why they ran into performance problems on an assessment, you should review these carefully and be prepared to discuss any problematic attributions with individual learners.

Students can use rubrics, checklists, or rating scales to refer to when they self-assess. Formats for checklists and rating scales were shown in Chapter 2. In Figure 3.10, we include an example of a guided questionnaire that students complete in order to self-assess their writing in a high school English class. Please note that not every learning goal and criteria of high school

---

Purposes: The purposes of this self-assessment are to have you reflect on and examine your essay and think about how to improve your writing.

Directions:
Step 1: Rate your work on each of the writing components from 1 (not well done) to 5 (very well done).
Step 2: Answer the questions A through G in complete sentences. Please record your answers on a separate sheet of paper.
Step 3: Date and keep your records. You will be reviewing your records from various dates.

Step 1

_____ *Thesis Statement, Introduction, and Argument:* Did my essay catch the reader's attention? Did it have a strong argument/thesis statement?
_____ *Clarity:* Overall, was this essay clear? Was it easy for the reader to understand what I was trying to say?
_____ *Evidence:* Did I use evidence to support my ideas? Were these the best examples to support my argument?
_____ *Organization and Structure:* Was my essay divided into paragraphs? Did each paragraph have a purpose that helped to support my argument?
_____ *Editing and Proofreading:* Was this essay proofread? Did I take the time and effort to correct the simple errors and misspellings that detract from the reader's experience?

Step 2

A. Which writing component did you score yourself highest in? Why did you give it a high score?
B. Which writing component did you score lowest in? Why did you give it a low score?
C. If peer assessment and feedback were provided, read your peer's comments on your essay; what did they have to say about my essay?
D. If peer assessment and feedback were provided, what do you think about your peer's comments? Do you have any questions for them?
E. Overall, do you think your essay was assessed fairly by your peers? Were their comments consistent with your own assessment of your essay?
F. After you have assessed your own essay and reviewed the rubric and writing guidelines, what do you think you might you have done differently in this essay?
G. What do you want to improve upon in your writing during this essay unit?

Figure 3.10 Example of Self-Assessment in High School Essay Writing

writing is on this self-assessment sheet. What you decide about the learning and writing needs of your students should govern what you include on the self-assessment sheet. Further, you may want to add a row for students to name their own writing component under Step 1, to allow students to self-differentiate according to their perceptions of their own needs and with individualized guidance from you.

Peer assessment and peer feedback help students see learning criteria through others' eyes. Peer assessment is like teacher assessment in that feedback comes from an external source, but quite unlike teacher assessment in that peers are working along similar learning progressions and can relate with each other in social-emotional ways that you as a teacher cannot. Peer assessment is also quite different from self-assessment. While self-assessment is a within-individual cognitive activity, peer feedback shifts students' responsibility for learning: they learn not only for themselves but to help others to learn. During Stage 2, students are actively engaged in a classroom community. In recent years, practitioners and researchers in the field of education have routinely advocated the inclusion of peer assistance as a supplemental tool for instruction and as a way to provide additional feedback to learners (Topping, 2013). Research has shown that when students are asked to explain their understanding to others (i.e., teach others), such overt action and covert cognitive processes make their explanations "stick" to themselves and improve performance (Chi, de Leeuw, Chiu, & LaVancher, 1994; Dunlosky, Rawson, Marsh, Nathan, & Willingham, 2013; Wong, Lawson, & Keeves, 2002).

Methods for peer assessment and feedback are similar to the assessment format for self-assessment, with a few distinctions. The criteria should be the same for all students in your classroom, unless some have particularly differentiated needs, in which case you should consult the special education or ELL teacher you work with about how best to structure peer assessment when general students may not be aware of special needs. Even with differentiation, you should make the objective and the criteria for success explicit to the class, and show examples of what various qualities of work look like.

Peer assessment is also interactive, and you as a teacher will need to explicitly teach students how to provide feedback to their peers. Students must learn that good feedback is focused on learning and is respectful to the individual receiving the feedback, at all levels of performance, or you risk a lack of trust in the classroom. For this reason, you may want to insert peer assessment gradually into your classroom routines, rather than starting peer assessment at the beginning of the year when your classroom culture has not been established.

In Figure 3.11, we provide suggestions and guidelines for you and your students to provide peer feedback. We urge you to state these or similar guidelines clearly and review them with all students before setting them loose. After peers give feedback, we advocate asking the following three questions to check whether students perceived that the feedback they received was adequate: "Is that enough help or information?", "Is the information/feedback clear to you?", and "Do you know what to do next?" These questions basically allow students to give feedback on feedback. In fact, you really should ask students to respond to your own feedback this way as well. Receivers of feedback need to be able to use the information to help them move forward with their learning.

Blending Methods

You take a two-pronged approach to Stage 2 assessment when you combine non-interactive and interactive methods. Because the bulk of instruction occurs in Stage 2, it is critical for you to have an in-depth understanding of your students' learning, changes in their conceptual perceptions, and skills acquisition. Even though non-interactive assessment tools elicit and

For peer reviewers:	For teachers:

• Read through your peer's work carefully, without making any interpretations.
• Make sure you understand the components in the rubric and criteria.
• Compare your peer's work with the rubric and criteria (only make comparison if you have completed guidelines 1 and 2).
• Do not judge (don't say "that's bad work"); instead:
  • Describe what you see or read
  • Ask questions for clarifications or explanations
  • Make specific suggestions
  • Refer to the rubric or criteria
• Ask your peer if your suggestions are clear to them for moving forward to the next step.
• Ask the teacher for support if neither of the peers can move forward in the process.
	• Be selective about what aspect of the student work should be assessed.
	• Have a set of guidelines for the students before engaging in peer assessment.
	• Go over the rubric and criteria with the class.
	• Teach students explicitly how to apply and use the rubric and criteria.
	• Show a couple of peer-feedback examples to demonstrate to the class the appropriate questions or comments to post to peers.
	• Remind students that peer assessment and providing peer feedback is not evaluation or making judgments about their peers' work.
	• Allow enough time for students to engage in peer assessment and give them opportunities to reflect on the feedback they receive.

Figure 3.11 Guidelines for Peer Feedback

measure student learning objectives, it is unlikely that you can form an accurate picture of students' conceptions of the content until you have a chance to interact with them and hear or observe them through conversations and observations. Scores on M-C items or short-answer questions generally give you information on whole-class trends, but not the in-depth information you need to address individual learners' needs and differentiate. When you interact with your students during an assessment process, you can clarify your interpretations of student learning and make adjustments in your teaching at the individual level.

When you combine methods, you can start at the non-interactive end, examine the evidence, and then follow up with interactive methods. This approach to combining methods means that you will end up using evidence elicited from a non-interactive method to guide the next step of assessment and instruction through interactive assessment. Imagine that you regularly administer a brief in-class assessment with a few M-C items (perhaps administered through technology, see Chapter 9). You see that several students exhibit the same pattern of error on repeated occasions. You then can use a structured interview with each of these students to ask them to demonstrate how they answer a question or solve a problem related to the same content. Multiple iterations of differentiated assessment and quick instructional responses may be necessary to help these individuals move along the learning progression.

Or you can go the other way around. You may wish to do on-the-spot interactive observations of student performance in the laboratory, during arts practice, or during group work, questioning each student or student group and making notes. When you are satisfied through multiple, brief interactions that each student has had an opportunity to learn and that you've appropriately differentiated instruction for their individual needs, you may find that a checkpoint in the form of a set of M-C items is a good way to obtain evidence about how the class as a whole is progressing.

References

Bangert-Drowns, R. L., Kulik, C. C., Kulik, J. A., & Morgan, M. T. (1991). The instructional effect of feedback in test-like events. *Review of Educational Research, 61*, 213–238.

Black, P. (2013). Formative and summative aspects of assessment: Theoretical and research foundations in the context of pedagogy. In J. H. McMillan (Ed.), *Sage handbook of research on classroom assessment* (pp. 167–178). London: Sage Publications.

Butler, D. L., & Winne, P. H. (1995). Feedback and self-regulated learning: A theoretical synthesis. *Review of Educational Research, 65*, 245–281.

Chi, M. T. H., de Leeuw, N., Chiu, M. H., & LaVancher, C. (1994). Eliciting self-explanations improves understanding. *Cognitive Science, 18*, 439–477.

Chi, M. T. H., & Menekse, M. (2015). Dialogue patterns that promote learning. In L. B. Resnick, C. Asterhan, & S. N. Clarke (Eds.), *Socializing intelligence through academic talk and dialogue* (pp. 263–274). Washington, DC: AERA.

Dunlosky, J., Rawson, K. A., Marsh, E. J., Nathan, M. J., & Willingham, D. T. (2013). Improving students' learning with effective learning techniques: Promising directions from cognitive and educational psychology. *Psychological Science in the Public Interest, 14*, 4–58.

Gan, M. J. S., & Hattie, J. (2014). Prompting secondary student' use of criteria, feedback specificity and feedback levels during an investigative task. *Instructional Science, 42*, 861–878.

Haladyna, T. M., Downing, S. M., & Rodriguez, M. C. (2002). A review of multiple-choice item-writing guidelines for classroom assessment. *Applied Measurement in Education, 15*(3), 309–333.

Hattie, J., & Timperley, H. (2007). The power of feedback. *Review of educational research, 77*(1), 81–112.

King, A. (1998). Transactive peer tutoring: Distributing cognition and metacognition. *Educational Psychology Review, 10*, 57–74.

Kluger, A. N., & DeNisi, A. (1996). The effects of feedback interventions on performance: A historical review, a meta-analysis, and a preliminary feedback intervention theory. *Psychological Bulletin, 119*(2), 254–284.

Nelson, T. O., & Narens, L. (1994). Why investigate metacognition? In J. Metcalfe & A. P. Shimamura (Eds.), *Metacognition: Knowing about knowing* (pp. 1–25). Cambridge, MA: The MIT Press.

Pashler, H., Bain, P., Bottge, B., Graesser, A., Koedinger, K., McDaniel, M., & Metcalfe, J. (2007). *Organizing instruction and study to improve student learning (NCER 2007–2004).* Washington, DC: National Center for Education Research, Institute of Education Sciences, U.S. Department of Education. Retrieved from http://ncer.ed.gov.

Topping, J. K. (2013). Peer as a source of formative and summative assessment. In J. H. McMillan (Ed.), *SAGE handbook of research on classroom assessment* (pp. 395–412). Thousand Oaks, CA: SAGE Publications.

Wong, R. M. F., Lawson, M. J., & Keeves, J. (2002). The effects of self-explanation training on student's problem solving in high school mathematics. *Learning and Instruction, 12*, 233–262.

Chapter 4

Formally Assessing Student Learning

This chapter focuses on the formal assessment of student performance and teacher activities that follow formal assessment administration, like analysis of tasks and teacher feedback. In the four-stage CA:SRL framework, we differentiate between assessment of student performances that happen simultaneously with teaching and learning (Stage 2) and those that take place at the end of a unit or well-defined sequence of instruction (Stage 3). You and your students' peers offer much support in Stage 2, while students perform behaviors that help you all interpret learning progress. But inevitably there comes a point for you to pause from instruction and appraise. When students have had multiple opportunities to learn and are ready to show their learning independently of others' support, more formal CA should take place. Stage 3 allows learners to demonstrate the achievement level they have reached at this point of closure. There will likely be multiple places in your curriculum where it is appropriate to ask your students to take off their training wheels, try their skills on their own, and see how they can do independently.

In terms of methods for designing assessment tasks, in this chapter we highlight the methods of performance assessment and essay tasks. We present item analysis, a quantitative method of interpreting assessment results. More qualitative interpretations mostly focused on close analysis of student work are illustrated through the case studies in Section 3 of this text. Stage 3 also gives you the crucial opportunity to give your students feedback in a formal way, so we present feedback guidelines in this chapter. Teacher feedback is central to learning through assessment (Brookhart, 2008). It is critical for supporting student SRL (Butler & Winne, 1995; Clark, 2012) and co-regulating learning.

Why Make Assessment Formal?

Why do we say that assessment at this stage should be formal? First, let us be clear that informal Stage 2 assessment is no more or less important than the formal assessment methods you will administer and review in Stage 3. Formal assessment does not replace the need for informal assessment, or vice versa—the two serve different purposes. Informal assessment provides evidence that can be rapidly turned around into instructional actions and can build a classroom community where all members engage in shared regulation about learning. Formal assessment provides you as a teacher with information about multiple SLOs and complex integration of learning, and uses carefully designed tasks and systematic scoring procedures to generate the best interpretations and feedback you can provide. Stage 3 assessments should be designed with particular care, so that you will have high confidence in the information you derive from them and be able to use that information to make the kinds of formal decisions that will be necessary at the next stage. If you do not feel confident that the results of your Stage 3 assessments give you sufficient information about student learning, you should revise your

Formally Assessing Student Learning 57

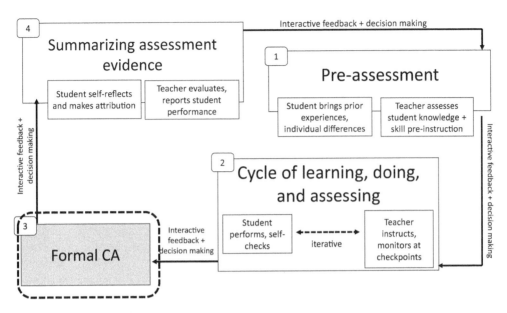

Figure 4.1 Four-Stage CA:SRL Framework, Stage 3: Formally Assessing Student Learning

assessment methods. Also, if you are confident in the quality of the results, but those results indicate that many students need more instruction and support, you should go back to Stage 2 for further instructional adjustment.

What Are We Formally Assessing?

At Stage 3, you should carefully select learning outcomes that are most important to the content and assess them for all students, so that each student's learning and skills can be exhibited to demonstrate the same competencies. By the end of multiple iterations of Stage 2, over the course of which students make learning progress toward the goal, you will be ready to assess complex learning outcomes that are critical to a conceptual understanding of the whole unit and involve complicated cognitive processes. The assessment tasks in Stage 3 should allow you to assess each student individually without group effects, even if they perform ensemble, for instance in a theatrical or band performance.

We suggest that you think back to DOK levels when selecting learning outcomes for Stage 3 assessment, particularly the outcomes that are considered to be at DOK levels 3 and 4 (see Figure 4.2). Learning outcomes at DOK level 3 (i.e., strategic thinking) are complex and abstract. They require deep understanding of the content, which is exhibited through planning, the use of evidence, and more demanding cognitive reasoning. Examples of learning outcomes at DOK 3 include having students draw conclusions, make inferences, or present multiple arguments. DOK level 4 (i.e., extended thinking) learning outcomes have high cognitive demand and are complex; students are expected to make connections, relate ideas within the content or among content areas, and select or devise one approach among many that would solve a problem. Due to the complexity of cognition, DOK 4 learning outcomes often require an extended period of time to assess. However, increasing the length of an activity or assignment does not, by itself, necessarily stimulate complex thinking or relate to a learning outcome

58 Section I Chapter 4

at DOK level 4. Learning outcomes at this level involve developing plans from various sources, making generalizations from data sets, and constructing models using computerized tools. For more description of DOK levels and appropriate SLOs, you may refer back to Chapter 2.

How Are We Formally Assessing?

Before we begin this section, we remind you that your selection of a particular assessment method should be governed by consideration of whether it can suitably measure the cognitive processes and behaviors most relevant to the SLOs. Two methods that we have not yet discussed, which are often used to measure complex learning outcomes, are performance assessments and extended-response writing tasks such as essays.

Performance Assessment

We design performance assessment (PA) tasks to focus on use of knowledge and skills in action. Performance assessments can measure a simple, single learning outcome, such as the ability to demonstrate a plié in dance. This kind of PA is relatively easy to administer, observe, and score. Many SLOs in the arts, physical education, and sciences—such as the ability to locate notes on a keyboard, use a balance beam, or dribble a ball—cannot be assessed well through any other means. It is relatively easy to construct, administer, and rate student performance on these kinds of PAs, which are essential in their disciplines. Therefore, we will not discuss them further, except to note that it is important to assess each of these isolated skills not just once, but several times, to be sure the student's one-time performance is not a fluke.

PA is also a useful method to assess complex learning outcomes. For example, PA can measure students' ability to use language, movement, and space to perform a monologue from a choice

Assessment Tasks	Thinking Processes
• Collecting numeric data over several weeks or months in notebooks • Organizing the data in a computerized spreadsheet	• Deciding how to record numeric data • Arranging data in a certain order with proper units and names • Using skills to enter and manage data on spreadsheets such as Excel
• Summarizing the data in charts or graphs • Presenting data in figures • Making and justifying predictions based on a chart, graph, or figure	• Determining the types of forms to best represent the data in a way that tells a story • Deciding which pieces of evidence can support a justification or prediction
• Developing a generalizable framework or model from the data and applying it to a new situation	• Looking for general patterns in data • Formulating a sufficient framework or model based on the existing data • Transferring the thinking processes and testing the framework or model with a new set of data or in a new learning context

Figure 4.2 Examples of Assessment Tasks and Thinking Processes for DOK Levels 3 & 4

of plays. This kind of multicomponent task requires students to understand and interpret the monologue they chose, and to incorporate elements of dramatic performance to create a scene that embodies their interpretation. Assessment of such complex groups of learning outcomes is only appropriate after students have been given learning and informal assessment opportunities to practice and receive feedback on the integration of the several learning components. Also, when you assess any complex combination of SLOs at Stage 3 in the CA:SRL framework, you should be sure that students show the processes they have used in making choices and interpretations. For instance, in addition to the performance of the dramatic monologue, students can introduce their work or reflect on it in writing. Adding evidence of process will support your ability to interpret their thinking and their SRL.

PA tasks can be authentic, meaning they directly involve behaviors that are desired and expected for individuals in society beyond the classroom. Outside of schooling, no one much values the ability to bubble in answers on a Scantron. On the other hand, many people do value the ability to perform a monologue on stage, to write an editorial, and to create a web application. While performance assessment, essay assessment, and authentic assessment are far from synonymous terms, they have significant overlaps in that they provide opportunities for direct assessment of real-life skills (Palm, 2008).

A well-designed PA consists of the following components, which you should be able to explicitly state and which happen to align neatly with the questions we pose in each chapter on Stages 1–4: 1) the purpose of the task (*why*); 2) the SLOs and learning standards (*what*); and 3) the task, instructions to the learners, and scoring guidelines (*how*). Each of these components of a PA should be addressed from two perspectives: the designer's (yours) and the users' (your students'). Designing a good PA means not only that you think through why, what, and how, but that you communicate information on all three points to your students through the task directions. For students in lower grade levels, the information you tell them need not be in great detail, but all students should be able to identify from your written or oral directions the answers to these questions: Why am I doing this? What skills and concepts am I supposed to show? What steps am I supposed to follow? How will I know how well I've done? Your directions should include information about the resources students can use, the timeframe, whether they can receive help at intervals, and so on. Figure 4.3 presents questions you should take into consideration when designing each component of a PA. If you involve your students in designing the process or product, you should share these questions with them. For more detail on the steps, we refer you to the excellent guidelines of Stiggins (1987).

You can assess two kinds of student performance: those that should occur *naturally* given the structures and expectations of your discipline, and those that you have *structured* to occur. The purpose of assessing naturally occurring performances, which happen organically as part of students' participation in the classroom setting, is to evaluate progress on the routines of learning: taking notes, following lab safety procedures, collaborating appropriately with peers, and so on. Figure 4.4 shows two examples of naturally occurring performances: students in science labs and students in dance class.

The structured PA can be thought of in terms of its timeframe (short-, mid-, and long-term) and its level of structure (high, moderate, and low). What we mean by timeframe is the amount of time needed to complete the performance. A short-term task means students will be able to perform the task within a few minutes, mid-term means approximately one class session, and long-term tasks require several days to complete. Levels of structure indicate how much variation in the process and product are allowed when students engage in the task. A highly structured task requires all students to demonstrate their learning in the same sequence and in the same forms. That includes applying the same standards for assessing students' performance.

60   Section I Chapter 4

What should YOUR design for a PA include?	What should STUDENT directions for a PA include?
Purpose of the task	*Purpose of the task*
• (Why use this task?)	• (Why do I perform this task?)
SLOs and Standards	*Outcome expectations*
• (What processes and/or products should be elicited and assessed?)	• (What knowledge and/or practices should I show?)
Task Design	*The Task*
• (How should students complete this task? If possible, you can adapt tasks from existing sources. If not, you should pilot it—then modify the new task.)	• (How can I complete the task? This includes the directions for completing the task and the steps to use; the tools and resources needed, if any; the length of time needed to complete the task; and consultation with the teacher at the designated time.)
Scoring guidelines	*Scoring guidelines*
• (How can the guidelines be used by my students and me? The rubrics include descriptions of criteria and various levels of quality.)	• (How should work look, according to different levels of quality?)

Figure 4.3 Components of Performance Assessment

Science lab safety	Yes/No	*Dance class readiness*	Yes/No
On time		On time	
Hair back		In appropriate attire	
No dangling jewelry		No gum	
Lab notebook		No heavy jewelry	
Goggles on		Bag stowed	
At assigned station		In formation	
Materials in place		With partner	

Figure 4.4 Examples of Naturally Occurring Performances

Moderately structured tasks are those in which students engage in similar cognitive processes, but are allowed to vary how they go about completing the task. Low-structured tasks allow students the most choice about form, process, and product. Figure 4.5 shows examples of PA tasks for various timeframes and levels of structures. For simplicity, we show examples in categories according to time requirements and level of structure. However, time and levels of structure are relative terms.

	TIMEFRAME			
LEVEL OF STRUCTURE		Short	Mid	Long
	High	Perform on-demand a pas de *bourrée*	Edit writing samples	
	Moderate	Interpret figures in a table, graph, chart, or map	Create a proposal for a large urban-expansion project	
	Low			Write a senior thesis or research paper

Figure 4.5 Examples of PA According to Timeframe and Level of Structure

---

- Is the amount of time that students will spend on the task appropriate for its relevance to the curriculum?
- Does the task assess important higher-order learning targets or skills in combination?
- Can the task be made more authentic?
- How can individual achievement be assessed if the student does work at home or in a group?
- Have all students had an equal opportunity to learn all the skills required?
- Do all students have equal access to resources?
- Does the task favor one group over another?
- Do you have biases or preferences about certain responses or styles?
- Have students been adequately informed of and prepared for your expectations?

Figure 4.6 Questions to Ask About a Proposed PA

After you have designed a PA task, and before you ask students to perform, ask yourself a number of questions to ensure that the tasks are appropriate (see Figure 4.6).

If you have adapted tasks that others have designed, ask yourself the same questions and prepare to revise the given task. In these questions, we draw your attention to authenticity. Tasks can require various levels of authenticity; it is not an all-or-nothing construct. For example, we can assess ability to drive a car through more or less authentic methods. We can ask would-be drivers to answer multiple-choice questions about their knowledge about driving and vehicular rules and regulations. Knowledge of the rules of the road is important, but far from an authentic measurement of driving skill. To assess driving skill more authentically, we can require the student-driver to operate a car simulator or drive around a parking lot. Still, operating a car simulator or driving a car in an empty parking lot is not as authentic as driving a car on a street with other motorists in real traffic. The most direct and authentic test of driving is to put the driver behind the wheel. However, there are often very good reasons to use less authentic methods in the classroom or while skills are still in development. Authenticity is a matter of degree, and a performance assessment need not be 100% authentic to result in strong evidence about student skills.

In addition to questions that guide your design of a PA, reminders for improving performance assessment are listed in Figure 4.7. To improve PA, make sure that the problem or task to be solved is specific and clearly defined. Like M-C stems, we suggest that you ask direct questions in your instructions when possible. Be certain that you share with your students how their work or performance will be assessed throughout the PA experience. Please note that when you assess student processes, you are actually assessing their work in progress or at various stages of development. Performance assessments can be interactive, and you can provide students with prompt feedback and self-assessment as they demonstrate their knowledge and practices, and with opportunities to revise earlier work before they move on to the next stage toward completion of the entire task.

As with any assessment method, PA has strengths and weaknesses. The strengths of PAs are that they can assess divergent thinking as well as combinations of knowledge and skills sets, and they have a higher level of authenticity. Complex performances can be broken down into small sub-tasks for students according to their individual needs or IEPs. Any such sub-tasks should be conceptually and developmentally aligned to the expected learning progression. Another strength of PA is its consistency with learning theories. For example, research on situated cognition and enculturation has posited that knowledge is embedded within the culture and that learning is a process of enculturation. Learners are like apprentices and are immersed in the doing, like masters in the field (Brown, Collins, & Duguid, 1989). Another learning theory that supports that PA is a constructivist approach to learning, which focuses on students being active seekers and builders of knowledge.

However, PA has a number of weaknesses. First, PAs can require considerable time, especially assessments that require the synthesis of multiple behaviors, such as research, organization, and presentation. You must decide whether the synthesis of learning into an integrated whole is important enough to justify the trade-off with instructional time. Also, PA tasks involve a limited sampling of content, compared to other objectively scored items that can efficiently cover a breadth of content. Often students' performances on these kinds of assessments are highly influenced by conditions in the context in which they are assessed, so the results of any individual PA may not generalize well to other complex behaviors or even to other assessments of highly related SLOs. Performance assessment may put students with special needs at a disadvantage, if such students specifically need assessments to be conducted in small "chunks." Finally, if students lack choice in topics—for instance, if they have to perform a speech from a particular play—the task may disadvantage students whose language or cultural or individual perspectives do not match that of the playwright. It is therefore important to have a balanced

---

- Define the problem to be solved. This is key, so be clear, specific, and focused. Ask direct questions if possible.
- Share information with students about the dimensions of the work that will be assessed.
- Structure tasks in a way that makes it easier for teachers and students to keep expectations in mind.
- Construct opportunities to assess work in development to assess student processes.
- Give prompt teacher feedback and involve students in self- and peer feedback.

Figure 4.7 Improving Performance Assessment

menu of different methods of assessment to elicit and measure the learning outcomes that are stated in your SLOs.

Perhaps because of these drawbacks, the national enthusiasm for performance assessment has waned since the 1980s, although it still is used extensively in some disciplines, as stated previously. At one time in the U.S., several states adopted performance-based portfolio assessment systems for statewide accountability. Such a system proved to be untenable, especially in the early twentieth century under the framework of high accountability through large-scale testing. However, many researchers believed performance assessment could help blend instruction and assessment in ways that are compatible with the four-stage CA:SRL framework, and it could improve student motivation, sense of value for classroom learning, and achievement. We agree with Haertel (1999) that such "benefits of assessing students using complex, integrative, hands-on tasks that blur the lines between testing and teaching can in fact be realized when teachers themselves make skillful use of sound performance assessments in their own classrooms" (p. 663).

Essay Tasks

Writing well requires complex cognitive processes and strategic planning. As we described in Chapter 2, written responses may range from a few sentences (restricted constructed-response or supply-type questions) to several pages (extended constructed-response). Restricted constructed-response writing tasks are highly appropriate for the assessment of conceptual understanding and application of principles, whether in Stage 1 pre-assessment, Stage 2, or formal Stage 3 assessment. You should review the guidelines for supply-type tasks that were given in Chapter 2 if this format matches well to the SLOs you need to assess formally in your content area. Extended-response essay tasks can be used to assess a wide range of thinking skills, including factual knowledge, argument organization, interpretation and evaluation of evidence, and synthesis of ideas from many sources to reach a decision.

An essay assessment task consists of a prompt or set of questions, any interpretive material the student is required to use to respond to the prompt or questions, directions about how the essay should be completed, and its scoring method. Depending on the length of an essay task and the time required for its completion, students can write essay assessments in class or be allowed to work both in class and at home. If you allow work on any assessment to be performed at home, you must take steps to ensure that the work students turn in is their own and that all students have a fair opportunity to complete homework. One way to approach this is to have students begin to write in class, allow them to revise at home or after school, and require them to complete the work in class. In this way, you will find evidence of any discontinuities between the in-class and at-home portions of the work that may indicate the student has had outside help or has a home situation that makes it difficult to complete projects outside school. In the latter case, you will need to revise your guidelines to provide all students space and time for work in class.

In Figure 4.8, we present an example of an extended-response task that measures students' abilities to cite appropriate evidence, make inferences, and draw conclusions. We also present the SLO and DOK level to show you why the task is appropriate for measuring the targeted learning outcome. Although this essay task is intended to measure interdisciplinary content knowledge and skills in science and mathematics, it can be modified to measure the same cognitive processes and skills in other subject areas.

SLO: Given both quantitative and qualitative data on U.S. wheat exports from the past decade, students will be able to draw conclusions.

DOK Level 3: Draw conclusions from observations or data, citing evidence.

> **Directions**: For the next hour, you will analyze the data and information provided on wheat exports for the years 2000–2010. Based on the data and information, you will make inferences. Please answer the following two questions by:
> (1) Writing at least one full paragraph to answer each question,
> (2) Writing complete sentences,
> (3) Including evidence from the given data and information to support your statements,
> (4) Explaining your positions and assumptions fully, and
> (5) Checking the accuracy of any calculations.

Essay questions:
(1) Study the data and information provided. What would you expect to happen to our wheat exports during the next 10 years?
(2) Explain the assumptions you made for your predictions in question (1) to be valid.

Figure 4.8 Example of Extended-Response Essay Assignment

Like performance assessment, essay tasks have strengths and weaknesses. Like PAs, essay tasks can elicit and be used to measure complex learning outcomes, as well as skills in combination. To construct responses to an essay question, students often need to integrate various pieces of knowledge, use multiple cognitive processes, monitor progress, and apply writing strategies to create a coherent work. Another strength of essay tasks is that they provide opportunities for you to evaluate students' ability to communicate their content knowledge in writing, using the language of the discipline or topic. Developing and putting academic language into use is essential for further learning acquisition.

In terms of disadvantages, essay tasks take a long time to score, which can be daunting for busy teachers. Another limitation is that essay tasks, like PAs, assess depth of knowledge more than breadth. Any particular essay only addresses a limited number of concepts related to its topic, although it may involve multiple skills. You need to consider using other methods of assessment if breadth of content knowledge is also important to assess. Finally, the scoring of essay tasks involves a lack of reliability. To improve the scoring and reliability of rating students' responses, we suggest using scoring rubrics, which are addressed next.

For English language learners, essay tasks pose an interesting conundrum. An over-reliance on essay tasks can be an unnecessary burden to English language learners, who may need more time to respond and may be challenged more by the mechanics of writing than by the "big" skills the essay is intended to assess. We consider this a particular problem when essay tasks are used to assess SLOs in disciplines that are not traditionally associated with extensive writing, such as mathematics and the sciences, although of course writing across the curriculum is an essential skill. Although English language learners may struggle with essay assessment, failure to give them rich opportunities to develop and receive feedback on their use of written language may hinder their advancement in any content area. You may choose to differentiate your assessment of the mechanics of writing for the English language learners in your classes, offer more liberal timelines, or allow English language learners to use technology in their writing that allows them to check spelling and grammar.

Scoring Rubrics for PAs and Essays

Many teachers find it more difficult to evaluate students' responses to PAs and essays than to construct the task prompts and procedures. These are assessments without "correct" or "incorrect" responses, and high-quality responses can diverge widely in form and content. Therefore, you need to create rubrics or scoring guidelines to structure your ratings of student work. Rubrics are tools to guide the rating of responses to open-ended essays, tasks, or performance assessments. They list the specific, pre-established criteria that will be rated in each work sample and provide a scale for rating the quality of work for each criterion. We discussed using checklists to rate whether a behavior or skill is present in Chapter 2; these checklists are very simple scoring rubrics. Each behavior is a criterion, and "present" or "absent" are the simple rating scale. For essays and PAs, you are much more likely to use rubrics with more scoring levels and corresponding descriptions of various qualities of performance. Scoring rubrics permit teachers to indicate the frequency or degree to which a behavior or skill is exhibited, and they can be either holistic or analytic. Figures 4.9.1 and 4.9.2 show examples of holistic and analytic rubrics used to score teacher candidates in a school of education on their assessment knowledge and skills. You as a teacher can also use these to rate your own understanding about CA.

A holistic scoring rubric consists of a single dimension on which performance is rated at several levels. For instance, overall skill in oral presentation might be rated 1, 2, 3, or 4. A holistic rubric will typically have descriptors for each level, with several characteristics all clustered together. With a holistic rubric you will render a single score for the performance, which makes the scoring process quick. Holistic rubrics are not very useful for giving students feedback since a general score does not communicate about specific strengths or weaknesses.

To provide more useful and focused feedback, an analytic scoring rubric is appropriate because it includes all the criteria (or attributes) and each criterion is evaluated separately. Analytic scoring rubrics are useful if you want to be sure that each attribute is evaluated and that the corresponding score is correctly rendered. Such judgments of students' work require you to be detailed in considering every aspect of a response and to take care to evaluate each criterion separately, without consideration of other criteria that affect the work as a whole. Feedback derived from an analytic scoring rubric is more detailed than holistic feedback and is more helpful to your students for improving specific dimensions of their performance.

Having well-defined scoring rubrics is a good start to maintaining consistent standards of evaluation of all student work. However, if you modify the rubric or change the way you interpret it at any point during the scoring process, you need to re-evaluate all students' work so that every student's work is judged fairly. If possible, we encourage you and those of your colleagues who use the same assessment to collaboratively decide on standards of student work or what quality of responses constitute your standards for low levels of achievement versus high levels. To do this, select samples of student work that represent different levels of achievement and calibrate your judgments to one another's.

This calibration among teachers' judgments is particularly crucial in schools where multiple classes of the same content are taught by different teachers. Poor calibration among teachers on scoring standards means that teachers will vary in leniency or severity. This is most concerning when the same tasks are assigned to students in many classrooms, but each task is evaluated by only one teacher. Students should know that no matter who their classroom teacher is, you all share common criteria for success.

	Unsatisfactory 1	Marginal 2	Proficient 3	Excellent 4
Teacher Candidate's Overall Performance	Quality very incomplete or characterized by pervasive major misunderstandings of essential concepts.	Quality sound in parts, but significantly marred by some major misunderstandings of essential concepts.	Sound quality throughout, possibly with minor or occasional misunderstandings of essential concepts.	Very high quality throughout, with no misunderstandings of essential concepts shown and some conceptual richness.

Figure 4.9.1 Holistic Rubric for Rating Teacher Candidates in an Assessment

RATING DIMENSIONS	Unsatisfactory 1	Marginal 2	Proficient 3	Excellent 4
Consideration of School, Family, and Community Context, and the Prior Experiences of Students Relevant to Assessment	Qualitative and/or quantitative data to describe assessment context are lacking from description.	Qualitative and quantitative data are insufficient or not synthesized to describe assessment context.	Data from qualitative and quantitative sources are synthesized to adequately describe assessment context.	Data from qualitative and quantitative sources are synthesized to describe assessment context in-depth.
Use of Appropriate State or National Standards and Specific Learning Objectives in the Content Area	Many learning goals and objectives are missing, inappropriately stated, instructionally unimportant, or not aligned with standards.	Several learning goals and objectives are missing, inappropriately stated, instructionally unimportant, or not aligned with standards.	Almost all learning goals and objectives are appropriately stated, instructionally important, and aligned with standards.	All learning goals and objectives are well stated, instructionally important, and well-aligned with standards.
Plans for and Use of Multiple Assessment Methods Aligned to Standards and SLOs	Methods frequently show technical flaws, assess trivia, or lack alignment to SLOs and standards.	Methods occasionally show technical flaws, assess trivia, or lack alignment to SLOs and standards.	Methods are usually technically sound, assess important aspects of instruction, and are aligned to SLOs and standards.	Methods are all technically sound, assess important aspects of instruction, and are well-aligned to SLOs and standards.

Assessment Methods Promote Each Student's Growth in the Content Area	Analysis of student data is very limited and/or used to draw inappropriate conclusions about teaching effectiveness and student learning.	Analysis of student data is limited and/or conclusions about teaching effectiveness and student learning are weakly supported by data.	Student data are analyzed quantitatively and qualitatively, and conclusions about teaching effectiveness and student learning are mostly supported.	Student data are analyzed quantitatively and qualitatively, and conclusions about teaching effectiveness and student learning are well supported.
Use of Assessment in Ways That Show Fairness to All Students and Belief That All Students Can Learn	Issues of fairness in assessment for all students are not addressed in descriptions of assessment procedures, interpretations, or instructional responses.	Issues of fairness in assessment for all students are inadequately addressed in descriptions of assessment procedures, interpretations, or instructional responses.	Issues of fairness in assessment for all students are adequately addressed in descriptions of assessment procedures, interpretations, or instructional responses.	Issues of fairness in assessment for all students are thoroughly addressed in descriptions of assessment procedures, interpretations, or instructional responses.
Results of Assessments Used to Guide and Modify Further Instruction or Assessment	Plans for instructional responses to assessment results are not given or are not based on data or evidence in student work.	Plans for instructional responses to assessment results are given that relate weakly to data or evidence in student work.	Plans for instructional responses to assessment results are given that in most cases draw on data or evidence in student work.	Plans for instructional responses to assessment results draw on in-depth analysis of data or evidence in student work.

Figure 4.9.2 Analytic Rubric for Rating Teacher Candidates in an Assessment Course

Item Analysis

Item analysis involves examination of student scores to gain information about the effectiveness of different prompts for their intended purposes. Results of item analysis can suggest whether individual subcomponents of a complex task, like the separate criteria assessed on a rubric or individual M-C items, function as intended. You can use item analysis to help you identify specific content where your class as a whole needs feedback and to revise and improve the tasks. Here, we take you through the process of quantitatively analyzing and determining the effectiveness of M-C items and rubric-based tasks after students have provided their answers. As stated previously, you can read teachers' qualitative interpretations of student work on individual tasks and items in Section 3 of this text.

Item analysis is not highly appropriate if only a small number of students have been assessed, so we advise you to be careful about using this method with small groups. However, if you have a test or a rubric-scored PA or essay task that you or your school administer to all students at a certain grade level or who take a particular course, item analysis can give you useful information. Also, item analysis methods work best when students are heterogeneous in terms of performance, such as when there is great variation in scores. With homogeneous groups, item analysis is less useful.

Two numeric indexes that are readily obtained are the item difficulty index (p value) and the item discrimination index (D). Item difficulty shows the percent of students who answered an item correctly: the larger the p value, the easier the item; the smaller the p value, the more difficult the item. The item discrimination index (D) distinguishes between students who do well on the overall task and those who do not do well overall. In other words, the D index for a particular item (M-C) or criterion (essay, PA) indicates how well the task differentiates between students with overall high scores and those with low scores. The usefulness of D is that it can detect various problems with items or task components and can direct your attention to parts of your Stage 3 assessment that might merit additional examination before you use the results for feedback and further instruction and assessment.

Item Analysis With M-C Items

In Figure 4.10, we show the steps and equations used in computing p and D, using basic formulas for M-C items on a test. We will show the way to calculate p and D for tasks that are scored with rubrics in a subsequent section; the methods are similar and the interpretations of the values are the same.

A few caveats about the differences in our CA methods for p and D and those used by professionals:

1. In our equation for p in M-C items, the value in the denominator is the number of students who took the test. In professional practice, this value should be the number of students who answered each particular item, which might vary item by item.
2. In professional test development and analysis, D is not calculated as a difference between "upper" and "lower" groups, but as the correlation between item-level scores and test-total scores.

We present calculated examples of the item difficulty index (p) in Figure 4.11. In Figure 4.11, you can see that M-C item 1 has a p of .80 and M-C item 2 has a p of .30. The values of p can range from 0.00 to 1.00. The closer the p is to 1.00, the easier the item was for the group of test-takers (in other words, the more students chose the answer). In this example, 120 of 150

1. Score every student's test by marking the correct answers and putting the total number of correct answers on the test (or on the answer sheet).
2. Rank all test papers in numeric order according to the total score on the test.
3. Determine the upper-scoring, middle-scoring, and lower-scoring groups.
4. Tally the number of students across all three groups who chose each M-C option in all groups.
5. Calculate the difficulty (p) for each M-C item.

$$p = \frac{\textit{total number of students choosing the correct answer}}{\textit{number of students who take the test}}$$

6. Calculate the discrimination index (D) for each M-C item. *Use only the upper and lower groups for determining the D index.*

$$D = (\textit{fraction of upper group choosing the correct answer})$$
$$- (\textit{fraction of lower group choosing the correct answer})$$

7. Use the results from Step 4 to check each M-C item for
   • Poor distractors
   • Ambiguous options
   • Incorrect keying
   • Random guessing

Figure 4.10 Steps in Item Analysis of Multiple-Choice Items

Example: Computing p Value

Scenario: Ms. James taught 150 ninth-grade biology students this year, and they recently took the midterm exam. She computed p values for the following two items to check their difficulty levels:

M-C Item 1: Of the group, 120 students answered the M-C item #1 correctly. The p value of M-C item # 1 is .80. The proportion of .80 can be represented as 80%.

$$p = \frac{120}{150} = .80 \; or \; 80\%$$

M-C Item 2: Of the group, 45 students answered the M-C item #2 correctly. The p value of M-C item # 2 is .30. The proportion of .30 can be represented as 30%.

$$p = \frac{45}{150} = .30 \; or \; 30\%$$

Figure 4.11 Calculation of Item Difficulty Index (*p* value)

---

students—or 80% of Ms. James's students—answered M-C item 1 correctly. It has a p of .80 and is considered a relatively easy item. On the other hand, Ms. James's students did not do so well with M-C item 2, which only 30% of test-takers answered correctly. This item has a p of .30.

Continuing with the same scenario but with three different M-C items, we show examples of the discrimination index D in Figure 4.12. To compute D, we use the upper and lower

70　Section I Chapter 4

Example: Computing D

Scenario (continues): After scoring all the tests, Ms. James ranked the total scores from the highest to the lowest. She then selected the test papers of the 50 highest scorers and the 50 lowest scorers from the 150 test papers to check discrimination of M-C items.

The tables show data on different M-C items in terms the number of students in each of the upper-scoring and lower-scoring groups who selected each option, A, B, C, or D. The * represents the key or correct response to the item.

M-C Item 3:

	A	B*	C	D
Upper group (50)	3	45	1	1
Lower group (50)	10	20	10	10

$$D = \frac{45}{50} - \frac{20}{50} = .9 - .4 = .50$$

M-C Item 4:

	A	B	C	D*
Upper group (50)	5	5	20	20
Lower group (50)	6	6	8	30

$$D = \frac{20}{50} - \frac{30}{50} = .4 - .6 = -.20$$

M-C Item 5:

	A*	B	C	D
Upper group (50)	30	0	10	10
Lower group (50)	30	0	12	8

$$D = \frac{30}{50} - \frac{30}{50} = .6 - .6 = 0.00$$

Figure 4.12 Calculation of Discrimination Index for Multiple-Choice Items

groups of scores. The idea is whether the items can separate out students who "know" their content, versus those who do not. A common way to define "upper" and "lower" groups for the purpose of calculating D is to use the total score on the test as a basis. You can define "upper" as the top third of scores, and "lower" as the bottom third scores. The middle scores are not used in the calculation of D. The D index can range from −1.00 to 1.00. A positive discrimination index, as found with M-C item 3 ($D = .50$), indicates that those who performed well on the overall test chose the correct answer for this item more often than did students

Formally Assessing Student Learning   71

who performed poorly on the overall test. A negative discrimination index, as found with M-C item 4 ($D = -.20$), indicates that students who did poorly on the overall test chose the correct answer for this item more often than did those who performed well on the overall test. When considering D indexes for CA purposes, we focus on whether the D is positive or negative. Items that have negative D indexes merit further investigation, because the result is counter-intuitive. We expect that, on average, more top-performing students will answer any particular item correctly than will much lower-performing students.

The example of M-C item 5 shows a zero discrimination, indicating that students who did well and those who did poorly on the overall test chose the correct answer on this item with equal frequency. In other words, M-C item 5 is a non-discriminating item. This means that it is not able to separate out those who have a good understanding of the content from those who do not. Such occurrences are likely due to the item being either extremely easy or extremely difficult.

Thus far, we have presented how to identify whether an M-C item is discriminating based on its key or correct answer. We also need to consider whether the alternatives or distractors in an M-C item are discriminating in the way we expect. In the case of the distractors, we look for negative D indexes—students with overall high performance should be *less* likely to choose the distractors than those with overall low performance. The main function of distractor analysis is to spot students' misconceptions, incomplete understandings, or weaknesses in skill. Example M-C item 3 has negative D indexes of the three distractors (options A, C, and D). Such an item appears to be functioning well.

In Figure 4.12, item 4 has the negative D for the keyed or correct response (option D), which is not what we expect, and a positive index of one of the distractors (option C, $20/50 - 8/50 = 12/50$ or $.24$). This indicates that either the key or the distractor may need to be revised, although it is impossible to be sure without reviewing the content of the item. Looking further at response patterns on the same item, the upper group has an equal number of students who selected the key (option D) and the distractor (option C). For CA purposes, you should discuss with students how they interpret the two options of this item. It is possible that test-takers have similar interpretations of option C and the key (option D); in other words, these two options ambiguous and their underlying ideas may be conceptually undistinguishable for even the highest-achieving students in the class.

M-C item 5 in Figure 4.12 has two problems: the keyed response has a D index of 0.00, and no one selected one of the distractors (option B). With such an M-C item, you should review the content of the item to decide whether option B is too implausible to be included among the options and consider whether the item was too easy overall to be needed as part of your overall assessment.

To interpret a p value, we suggest using quartiles as a general guideline. The difficulty levels of $p > .75$ would be considered relatively easy, and $p < .25$ would be considered difficult. The items with p values between .75 and .25 would be considered moderately difficult. As for the discrimination index, we first check whether the D is positive or negative, and then consider the magnitude of the value. For the M-C items, we first looked for a positive D index for the key and negative D indexes for the distractors. The discrimination index of $D > .75$ indicates very good discrimination by an item, while $D < .25$ indicates a not-so-good discrimination. However, it is not at all uncommon for M-C items to have low discrimination, especially when students perform in homogeneous ways.

Bear in mind that what we do with the information that scores provide, including analysis at the item level, is just as important as the results themselves. Discussing students' performance results with them and going over their reasons for selecting the M-C item keys or distractors

72 Section I Chapter 4

after a test offers another opportunity to learn about students' interpretations of the test items and to receive feedback about their thinking processes when they rendered their selections on the M-C items. Review of item responses with the whole class should be conducted strategically, with an emphasis on items that are difficult or where it appears from the distractors that there are common misconceptions among students.

Item Analysis for Items Scored With Rubrics

We can also use the method of item analysis to assess how well essay and PA tasks function, or any task scored on a rubric, with a few minor revisions to the formulas, as shown in Figure 4.13.

To do this, compute the difficulty (p) and the discrimination index (D) after students' responses have been evaluated based on a scoring rubric. You can use individual short essay items from a single assessment or the scores on each dimension of an analytic rubric as data for the analysis. Figure 4.13 shows an example of how the p and D indexes are computed for one

---

Scenario: The English department administered an essay exam to 400 students. Based on students' overall scores on the exam, their scores were ranked into upper, middle, and lower groups. The following table shows the breakdown of frequency on essay item I, based on a 5-point scoring rubric (5 = highest level of achievement to I = lowest level of achievement on the essay).

Rubric Points	Upper	Middle	Lower
5	40	10	0
4	45	50	0
3	15	80	15
2	0	50	45
I	0	10	40

$$p = \frac{\overline{X} - X_{min}}{X_{max} - X_{min}} = \frac{3 - 1}{5 - 1} = \frac{2}{4} = .50$$

$\overline{X}$ = the average of item score for all stuents

X_{min} = the smallest item score

X_{max} = the highest item score

$$D = \frac{\overline{X}_U - \overline{X}_L}{X_{max} - X_{min}} = \frac{4.25 - 1.75}{5 - 1} = .63$$

$\overline{X}_U$ = the average of item scores for the upper group

$\overline{X}_L$ = the average of item scores for the lower group

---

Figure 4.13 Computing the p Value and D Index for a Single Essay Item

essay-based assessment. In this example the p of essay item 1 is .50, which has a moderately difficult level. Remember that the range of p is always 0.00 to 1.00, with indexes closer to 1.00 being easy items and closer to 0.00 being more difficult. The discrimination index (D), the difference between higher-performing and lower-performing groups, is taken, as before, as a comparison between the scores of the highest-scoring third and lowest-scoring third of the group, omitting the middle. In the example, the "upper" and "lower" groups are determined by their overall score on the essay-based assessment. The D index of essay item 1 is positive .63 (with rounding), indicating that students who were higher-performing overall produced responses to this essay item that earned higher scores than did lower-performing students, whose responses tended to earn lower scores. In other words, the indexes for essay item 1 show that this essay item is moderately difficult and indicate that high-scoring students obtained higher scores on average for this essay than did the low-scoring students.

If you use an analytic scoring rubric to evaluate a single essay or PA, you can compute p and D in the way described above either for using an overall holistic score, or for subscores by criterion from an analytic rubric. Types of scoring rubrics do not affect how you calculate p and D.

Remember that this type of quantitative analysis is by no means definitive, and statistical qualities of items or tasks should not drive your decisions about their inclusion in an assessment. In CA, the most important consideration of any M-C item or task is that the item aligns with what was taught and measures a particular learning outcome. Also, bear in mind that there is nothing wrong with writing items that are either quite easy or quite challenging for students, or that have poor discrimination. Your assessments should be designed with your objectives and a range of achievement along the learning progression in mind. An item that is very easy will have a p value close to 1.00 and a D index close to zero. Statistically, it will look like a poor item, and you probably should review its content before giving students feedback. However, the fact of the matter may simply be that all your students had learned that material well—a piece of information you surely want to know to plan your next steps. Similarly, an item that is very difficult will have a p value close to 0.00 and a D that is also close to zero. You should look at the content of this item and students' responses carefully. Was it so difficult for students because of item-writing flaws like excess verbiage or unclear directions, or was it a particularly challenging concept or skill that you and your students need to continue to tackle?

Giving Formal Feedback to Students

Your students will have been receiving feedback throughout the entire cycle of CA, from you and from their peers. In Stage 2, much of that feedback will have been in the moment and informal, and may have been based on individualized goals set between you and your students during their learning progression. Such feedback information should be non-evaluative, supportive, timely, and specific. Timeliness is particularly important during Stage 2's iterative, informal, and often interactive assessment. But teacher feedback does not always have to be immediate, informal, or given in relation to a short episode of instruction learning. When it comes to Stage 3, your feedback will be more formal, slightly less specific, and less in the moment. It should still very much help students understand their performance in terms of the learning criteria and internally plan for the next instructional cycle, moving through the SRL performance phase toward self-reflection. Generally speaking, assessment without feedback and actionable steps for individuals is associated with large-scale assessment, not classroom assessment (Heritage, Kim, Vendlinski, & Herman, 2009).

Providing feedback is both an art and a science. To provide good feedback, a teacher not only must draw correct inferences from the evidence of student work, but also must artfully provide targeted information that guides students to continuous learning improvement.

Feedback should address the accuracy of students' responses to tasks that may contain particular errors and misconceptions (Shute, 2008) so they can bridge the gap between their present understanding of learning tasks or performance and the level of understanding they aim to possess (Hattie & Timperley, 2007). According to Hattie and Timperley (2007), feedback to close this gap should address the following three questions: "Where am I going?" (what direction has been set or what are the learning goals), "How am I going?" (what strategies do I need to adopt to get there), and "Where to next?" (what subsequent goals follow from the previous goal). Feedback should be non-evaluative and focus on the task, on the strategies and processes that students employed in solving problems, and on developing their metacognitive capacity.

Feedback, external and internal, is critical to promoting SRL processes and can be a turning point for knowledge and skill acquisition. To promote students' SRL during Stage 3, you can 1) identify and describe students' strengths and specific errors in their work; 2) provide verbal feedback to the whole class about the errors; and 3) provide students with written individual feedback (e.g., specific guiding questions, error flagging, or showing specific examples), depending on student needs. There are many different types of feedback, and researchers have attempted to delineate how different types of feedback influences students' learning (Kulhavy, 1977; Shute, 2008). Sometimes feedback provides the student with a simple indication of correct or incorrect performance. Other times feedback more elaborately apprises the learner of what to do next to make progress to their learning goal. However, merely increasing the amount of elaboration or the complexity of information in feedback does not necessarily increase student learning (Bangert-Drowns, Kulik, Kulik, & Morgan, 1991; Kulhavy, 1977). The following is an adapted and simplified version of Shute's (2008) work, which we find user-friendly for identifying the types of teacher feedback that can be provided to students. To move learning forward, it is essential that you take the needs of your individual students into consideration and provide the differentiated feedback that each student needs.

Type	Description
1. No feedback	No indication of the student performance.
2. Verification	An indication of the performance such as right or wrong.
3. Correct response	The correct response of the performance is given.
4. Try again	Knowledge of results is given, and another performance attempt is required.
5. Source of errors (error flagging)	The location of errors is shown, but the correct performance or response is not given.
6. Elaboration	The learner is provided prompts, cues, strategies, or scaffolding toward making changes.

We see feedback as another opportunity to have a conversation with students, where you not only give but receive feedback from students about their perceived usefulness of your assessment interpretations and instruction. Students should have opportunities at Stage 2 to put the information they receive from feedback into action—it is imperative at Stage 2 that students get another opportunity to learn and be assessed after feedback. At Stage 3, you can also elicit student self-feedback with simple checklists that initiate self-reflection on the quality of their work or with guided questions that prompt students to learn from their performance at this stage.

When it comes to providing students with feedback on their performance, we have the following suggestions to help formulate effective feedback. Teacher feedback should focus

Formally Assessing Student Learning   75

on what is being learned (tied to SLOs) and how students should go about meeting the objectives (tied to success criteria). If you are providing feedback during Stage 2, your feedback should occur very close to the time when students are engaged in learning. If you are providing formal or summary feedback during Stage 3, your feedback can wait until students have completed their performance. Next, you can provide explicit information on how and why students have or have not met the criteria. Last, you can offer your students strategies and tools if you noticed that they need them. Our suggestions serve to help frame teacher feedback. We have compiled a list of questions and suggestions for decision-making about feedback in Figure 4.14.

Feedback is only useful if students use it. Therefore, whether you do or do not provide feedback, and how much of it is appropriate for students, should involve a conversation between you and the students. Feedback should be a conversation between you and students. Teacher and students should make the decisions about the level of support that is needed for them to be able to move forward. When feedback is not enough for students, they will stay in a fog, with no clear direction about how to improve. However, too much feedback can be overwhelming and students might give up trying to learn. To check the adequacy of your feedback to

---

How Much?
 1. How many points/issues to address?
 2. How much detail to write/say about each point?

Suggestions
 1. Prioritize: Pick the most important points that are related to the SLO.
 2. Consider the student's developmental level so they are not overwhelmed with feedback.
 3. If the student work needs lots of feedback, you can start with a few points and let students know that this is the first round of feedback and another round of feedback might be provided after they have addressed the first round of feedback and made changes.

On What?
 1. The work itself
 2. The process and strategies that the student used to do the work

Suggestions
 1. Align the feedback to the content and SLO.
 2. Describe what students have done on the work and their process.
 3. Pose questions and prompts to guide students to move forward another step.
 4. Avoid personal comments (particularly negative ones).

To Whom?
 1. Individual student
 2. Group or the whole class

Suggestions
 1. Individual feedback conveys to students that you value their learning and pay attention to their needs.
 2. Group feedback works if most of the class missed the same concept on an assignment and the opportunity to re-teach it presents itself.

Figure 4.14 Decision-making About Providing Feedback

students, ask them: 1) Is my assistance (i.e., verbal or written feedback) clear to you?; 2) Is it enough feedback to get you started?; 3) Do you know what to do or how to move forward?; 4) Can you tell me what you will do next?; and 5) What will you do if you get stuck again?

References

Bangert-Drowns, R. L., Kulik, J. A., & Kulik, C. C. (1991). Effects of frequent classroom testing. *Journal of Educational Research, 85*(2), 89–99.

Brookhart, S. (2008). *How to give effective feedback to your students.* Alexandria, VA: Association for Supervision and Curriculum Development.

Brown, J. S., Collins, A., & Duguid, P. (1989). Situated cognition and the culture of learning. *Educational Researcher, 18,* 32–42.

Butler, D. L., & Winne, P. H. (1995). Feedback and self-regulated learning: A theoretical synthesis. *Review of Educational Research, 65*(3), 245 281.

Clark, I. (2012). Formative assessment: Assessment is for self-regulated learning. *Educational Psychology Review, 24*(2), 205–249.

Haertel, E. H. (1999). Performance assessment and education reform. *Phi Delta Kappan, 80*(9), 662–666.

Hattie, J., & Timperley, H. (2007). The power of feedback. *Review of Educational Research, 77,* 81–112.

Heritage, M., Kim, J., Vendlinski, T., & Herman, J. (2009). From evidence to action: A seamless process in formative assessment? *Educational Measurement: Issues and Practice, 28*(3), 24–31.

Kulhavy, R. W. (1977). Feedback in written instruction. *Review of Educational Research, 47,* 211–232.

Palm, T. (2008). Performance assessment and authentic assessment: A conceptual analysis of the literature. *Practical Assessment, Research & Evaluation, 13*(4), 1–11.

Shute, V. J. (2008). Focus on formative feedback. *Review of Educational Research, 78,153–189.*

Stiggins, R. J. (1987). Design and development of performance assessments. *Educational Measurement: Issues and Practice, 6*(3), 33–42.

Webb, N. (2002, March 28). *Depth-of-knowledge levels for four content areas.* unpublished paper. Retrieved from http://ossucurr.pbworks.com/w/file/fetch/49691156/Norm%20web%20 dok%20by%20subject%20area.pdf

Chapter 5

Reflection on Overall Performance

This chapter focuses on ways to consolidate overall reflections on students' achievement and report student learning progress after they have completed multiple cycles of instruction, assessment, and learning. Stage 4 is the last part of the four-stage CA:SRL framework, although it also marks the transition to a new cycle (see Figure 5.1).

People often use the term *summative assessment* to mean assessment with a purpose of communicating evidence of achievement with those outside the classroom. We generally avoid using the word *summative* in this text because it has a somewhat negative connotation in CA, being associated with assessment as a thing apart from learning. We will refer to assessment at Stage 4 as a reflection and evaluation on combined results, or simply Stage 4. Nonetheless, you will probably hear the term *summative* used in the profession.

Traditionally, the work of reflecting on student overall achievement and learning at the end of an instructional cycle falls almost entirely on the shoulders of teachers. However, in a classroom where learning from assessment information is a shared process, students should still be involved in Stage 4. While you compile and evaluate the evidence from students' work for communication outside your classroom, students should reflect on their overall performance and evaluate the effectiveness of the strategies they used in completing the formal assessments.

In this chapter, we also remind you of the vast world of educational assessment beyond your classroom. Assessments administered by external authorities that affect individual students in your classroom are at the far border of Stage 4 in the CA:SRL framework. They are certainly not altogether CA, because you and your students don't control their methods, interpretations, or use. But externally designed or administered assessments fit partially into the CA:SRL framework because they provide information about the learning of individuals in your classroom, and they are intended to promote learning, as are your CA practices. We include a brief discussion of assessments that are administered by external authorities like state and federal government to report on your students' achievement. Whether or not you are directly involved in collecting, reporting, or responding to this type of large-scale assessment data, you, as a classroom teacher, have a professional responsibility to know and be able to understand information derived from this type of assessment.

Why Assess Cumulative Learning?

In schools, we summarize student performance and report it to others to support decision-making that takes place beyond the classroom. When a teacher meets with other teachers in their school to report and compare student performance for the purpose of mapping curriculum, that's Stage 4, because the teacher's interpretations are being extended to an audience beyond the classroom. When student work at the end of instruction is presented on a parent

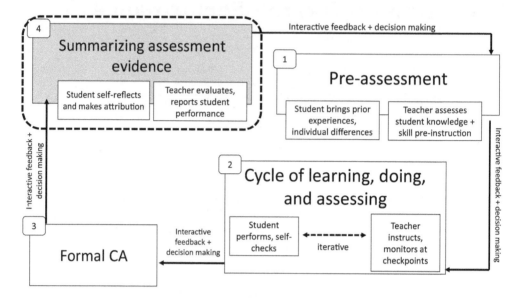

Figure 5.1 Four-stage CA:SRL Framework, Stage 4: Summarizing Performance of Learning

night or school open-house, that's also Stage 4. The students' performance has, in some way, become public. Cumulative reports of achievement testing may be sent to school districts or a state's Department of Education as part of an official reporting process. In short, the interpretations made at Stage 4 are more broadly distributed and consumed than are other interpretations of CA.

Grades and test results are types of Stage 4 assessment that come most readily to mind for most of us. Course grades have immediate and long-term academic consequences for students. They influence students' placement into classes (e.g., advanced placement, remediation) and grade promotion. They affect selection for awards and honors, which in turn affect post-secondary opportunities (Tyson & Roksa, 2017). Grades are the most important factor used by colleges and universities in selecting students for admission (National Association for College Admission Counseling, 2016). Grades are also significant at the administrative and school leadership levels. Because they influence school and course promotion, grades affect graduation rates and school performance indices. For instance, in New York State, metrics of school accountability include the four-year graduation rate, which is determined by the rate at which students pass courses to achieve the required credits for graduation. Finally, students and families make decisions based on school grades, which carry an emotional valence that can affect student self-image (Thomas & Oldfather, 1997). After seeing poor grades, parents may chide their children to perform better, hire a tutor, or contest a grade if they believe it is inaccurate or unfair. Because cumulative assessments like grades communicate information not just between the teacher and the student but to people outside the classroom, they have greater consequences than typical classroom assessments. This quasi-official nature of cumulative assessments is important, because cumulative assessments are very often used to make important decisions for the future.

While the function of Stage 4 for communication beyond the classroom distinguishes it from other parts of the four-stage framework, it is also important for both teachers and students to communicate about summary results internally, within the teaching and learning context of the classroom. Concluding Stage 4 begins a whole new cycle in the CA:SRL framework. We continue to support SRL as we move into the next cycle, whether it is a new topic, unit, chapter, marking period, semester, or year. You as teachers should be transparent with students about your evaluation of their performance, giving them another opportunity to reflect on the outcomes of multiple formal performances, which have now been graded. Part of being self-regulated is being able to make decisions about the extent to which goals were met, the effectiveness of learning strategies, and individual satisfaction with performance. At Stage 4, students should be encouraged to participate in reporting and highlighting their achievement at this time. An important component of being self-regulated learners is the ability to reflect on one's learning and provide feedback at every stage of the process. Whenever assessment occurs, it signals an opportunity for you and your students to review and reflect on their assessment outcomes.

Just as importantly, you, the teacher, should carefully examine how students react to your interpretations of their performance and the reasons they attribute to their success or failure. This can help you calibrate your teaching and expectations to student strengths and weaknesses in the next cycle of instruction. It can help you check on the fairness and quality of your assessment practice. You should take this time to reflect back on and evaluate your own instructional effectiveness, make decisions about teaching strategies for next time, and thoughtfully appraise your own strengths and weaknesses in your profession.

What Students Do in Stage 4

For students, Stage 4 is aligned with Zimmerman's third phase of the SRL model, which includes processes such as self-evaluation and self-reflection. After any Stage 3 formal performance, students can compare their performance to external standards to identify learning gaps and reflect on the effectiveness of their learning strategies. At Stage 4, students look inside, and look at the accumulated evidence, and ask themselves, "Have I met my learning goals?" In accordance with Zimmerman's SRL theory, self-regulated students make self-judgments and self-reactions about their performance outcomes that they have achieved and that they have demonstrated, likely multiple times over the course of a period of study.

To aid self-reflection, students can refer back to initial goals or any rubrics that were used to evaluate their performance, as well as the feedback they have received. If you pre-assessed their confidence, goals, prior knowledge, or skills, they can compare their Stage 4 outcomes to where they started. With planning and organization, you can set up a portfolio system (see Chapter 9) that allows you and your students to curate and reflect on work samples accumulated over time. By helping students generate and maintain records of their achievements and struggles as they progress in learning, you provide them rich material for reflection. Rather than looking at your evaluation as a point of finality and something that is foisted upon them, through co-regulation you and your students can use any observed discrepancies between the learning goals and performance to plan for the next go-around of the four-stage framework.

Also, we advocate that self-assessment at this stage not focus on academic performance alone. At this point, students can self-reflect on their own SRL. What do they think about their own planning and their use of resources? Do they find goal-setting helpful? What learning strategies do they want to use better, next time they embark on an academic challenge? In addition, we suggest that students reflect on the reasons they attribute to the outcomes of their formal assessment. In short, this is a good point in time to have students identify what sources contributed to their success or failure of performance, and what they think they can do differently for the next cycle of instruction and learning.

80 Section I Chapter 5

In Figure 5.2, we show simple items and prompts that are aligned with self-reflection processes and are designed to elicit students' thinking when they have accumulated a body of work. Reflection items are shown in both Yes/No/Plan form and in a more open-ended version. These prompts could be used with minor modifications for reflection on a single formal task performance at the end of Stage 3.

What Teachers Do in Stage 4

Given the vast amount of student information that can be considered for grading and reporting purposes, you need to make decisions about what student information should be summarized and what should be reported in advance of starting the marking period. You manage student data and keep records of many classroom activities and small daily performances, but not all data should be turned into student grades. Some student data are used to monitor student learning, and other data are used for grading purposes. Thus, we will go through each

Directions to students (Survey Version): You have completed several tasks and assessments over the last period of study, and seen the scores on your performance. At this time, please answer the "How Did I Do?" survey by checking *yes* or *no*, and write in your plan of change.

How did I do?	YES	NO	What is my plan of change?
1. My performance over the period of study met my goals.			
2. I know what I did well on the tasks.			
3. I know what I did poorly on these tasks.			
4. I know what strategies worked.			
5. I know what strategies did not work.			

Directions to students (Open-Ended Version): You have completed several tasks and assessments over the last period of study, and seen the scores on your performance. At this time, please answer the "How Do I Feel about My Performance?" questions or complete the sentences.

How do I feel about my performance?	Your answer:
1. After knowing how I performed over this period of study, I feel . . .	
2. I am satisfied with my performance because . . .	
3. I am *dissatisfied* with my performance because . . .	
4. What are the reasons that I did well over this period of study?	
5. What are the reasons that I did *not* do well over this period of study?	

Figure 5.2 Student Self-Reflection and Corresponding Prompts

stage of the CA:SRL framework and think about whether the information compiled should be considered in the summary and reporting of student achievement and learning. We also discuss whether non-achievement factors such as effort and classroom conduct should be considered in grading and reporting.

The Place of Stage 1 Pre-assessment Evidence in Stage 4 Grading

You use pre-assessment to elicit information on students' prior knowledge, beliefs, and attitudes about the topics that you will address in upcoming instruction. Pre-assessment informs you about your students' beliefs, conceptions or misconceptions, and attitudes toward topics to help you decide what to emphasize in teaching; it makes students more aware of these factors, as well. Further, through pre-assessment you as a teacher become more systematic in your thinking about the cycle of assessment. You think about your objectives not as isolated bits, but as part of the learning trajectory that spans the distance between students' prior learning experiences and your broader goals, and you can situate your instruction at the right point of the trajectory between where students are and where they need to be next.

Should the results of pre-assessments be summarized and included in a student's evaluation? They should not. We consider a policy of scoring and reporting pre-assessment results unfair because it penalizes students who begin with lower achievement. If pre-assessment shows that many of your students have very little prior knowledge of a topic, your inference should be that they have much to learn and that you have much to teach them. Pre-assessment results have no place when it comes to your evaluative decisions.

The Place of Stage 2 Evidence in Stage 4 Grading

Results that are collected in Stage 2 emphasize assessment as part of learning and also have no place in the gradebook. Some teachers want to score Stage 2 assessments such as quizzes, interactive assessments like student interviews, and classroom exchanges during questioning, at least in terms of whether or not the student participated. However, marking something as a "1" if it was performed and a "0" if it wasn't communicates misleading information about the quality of achievement. A "1" indicates compliance on an assignment, not your interpretation of the results of the student's work. If you did not record your inferences based on the quality of the work, how can you record a number for it? It would be better to keep personal notes to guide you in classroom planning.

The same principle applies to homework assignments, which are good ways for students to monitor their learning progress and to prepare and practice. If you intend homework to show evidence you will communicate with others, you need to design your homework assignments quite carefully. Have you taken steps to make sure that all students have opportunities to complete work outside of class? The quality of homework can be affected, for instance, by whether or not a student has a job or other duties outside the classroom. Using homework as a grading criterion can bias grades in favor of compliant students with few obligations outside school. Also, have you designed homework to make sure that all students are completing the homework themselves? Different parenting styles can affect the work students do at home considerably. Homework, in our view, is best used for independent practice and self-monitoring, and should be reviewed as needed by the teacher, perhaps with the whole class or in small groups, and on an individual basis as needed for students who are struggling.

Other Stage 2 assessments, like interactive assessments and group work, are notoriously hard to evaluate. If you desire to assess these components of classroom behavior because they strongly relate to standards in your discipline, you will need to devise objective ways to measure them formally. A specific issue with these behaviors is the need to distinguish participation, individually or in groups, in a way that measures substantive rather than superficial participation, and a way to tease out your own emotions—including optimism—from your interactions with students over learning. For all these reasons, we do not recommend incorporating Stage 2 assessments into your grading plan.

The Place of Stage 3 Formal Evidence in Stage 4 Grading

In the four-stage CA:SRL framework, the results of Stage 3 assessments are appropriate for use in reflection on accumulated learning and evaluation. The evidence you gather in Stage 3 should be of high quality, should be aligned with your SLOs, and should represent the work students can do independently after adequate instruction. The rubrics or other systematic rating methods you used to communicate the results to students and help support them in SRL should yield scores you can include in a grading system, which we will describe in more detail below.

For formal performances in Stage 3, especially as a marking period progresses, teachers may periodically assign projects or tasks that synthesize multiple learning objectives and sometimes multiple units of study. Such assessments are more complex than most of the types of tasks we have discussed in this volume, although we touched on them in Chapter 4. For instance, a project may synthesize book learning, independent research, multimedia presentation skills, and collaboration. Ultimately, however, such a project is a combination and culmination of multiple, discrete SLOs. If students have practiced skills in all the relevant domains and have had opportunities to practice and receive feedback on synthesizing the skills, and if you have assessed their skills in relative isolation, you and your students are prepared for formal assessment that can be graded. Encouraging synthesis of multiple, inter-related objectives is an excellent idea, as long as students have had opportunities to work on the relevant skills throughout the marking period and to practice synthesis before the skills are assessed.

For general guidance on whether it is appropriate to include an assessment as part of your students' grades, always refer to the purpose of the assessment, its relevance to the SLOs, whether you have provided students with adequate instruction and opportunities for learning from formative assessments, and whether it yielded scores that provide meaningful information about accumulated learning.

What Else Counts in Stage 4?

Some teachers want to include social and motivational components in classroom grades, in addition to information collected from formal assessments in Stage 3. Throughout this text, we have recommended collecting information about factors other than academic achievement. We have recommended collecting this kind of evidence to support student SRL and to support your interactions with students and your ability to practice shared regulation. Now we come to the question, is there a place for such information in Stage 4, the summation and reporting of student achievement? Let us look at various factors that have been found to influence teacher grading and consider them each in turn.

Effort

Some teachers explicitly include effort and engagement as components in their grading calculations, irrespective of achievement. For instance, they might give points for extra credit assignments that do not strongly relate to core learning objectives, or they might grade class participation regardless of the substance of that participation. These teachers may believe that effort and engagement support lifelong learning and are valid educational outcomes in and of themselves. Some teachers have been found to raise the grades of individual students who demonstrated effort and engagement, especially students who had scores at the borderline between grades (Randall & Engelhard 2009). In our own research, we have consistently found that teachers are more likely to support including effort in a classroom grade compared to any other non-achievement factor (Bonner & Chen, 2009; Chen & Bonner, 2017).

Despite the likely good intentions of such teachers, there are several arguments against including effort and engagement as dimensions of grading. First, we know of no systematic way to measure these variables in classrooms without raising the possibility of bias and unfairness in our judgments. Second, while it is true that effort and engagement support learning, they do not substitute for learning. Grades communicate student achievement to a wide audience, beyond the confines of the classroom. Including information about factors other than achievement is like putting fruit punch in grape juice bottles. It looks the same from the outside, and may even taste good, but it's not truth in advertising.

To discourage some teachers' tendencies to mix together some achievement and some effort or engagement factors, some schools report academic and non-academic outcomes separately. For an example, see Figure 5.4. There are advantages to this practice, but if not executed carefully, it can convey undesirable messages to students, particularly at higher levels of schooling when students become strategic. What interpretations might be made when "Achievement" and "Effort" are graded separately? A student with a high grade in the "Achievement" area and low marks for "Effort" might infer that they can excel effortlessly, with the result that they may fail to learn to expend energy to meet goals. Another student with the same grade profile might perceive that their effort isn't recognized and appreciated. How might a student interpret a *low* mark in "Achievement" area and a *high* rating in "Effort"? They may perceive that effort doesn't "pay," and respond by lowering their motivation for future endeavors. Your interpretations of student characteristics like effort should be communicated cautiously; it is often better, as we advocate with the CA:SRL framework, to encourage students to make self-interpretations about such characteristics.

We know of numerous better ways to support student effort and behavior in classrooms than through grading. Classroom activities that have high utility and relevance to students' lives result in improved interest (Hulleman, Godes, Hendricks, & Harackiewicz, 2010). Giving students the opportunity to choose the activities or topics they study engages them and helps them become invested in their own learning (Stefanou, Perencevich, DiCintio, & Turner, 2004). Training students in SRL processes also has a positive effect on intrinsic motivation, effort, attention, and other factors. Indeed, it is one of the tenets of the CA:SRL framework that when students receive support for these non-academic factors, they are likely to improve in their independent learning as well as SRL (Schmitz & Wiese, 2006). Developing SRL in students promotes learning; however, students' practices of SRL should not be treated as a learning outcome and evaluated by teachers.

Classroom Conduct

Another irregular grading practice involves awarding points to encourage good behavior in response to an academic task, and/or reducing grades to discourage bad behavior. In multiple studies, a small but distinct number of teachers report using grades that relate to classroom conduct and discipline or to reinforce compliance with classroom rules (Sun & Cheng, 2014; Cizek, Fitzgerald, & Rachor, 1996). Teachers sometimes use grades to reward positive student behaviors such as "paying attention" and completing ungraded homework, and to punish students for misconduct. Teachers may consider such practices necessary to establish their authority and a classroom culture of respect. Others may take a utilitarian, behaviorist standpoint: "It works." However, evidence from a synthesis of studies indicates a negative effect on both intrinsic motivation and learning when teachers use grades to reward or punish. Therefore, using grades as a "carrot" to promote effort may defeat the purpose (Harlen, 2004).

Moreover, no one can predict how behavioral grades, which inevitably carry an official status and remain on a student's permanent record, might be misinterpreted and used inappropriately by other people to whom they are reported: parents, future teachers, school leaders, and researchers. Instead of reporting behavioral grades, we recommend that teachers have space to comment on students' report cards. This allows communication about engagement, effort, behavior, and so on, without giving the false impression that the information is objective and reliable.

Selecting Scores After the Results Are In

Many teachers endorse dropping a low score from students' grade average (Chen & Bonner, 2017). We see this most at the secondary school level. The usual rationale for this practice is to make allowances for the bad days we all have from time to time, but the practice is problematic if it leads to grades that are not all based on the same learning objectives. If students in a chemistry class take five tests, each on a different topic, and each student's grade is solely based on their top four test scores, their grades do not all convey information about achievement of the same content. Knowing that one grade will be dropped may also motivate students not to try as hard when they know an upcoming assessment will be challenging. On the other hand, failure to inform the students in advance of this kind of grading policy is unfair.

We suggest two alternatives to dropping assignments based on score alone. One, when a grade includes multiple assessments of a skill that students are developing, it makes sense to weight early scores less than scores earned toward the end of a cycle. Second, we support allowing students to select samples of their best work, within teacher guidelines, such that all key learning objectives are represented, and with evidence of self-reflection and self-appraisal. This is the general basis for portfolio assessment. The use of portfolios for cumulative assessment purposes has declined in the U.S. over the last 20 years due to state testing mandates and the complexities of organizing and analyzing portfolios. Portfolios are, however, becoming more manageable through technology (see Chapter 9). Using an assessment system wherein students select and self-evaluate multiple pieces of work each of which is aligned to core SLOs addresses the "bad day" concern and supports student self-regulation and autonomy.

In Summary, What Do We Include in Stage 4 Reports?

You can see from Figure 5.3 that we strongly recommend that assessment information gathered in Stages 1 and 2 of CA:SRL not be compiled into grades or other reports at Stage 4. An assessment with a purely learning purpose cannot and should not be used to evaluate whether students have accomplished learning goals and summarize their level of accomplishment. Indeed, summarizing student learning-in-progress can deflate the potential learning benefits of quality assessment throughout instruction, by over-emphasizing performance orientation over mastery orientation. Stage 4 summaries of performance take place only periodically, and

DO include ...
✓ Formal assessments at the end of Stage 3 ✓ Culminating performances, projects, or tests that synthesize multiple units

DON'T include ...
✗ Pre-assessments ✗ Formative assessments for developing learning ✗ Information about student behaviors, perceptions, and attitudes that are not direct indicators of achievement

Possibly include ...
? In-class assignments or quizzes that are regular and announced ? Homework, if you are sure students have equal opportunities to complete it and you assign it for purposes other than independent practice ? Group work, if collaboration toward a goal is a learning objective and you can gather evidence about individual contributions ? Participation, if it can be measured objectively and is intrinsically essential to learning in the domain

Figure 5.3 What Counts Toward a Student's Grade?

with full information provided to students. Moreover, you should convey to your students that a summary report is not a final statement of the student's achievement, and does not equate to their intellectual capability. It expresses what you know about the student's achievement for now. You should combine it or update it with more information as the term proceeds.

How to Summarize Performance in Stage 4

Most of the Stage 4 achievement reporting you do as a classroom teacher will be in the form of grades. Grades are the ubiquitous piece of information about student achievement that is reported to various stakeholders. You, as a teacher, are a grade developer, just like the Educational Testing Service (ETS) is the developer of examinations like the Graduate Record Examinations (GRE). When you assign students a score on an assessment or assign a grade, you employ a deliberate system to rate and classify the quality of their classroom performance into ordered categories. Your ratings or classifications—whether in the form of letters, levels, or numbers—make it possible to rank students on a continuum that summarizes your perceptions of students' performance in your classroom over a certain period of time. When you "make" grades, you are directly responsible for how educational outcomes are defined, related to behaviors, and reported.

For practical as well as ethical reasons, you as a teacher needs to decide in advance of the marking period which assessments will be recorded in the gradebook. We emphasize that the Stage 3 assessments you include in your grade should be of the highest quality possible. They should be tasks you have designed, administered, interpreted, and scored using more formal procedures than you do in everyday classroom practice (e.g., at Stages 1 and 2). When people outside the classroom will see and use the assessment results, you need them to be solid interpretations of learning. The importance of making quality decisions at this stage of assessment cannot be overemphasized. With some cumulative assessments, there is little chance for feedback and no do-overs. To make grades good, interpretable indicators of achievement, we suggest various practices below.

How Grades Are Reported

The most common grading scale ranges from A to F. An A is interpreted as achievement at a very high level; F is interpreted as failure to achieve at the most basic level of expectations. Many high schools and middle schools use this kind of letter-grade reporting. Elementary schools sometimes use it for upper elementary levels only. Letter grades are usually derived from some kind of average of the scores that have gone into the teacher's gradebook. The average—or weighted average, as we will see below—is compared against a scale; for instance, an average of 88% will correspond to a grade of B+ because the range for a B+ is 87.5% to 89.9%.

Letter grades are often translated into number values and averaged across courses to create a grade point average (GPA). When a student in high school applies to college, the GPA becomes important as part of the college admissions process. Some schools, especially high schools, report simple percent averages in lieu of letter grades. They may or may not report an average across all courses, which can be converted to a GPA. Many colleges re-calculate student GPAs, weighting courses at an advanced or honors level more heavily in determining GPA, and non-academic courses like physical education less heavily.

A school may have a policy of reporting only quality levels such as "Honors," "Pass," and "Incomplete," either for specific courses or schoolwide. These descriptors are usually accompanied by a written summary of the student's strengths and weaknesses in the subject. This approach to cumulative assessment is more holistic than traditional grading. It also communicates the value that failure is not an option; rather, some students have not yet met the requirements for passing. In some cases, students may be able to negotiate for an Honors designation by opting to perform advanced-level work. One of the authors of this book attended a school that used this system in all of its courses, elementary through high school. Students and parents found the narrative reports issued every nine weeks very informative. However, there was a problem when students at the high school level applied to colleges: they had no grades to report on their transcripts. Eventually, the school switched to a traditional reporting method.

A method of reporting achievement that we recommend is called standards-based grading. Figure 5.4 shows an excerpt from a standards-based report card on the Common Core ELA Listening and Speaking Standards for sixth grade. If your school uses this method, you as a teacher do not report a single overall mark, but a group of ratings related to a set of academic standards that are covered in your course. Typically, you rate each student at one of four levels for each academic standard: does not meet the standard, approaches the standard, meets the standard, exceeds the standard. Your decisions about a student's proficiency are not based on the accumulation of evidence across the whole course, but on evidence of work on each standard. In standards-based grading, your assessments need to be strongly linked to the academic standards. Also, your assessment of the student's proficiency should be revisited frequently throughout the grading, as students have new opportunities to learn and be reassessed.

The information that students and parents receive on a standards-based report card is much more detailed than that provided under the traditional A–F scheme. Many schools that use standards-based grading also give teachers a specific space in which to report behaviors such as effort, collaboration, and work habits. As you've seen, it's best not to include those kinds of behaviors in an academic grade. When you can report them separately, students and parents

Anywhere School District, Anywhere, NY

GRADE 6 REPORT CARD
John Doe Middle School
2019–2020

Student:	Peggy P. Chen	Teacher:	Sarah M. Bonner

Performance Indicators

4. Exceeds understanding of standard
Student consistently grasps, applies, and extends key concepts, processes, and skills; works **beyond** standards.
3. Meets standard
Student grasps and applies key concepts, processes, and skills. **Meets** standards.
2. Developing understanding of standard
Student is beginning to grasp and apply key concepts, processes, and skills. **Approaches** standards.
1. Does not meet standard
Student is not grasping key concepts, processes, and essential skills. **Area of concern**.

English Language Arts: Speaking and Listening	T1	T2	T3
Comprehension and Collaboration			
Engage effectively in collaborative discussions (CCSS.ELA-LITERACY.SL.6.1)	3		
Interpret information in diverse media and formats (CCSS.ELA-LITERACY.SL.6.2)	2		
Delineate a speaker's arguments and claims (CCSS.ELA-LITERACY.SL.6.3)	2		
Presentation of Knowledge and Ideas			
Present claims and findings logically (CCSS.ELA-LITERACY.SL.6.4)	2		
Include multimedia components (CCSS.ELA-LITERACY.SL.6.5)	1		
Adapt speech to a variety of contexts (CCSS.ELA-LITERACY.SL.6.6)	3		

Behaviors That Support School Success	T1	T2	T3
Asks for help when needed	1		
Stays engaged despite distractions	2		
Follows directions	3		
Works well with others	3		

Teacher Comments

Glow: You ask challenging and meaningful questions when your peers present.
Grow: Please remember to include a graphic to illustrate your argument.

Figure 5.4 Sample Standards-Based Report Card

88 Section I Chapter 5

perceive that you and your school value them, but also that they are not the same as academic proficiency.

Nowadays, many schools use electronic gradebooks as part of bigger information management systems. These systems help schools keep track of attendance, classes and scheduling, and many kinds of other student information. The teacher functions in these systems allow you to record students' grades, and enter other information about your evaluation policies for Stage 4, such as due dates, and points or weights for each graded assignment. Many of these programs allow parents and students to log in via mobile apps to see grades, assignments, and due dates. Sometimes assignment files can be attached for students or their parents to download from home. These programs do not take away your responsibility for grading decisions, but they make record keeping much more convenient and transparent. They also support SRL by allowing students to keep track of their own progress.

The Composition of Grades

You should decide your method of evaluating the accumulated evidence of student learning before a semester begins. Being able to tell students in advance what will "count," and how much, promotes fairness in communication with students and families, particularly in the upper grades. Even in the lower grades, you may find yourself fiddling with your grades as the term progresses if you do not make these decisions in advance, which can cause personal feelings to creep into your interpretations of student work and detract from students' perceptions that they participate in their own learning and achievement.

How you represent achievement numerically influences students' final grades more than you might think, as we shall see. The first decision that should be made—again, before the start of the marking period—is how much each kind of assessment should be mathematically weighted to calculate the final grade. It is probably obvious to you that not all assessments are created equal: some assess more crucial learning objectives; some require synthesis of multiple objectives; some are based on many instructional days with many opportunities for formative assessment; some are small snapshots of isolated bits of knowledge or skill.

We will not expand on every single approach to weighting student work for calculating final grades. Instead, we will focus on one common method: categorical weighting. If you use this method, you group your assessments by type (categories). Then you combine all the scores within a type, average them, and multiply them by a percent value you have assigned to that category. If you choose this type of grade calculation, most electronic gradebooks will take the raw scores you input for each assignment of a type and automatically link their average into the category field. They will also weight the category averages according to the percent value you assign to calculate the final grade.

To understand this better, let's consider an example. Imagine a science teacher who is looking at 9-week marking period scores from a biology class. The teacher has categorized the assessments into four groups: Performance Assessments (labs), Homework, a single Cumulative Test, and Group Work. This is illustrated for 10 students in Table 5.1.

The first thing we need to know to understand this table is where the scores in each column come from. With the exception of the test, they are composites of individual assessments, usually based on averaging across the number of assessments of that type. To show this, notice that Amy has an 85 in PA and a 95 in Homework. Kevin has an 80 in PA and an 85 in Homework. How did the teacher derive these scores? Look at Table 5.2, which shows those two grade categories broken down by individual assessment for these two students.

Reflection on Overall Performance 89

Table 5.1 Students' 9-Week Marking Period Scores in Biology Class

Name	Performance Assessment	Homework	Cumulative Test	Group Work
Amy	85	95	90	85
Kevin	80	85	70	95
Mike	85	85	70	90
Zoey	95	85	90	100
Richard	95	65	95	80
Luka	95	85	90	85
Kathy	70	95	60	95
Charlie	85	95	85	80
Tiffany	85	75	80	75
Skylar	75	80	70	90

Table 5.2 Break Down: Amy and Kevin's Homework and Performance Assessments

Name	PA1	PA2	PA3	PA Average	H1	H2	H3	H4	H5	H6	H7	H8	H8	H10	H Average
Amy	86	79	90	85%	10	10	10	8	10	8	9	10	10	10	95%
Kevin	79	83	78	80%	8	9	9	9	8	7	8	9	9	9	85%

You see that there were three performance assessments (science labs) and 10 formal graded homework assignments. The percent scores on each PA are averaged to yield that 85% value in the PA category on Table 5.2 for Amy, and 85% for Kevin. The individual scores from the homework assignments are added and converted to a percent and appear in the Homework category on Table 5.1. Note that each homework assignment was worth the same number of points (10 points). It is a good idea to have each assignment within the same category have the same number of points to avoid inadvertently weighting some assignments in the same category more heavily than others in the grade.

Now we will examine how different weights that the teacher might decide to assign to each category would influence grades. Table 5.3 shows exactly the same values as Table 5.1, but with two additional columns showing the results of weighting the categories differently.

In Weighting Scheme 1, the teacher decided to count each category of assessment equally toward the marking period grade. Since there are four categories, each category is worth 25% of the final grade. The teacher considered that all the different sources of evidence represented equally important and meaningful information about student achievement.

In Weighting Scheme 2, the teacher made a very different decision. They considered the performance assessments most important because these assessments required students to synthesize their learning, and much of the marking period's instructional time led up to each one. Therefore, labs counted as 60% of the marking period grade. Homework did not count at all because homework was considered purely formative in nature. The cumulative test counted 30%, which is quite a bit; group work counted 10%.

Note the effect of the different weighting schemes on students' final scores. Two extreme examples are highlighted: Richard and Kathy. Richard did very well on the formal

90   Section I   Chapter 5

Table 5.3 Ways to Weight the Final Grades

Name	Performance Assessments	Homework	Cumulative Test	Group Work	Weighting Scheme 1	Weighting Scheme 2
Amy	85	95	90	85	88.8	86.5
Kevin	80	85	70	95	82.5	78.5
Mike	85	85	70	90	82.5	81
Zoey	95	85	90	100	92.5	94
Richard	95	65	95	80	83.8	93.5
Luka	95	85	90	85	88.8	92.5
Kathy	70	95	60	95	80	69.5
Charlie	85	95	85	80	86.3	84.5
Tiffany	85	75	80	75	78.8	82.5
Skylar	75	80	70	90	78.8	75

assessments—PAs and the test—but not as well on homework and group work. Under Weighting Scheme 1, he achieved an 84% average, which would translate into a B in traditional grade conversions. However, under Weighting Scheme 2 he achieves a 94%, or an A. Kathy, on the other hand, performed poorly on formal assessments, but did well on homework and works very well in groups. Under Weighting Scheme 1, her letter grade would be a B–, but under Weighting Scheme 2, a C–.

The example above shows the importance of a teacher's decision about what should "count" in grades and how much. These decisions should be based on sound knowledge of assessment that takes into consideration the purpose of each type of assessment, the importance of the topics assessed relative to the learning goals of the marking period, and how well different sources of information represent substantive learning.

There are two additional ways that number values can change or distort the way you communicate about student achievement through grades. One way is when a teacher enters "zero" values in a gradebook to represent work that is not turned in. To understand this effect, let's look at the same set of scores as in Table 5.4, with a single exception: Charlie did not take the cumulative test. Table 5.4 shows two rows for Charlie, demonstrating two different reporting methods for a missed assignment, and their impacts on a weighted average.

As you can see from the Table 5.4, the teacher has used Weighting Scheme 2: 60% for PAs, 0% for Homework, 30% for the test, and 10% for Group Work. Charlie, a student who generally does well on formal assessments, does not take the test. If the teacher enters a score of zero (0), Charlie will receive a failing grade, based on the average. If the teacher enters a score that represents the highest failing score (55, below a D–), Charlie will receive a grade of C. This is because in averaging scores, a single score well beyond the typical range (called an outlier) can strongly influence the calculated average, especially when only a few scores are used to calculate the average. To avoid this result, many schools now use a policy called "minimum grading," in which teachers are expected to enter the highest failing score rather than a zero for missing assignments (Carey & Carifio, 2012).

Another way that simple mathematics can affect grades is through the use of unequal scales. Let us say you have decided that one component of your grading system will be based on essay assessments written in class. You assign six of these essay tasks. You put a score in your gradebook for each of the first five essay assignments on a scale of 1–6, based on a rubric of overall writing quality. For the last essay, you use a more analytic rubric, which breaks down your analysis of writing among six dimensions, each on a scale of 6. With six points in each of six

Reflection on Overall Performance 91

Table 5.4 Ways to Weight a Missed Test

Name	Performance Assessment	Homework	Cumulative Test	Group Work	Weighted Average	Grade
Amy	85	95	90	85	86.5	B
Kevin	80	85	70	95	78.5	C+
Mike	85	85	70	90	81	B–
Zoey	95	85	90	100	94	A
Richard	95	65	95	80	93.5	A
Luka	95	85	90	85	92.5	A
Kathy	70	80	60	95	69.5	D+
Charlie	85	95	0	80	59	F
Charlie	85	95	55	80	75.5	C
Tiffany	85	75	80	75	82.5	B
Skylar	75	80	70	90	75	C

Table 5.5 Comparing Essay Scoring Methods

	E1	E2	E3	E4	E5	E6	E7	Overall
	6pts	6pts	6pts	6pts	6pts	6pts	36pts	
Method A	4	5	6	4	5	6	24	75%, percent of total points available
Method B	67%	83%	100%	67%	83%	100%	67%	81%, average of percent earned on each task

dimensions, the total points available for scoring this essay assignment are 36, and you record the score out of 36 for each student in your gradebook.

Now let's look at the essay scores for Mia in Table 5.5. Mia scored between four and six points on each of the first six essay assignments. On essay 7, she scored 24 out of 36 points. Note that her percent score (bottom row) for essay 7 is the same score that she earned for essays 1 and 4. However, her cumulative score for essays changes, depending on how the score for the overall essay field is calculated. If you just add up all the simple raw scores and divide by the number of points available, the result is 75%. If you first convert each essay score to an average of the total points available for that essay, the overall score is 81%. This is because the overall score in row A is heavily influenced by the value for essay 7, which has six times as many points as any of the other essay assignments. It is as if that single essay were worth six others. If you want all essay assignments to be weighted equally, you need to use the same scale for each one, or at least convert to percentages before averaging.

Large-Scale Assessment: Stage 4 Writ Large

As we stated in the beginning of this chapter, when it comes to Stage 4 assessments, many more stakeholders are involved than you and the students in your classroom. Although state and national testing is not a part of CA, these assessment systems affect your schools, you, and your students and communities. Therefore, we summarize some of the key features of state and national testing systems next.

State Tests for Accountability and the "Nation's Report Card"

Since the 1990s, the U.S. government has implemented a system of accountability for school performance as measured by state tests, which are aligned to state standards. Test performance outcomes are tied to federal funding. Student proficiency on state tests is represented at different levels: from failing to meet the state's standards of proficiency to exceeding proficiency expectations. This is known as *criterion-referenced testing* (CRT). In CRT, score interpretations are based on each student's score relative to *cut scores* or points that demarcate benchmarks for proficiency levels. These benchmarks are set by panelists composed of content experts, teachers, school administrators, and university faculty. CRT is compared to *norm-referenced testing* (NRT), like the SAT and ACT, where student scores are reported relative to those of other students taking the same test. Policymakers who support test-driven school accountability believe a CRT system for educational accountability pushes schools to offer high-quality programs so that students can meet high performance expectations.

The logic of using state CRT tests for educational accountability has been controversial. There have been problems in interpreting results, because each state has its own tests and its own educational standards, which has led to poor comparability of results between states. State officials can adjust their benchmarks for proficiency to allow large percentages of students to "pass," rather than improve teaching so all students could learn and meet similarly high expectations.

To find out whether gains in passing rates on state tests are valid indicators of increasing achievement in the U.S., analysts use data from the National Assessment of Educational Progress (NAEP), which is sometimes called the "Nation's Report Card." The NAEP generates information about academic performance based on samples of students of different demographics, at different grade levels, and different regions of the U.S. Like state accountability tests, NAEP is a CRT test; it reports performance according to proficiency level. Unlike state accountability tests, NAEP is a national assessment, so can be used to make state-to-state performance comparisons. Using NAEP data, research have found mixed changes in student performance since the advent of the test-driven accountability system. Some gains have been shown in student achievement in mathematics, but there is no evidence that the test-based accountability system has impacted reading (Dee & Jacob, 2011). Negative effects have been reported, such as loss of instructional time, narrowing of the curriculum, and school resources being shifted from support of learning to test administration (Zellmer, Frontier, & Pheifer, 2006).

Although federal law only requires that states take action to improve schools that continually fail to make state proficiency benchmarks, some states have elected to make students accountable for their own scores, by using passing scores as a requirement for high school graduation. Some states have also experimented with using student state-test scores as part of teacher evaluation. Recently, however, a trend has emerged against the use of state tests for student-level or teacher-level accountability. Many states that initially elected to use tests for teacher evaluation have since shied away from this practice.

Educational accountability systems in the U.S. will continue to evolve. In 2015, the Every Student Succeeds Act (ESSA) allowed states more leeway in their choice of assessments. To emphasize college readiness, states are now permitted to use college admissions tests, as well as locally developed measures, to assess student proficiency. Several states have backed away from a strong emphasis on large-scale testing. For the time being, however, the main tenets of accountability remain in place. Schools continue to be held accountable for showing evidence of student cumulative achievement. Consistent failure to show progress in student performance outcomes puts schools at risk for reorganization or closure. The award of federal Title I funding to states hinges on performance at least partly measured by tests of standards-based outcomes.

References

Bonner, S. M., & Chen, P. P. (2009). Teacher candidates' perceptions about grading and constructivist teaching. *Educational Assessment, 14*(2), 57–77.

Carey, T., & Carifio, J. (2012). The minimum grading controversy: Results of a quantitative study of seven years of grading data from an urban high school. *Educational Researcher, 41*(6), 201–208.

Chen, P. P., & Bonner, S. M. (2017). Teachers' beliefs about grading practices and a constructivist approach to teaching. *Educational Assessment, 22,* 18–34.

Cizek, G. J., Fitzgerald, S. M., & Rachor, R. E. (1996). Teachers' assessment practices: Preparation, isolation, and the kitchen sink. *Educational Assessment, 3*(2), 159–179.

Dee, T. S., & Jacob, B. (2011). The impact of No Child Left Behind on student achievement. *Journal of Policy Analysis and management, 30*(3), 418–446.

Harlen, W. (2004). *A systematic review of the evidence of the impact on students, teachers and the curriculum of the process of using assessment by teachers for cumulative purposes.* London: EPPI-Centre, Social Science Research Unit, Institute of Education. Retrieved from http://eppi.ioe.ac.uk/cms/Portals/0/PDF%20reviews%20and%20summaries/ass_rv4.pdf?ver=2006-03-02-124724-997

Hulleman, C. S., Godes, O., Hendricks, B. L., & Harackiewicz, J. M. (2010). Enhancing interest and performance with a utility value intervention. *American Psychological Association, 102*(4), 880–895.

National Association for College Admission Counseling. (2016). *Factors in admission decisions.* Retrieved from www.nacacnet.org/globalassets/documents/publications/research/soca_chapter3.pdf

Randall, J., & Engelhard, G. (2009). Differences between teachers' grading practices in elementary and middle schools. *The Journal of Educational Research, 10*(2), 175–185.

Schmitz, B., & Wiese, B. S. (2006). New perspectives for the evaluation of training sessions in self-regulated learning: Time-series analyses of diary data. *Contemporary Education Psychology, 31,* 64–96.

Stefanou, C. R., Perencevich, K. C., DiCintio, M., & Turner, J. C. (2004). Supporting autonomy in the classroom: Ways teachers encourage student decision making and ownership. *Educational Psychologist, 39*(2), 97–110.

Sun, Y., & Cheng, L. (2014). Teachers' grading practices: Meaning and values assigned. *Assessment in Education: Principles, Policy, & Practice, 21*(3), 326–343.

Thomas, S., & Oldfather, P. (1997). Intrinsic motivations, literacy, and assessment practice: "That's my grade. That's me." *Educational Psychologist, 32*(2), 107–123.

Tyson, W., & Roksa, J. (2017). Importance of grades and placement for math attainment. *Educational Researcher, 46*(3), 140–142.

Zellmer, M. B., Frontier, A., & Pheifer, D. (2006). What are NCLB's instructional costs? *Educational Leadership, 64*(3), 43.

Part 2

Section 2 Introduction
Technical Quality and Technology in Assessment

According to the *Standards for Educational and Psychological Testing* (2014), reliability, validity, and fairness are the foundations of educational assessment. Each concept has been defined and refined over more than a century of theory and applied research in education. While the techniques for evaluating these concepts and their characteristics are mostly used in large-scale testing, the ideas that underpin reliability, validity, and fairness are tremendously important in classroom assessment. Throughout this section, we encourage you to think about how you can inquire into, self-reflect on, and co-reflect with your students on your own assessment practices. Feedback about your CA practices from multiple sources will help ensure that you are using assessment to obtain credible and sufficient information for classroom decision-making.

In the first three chapters of this section, we discuss these core concepts in depth, primarily through the lens of CA purposes and contexts. The section closes with a chapter on the use of technology in assessment. Digital technology affords students and teachers unique opportunities for real-time feedback and peer-to-peer, student-teacher, or whole-class interaction. In each chapter, we show the relationship of the topic to previously covered material and the four-stage CA:SRL framework, and where the topic is synergistic with promotion of SRL.

Reliability is consistency of assessment results and interpretations. It tells us how much we can trust our results. In Chapter 6 you will learn about how different sources of random error can affect one's ability to interpret observations of student performance. You will learn methods for maximizing the dependability of your interpretations at all points in a classroom assessment cycle. You will also learn how reliability affects interpretations of large-scale educational test results.

Validity is the quality of interpretations drawn from assessments: how well interpretations relate to the assessment purpose. Chapter 7 presents principles that classroom teachers can use to guide them when designing, administering, and interpreting assessments for the purpose of learning improvement. You will have the opportunity to study multiple examples of how teachers and other assessment developers judge the validity of classroom assessment processes as well as large-scale assessments.

Chapter 8 discusses the concept of fairness and its applications to classroom assessment and large-scale educational testing. We focus on three ways that fairness is interpreted in the educational literature: as a technical quality of an assessment tool, as a set of procedures and principles to guide an assessment system, and as a societal goal. You will learn essential concepts about different dimensions of fairness, legal standards for fairness in testing students with special needs, and practical techniques to improve fairness in K–12 assessment.

Chapter 9 discusses the use of technology in classroom assessment and large-scale testing contexts. Digital technology pervades the educational and life-experiences of students. This chapter will introduce you to ways teachers can use technology to promote quality assessment at each stage of the four-stage framework for CA. You will learn about an array of techniques for using technology in classroom, noting examples where digital technology can provide students with opportunities to engage in forethought, set their own goals, seek help with, and reflect on performance.

An Added Note on Technical Quality

Concerns about the technical quality of classroom assessments have often been raised as a reason to question the interpretability of teacher grades and other decisions made from evidence gathered in classrooms. On that basis, student assessment is sometimes taken out of teachers' hands, which can result in a perception that teachers are not the experts in their schools, or cause teachers to be concerned about lack of professional autonomy. We believe that when teachers put high-quality, reasoned, theoretically-based assessment practices into use in their classrooms, such as those we propound in the four-stage CA:SRL framework, and when they pay due attention to the technical quality of their interpretations and use of assessment results, their decisions will justify heightened respect for teacher professionalism.

Chapter 6

Reliability
Making Sure You Can Depend on Your Data

What is this thing called *reliability* in assessment? Think about it in terms of your own experience. You probably know someone about whom you can say, "They are pretty reliable!" What do you mean? Maybe you mean you can count on them. Count on them for what? As a friend? Think of a person who is always late. Time after time, they arrive late for coffee, for a meeting, for class. Is that person reliable? Yes. They are reliably late. You can count on them. Their behavior is consistent.

Reliability, you see, doesn't necessarily mean consistency in good behavior or in bad behavior; it's just consistency, free from any value judgment. A behavior can be reliably proficient or less than proficient—before we can judge it either way, we must be confident that we can trust our own interpretation. The quality of reliability drives how confident we are about any interpretation we make based on observational information. From now on, let's assume that the word *consistency* expresses the big idea of reliability.

Reliability is an essential characteristic of high-quality educational assessments. In fact, specialists in the field of educational measurement refer to reliability as a *sine qua non*—a Latin phrase which means "without which, nothing." In other words, if you don't have reliability to start with, you don't have anything to interpret. Without reliability, as far as you can tell, your scores may be random observations without interpretable meaning.

Why do we need to be concerned about reliability in classroom assessment? As we all know from experience, we can't always trust the judgments we make based on a single occasion of observation. A good example of this is body weight. One of the authors of this book has the habit of going to a large department store to check her weight. She goes to the section where scales are on display, takes off her shoes and coat, sets down her bag, and steps on one of the display scales. She reads her weight as displayed on the scale. But does she stop there? No. She steps off the scale, replaces it on the shelf, and tries another scale. This scale displays a slightly different weight. Once more she repeats the process. She obtains a third weight. This value is different again. The weights provided by the different scales are estimates—none of them is an exact measurement of her true weight.

As we see in this example, even measurements of exactly the same thing, measured very close together in time, are not all equal. Everything we measure is measured with some amount of error. This is a small concern when the author wants to measure her weight, but a big concern when a teacher wants to measure a student's academic achievement. The question is, how *much* error is in the measurement? That is what we try to understand when we estimate reliability.

Random Error and Its Sources

Experts organize the ways reliability is estimated according to different factors. These correspond to sources of random error, or what we call *measurement error*. By error, we don't mean the kind of error of getting something wrong on a test item. We mean measuring something incorrectly. In particular, we mean measuring something incorrectly by accident, in an unpredictable way. Logically and mathematically, the more measurement error, the lower the reliability of our observations—and thus, the less confidence we have in them, and the harder they are to interpret.

There are lots of ways random error can creep into our assessments of students and the scores or results we record. Below, we will briefly look at some ways experts have described these sources of random error. We'll discuss this issue in more detail with examples, and provide summaries (Figures 6.2, 6.5, and 6.8). As you read, remember that measurement error is the opposite of reliability. Therefore, the more measurement error, the less reliable or trustworthy are your scores, and the less you can be confident about interpretations you make from them.

Day-to-Day Fluctuations as a Source of Random Error

Explanation

Consider the case of a multiple-choice test on which some students guess. Some will have lucky guesses, and some will not. Some students will miss points even though they know the material, because they are distracted by something, like a person chewing gum. But luck and mischance fluctuate randomly. To the extent that luck or accident affects their scores, their scores are unreliable. If the student were to be assessed on another time, another day, it's very unlikely that this same luck or accident would occur again. So day-to-day fluctuations in chance occurrences is an issue having to do with reliability. We usually generally use the word *time* to refer to error that stems from individual day-to-day fluctuations.

It's important to realize that if you're a teacher and are scoring the test, you don't know about these random bits of luck or accident. When the student is lucky and bubbles in the keyed response, you score their answer "right." When the student makes an accidental mistake, you score their answer "wrong." You don't know that these were chance occurrences. You only see the result, which departs slightly from what it would be if there were no random fluctuations involved.

Time influences student scores on assessments in essay writing as well. A student's ability to express their ideas in essay format is not likely to change much from Tuesday to Wednesday of the same week (unless, of course, the student learns from self-reflection or intense overnight studying). However, even though their writing ability stays pretty constant, their essay performance will still fluctuate. Say that you give your students a generic essay prompt on a Tuesday: "Write a five-paragraph essay that persuades the audience to adopt a specific healthy habit." Some of the students are in bad moods, perhaps because they missed breakfast or argued with a friend. On the following day, if you assign a very similar essay, those students may be in better moods. Others who concentrated well on Tuesday may not do so on Wednesday for all different kinds of reasons of their own. Mood, energy, and personal experiences influence every individual's ability to demonstrate their skills from day to day. Because we have no way to predict when or how much these kinds of things affect individual performance, we consider them to be sources of random error.

Evaluating Day-to-Day Fluctuations in Classroom Assessment

As we discuss day-to-day random error in CA, we focus on Stage 1 in the CA:SRL framework. We use Stage 1 here only for the purpose of example. Random fluctuations affect reliability at all stages of CA.

We have shown in Chapter 2 that Stage 1, before instruction begins, is an important time to collect evidence of student prior knowledge and pre-conceptions. Sometimes the results of a pre-assessment indicate pretty clearly where students can begin and from what point to move ahead. When this happens, we can set a clear instructional direction. At other times, the evidence is fuzzier. This can very often happen with the assessment of young children, whose attention fluctuates from day to day more than does the attention of older students.

When we have reason to believe that our assessment of students' pre-requisite skills may be less than dependable or provide too little information on which to base our instructional decisions moving forward, we may consider obtaining what are called *multiple baselines*. Obtaining multiple baselines means making multiple, similar observations over a short period of time prior to the start of instruction.

For instance, prior to assigning students to reading levels for literacy instruction, you may want to ask the students to read similar passages and answer questions about them daily, for a few days in a row. This will help even out the effect of the basically random factors that sometimes make it hard to get a reliable estimate of reading comprehension: student mood, energy, attention, and so on. For young children, it may be useful to get multiple baselines of performance on everyday school routines, such as entering the classroom in an orderly way, taking a seat, or stowing a book bag under the chair. A teacher shouldn't make an interpretation about whether an individual student or all the students are ill- or well-behaved based on only one occasion of measurement.

In classroom teaching and assessment, the use of multiple baseline observations is most common among special educators. When working with students who may have disabilities, special educators frequently take multiple baselines before implementing an intervention and evaluating what is called the *Response to Intervention*, commonly referred to as RTI. The concept of RTI was developed to describe the process of obtaining highly specific assessments of an individual student's skill or behavior. Multiple observations are conducted to establish where the student is "at." Then an intervention appropriate to the student's skill level is planned and carried out. After the intervention, the behavior of the student is observed again to see if the intervention had its intended effect. Although multiple baseline observations are most typically made on individual students who are being considered for special services, the logic of multiple baselines and RTI in general clearly has applications to the CA:SRL framework, especially at Stage 1.

In Figure 6.1, you can see an example of a graphical display of results from a multiple baseline assessment process in a third-grade classroom. Each of four students is asked to read a short, grade-level passage every day for six days in a row. High values on the y-axis represent errors in reading, so the higher the point on the line, the less fluent the student's oral reading.

You see from the graph that Flora is consistently making multiple errors in reading, every day. The trend of Lily's performance is also consistent. Lily makes, on average, the fewest errors, and Lily's error scores from day to day are in a similar range. Violet varies a lot from day to day. On the first assessment day, Violet made very many errors; on the second day, relatively few. After those two days, her reading seems to stabilize and is more consistent over the next three assessments. Why did she show these results? It's not clear, unless you as the teacher ask Violet to self-reflect. Perhaps Violet was familiar with the second reading passage or distracted by a classmate on the first day. Now look at Rose—her scores fluctuate considerably every day. Even after six measurements, you would have a hard time knowing how to describe Rose's reading. This is a point where your information from this assessment is not reliable, and you might consider consulting a reading specialist.

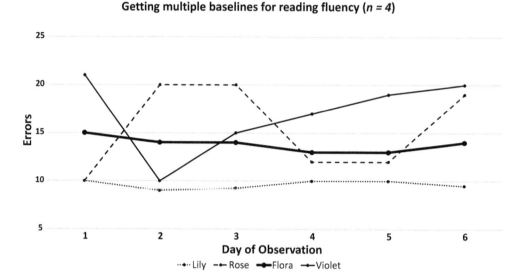

Figure 6.1 Getting Multiple Baselines for Reading Fluency

Large-Scale Testing Approaches to Estimating Day-to-Day Fluctuations: Test-Retest Reliability

Test developers sometimes conduct what is known as a test-retest reliability study in order to understand the extent to which the scores that their tests produce are consistent over time. They select a sample of students and administer exactly the same test to those students twice, often about two weeks apart in time—enough time so the students won't remember the test questions, but not so much time that the students will have substantially increased their knowledge. It's expensive to arrange a test-retest reliability study, and the timing can be tricky. But once the data are obtained, it's simple to analyze. One only has to calculate the correlation between the scores on the first administration (Time1) and the second administration (Time2). If the correlation between Time1 and Time2 is .90, the test-retest reliability coefficient is .90, and one can say that 90% of the variability in the test scores is due to a consistent knowledge or skill component that was measured, and 10% is due to random fluctuations over time or other random factors. (Note that correlations cannot usually be interpreted as percentages of variability; one can only make this kind of interpretation with a reliability coefficient.)

The *standard error of measurement* (SEM) is an interesting statistic that can be derived if you have a reliability coefficient and the standard deviation of a distribution of scores. The SEM expresses how many points on a scale, plus or minus, a score might likely vary due to random error. If the reliability term in the SEM is based on a test-retest study, the SEM expresses how many points a score might likely vary due to day-to-day fluctuations. The formula for the SEM is given below, where the notation *SD* represents standard deviation, and *r* represents the reliability coefficient.

$$SEM = SD\sqrt{1-r}$$

Let's take one of the SAT tests as an example. According to the College Board (2015), the test-retest reliability coefficient of the Critical Reading test ranges from .91 to .92 over studies.

Explanation	Techniques	In large-scale testing
• Different random factors shape students' performance, day to day. • They may guess differently or be in a different mood. • We can't predict or control how these factors shape their performance.	• To make strong decisions based on pre-assessments, you need a baseline. • Similar multiple baseline measurements show more reliability than highly fluctuating multiple baselines.	• When developing a test, administer the same test to the same sample twice. • Correlate results to yield a test-retest reliability metric. • Calculate the standard error of measurement to see how much score points might fluctuate due to differences, day to day.

Figure 6.2 Source of Random Error: Time

Based on reported statistics, the standard deviation of the test was approximately 103. Given the SEM formula, one SEM is therefore equal to approximately 30 points.

How do we interpret this? SEMs correspond to standard deviation units, and under the assumption of a normal distribution (which is appropriate for large-scale tests), 68% of test scores are likely to fall within 1 standard deviation, or plus or minus 1 SEM, of a sample score. Therefore, we predict that an individual test-taker's score on this test might vary by plus or minus 1 SEM due to day-to-day random fluctuations alone. If a student took the SAT Critical Reading test on one occasion and obtained a score of 620, it would not be surprising for the student to score anywhere between 590 and 650 on taking the test again, with no additional learning experiences. This may put into perspective the apparently astonishing gains that some students make on the SAT with expensive test preparation. Some portion of score changes are simply due to random effects.

You might also be interested in thinking about test-retest error in the context of high-stakes pass-fail decisions, such as licensure testing. In a licensure or certification test, the decision about whether or not a test-taker passes is based on their score, which is compared to what is known as a *cut score*—the minimum score for passing. A person with a score one point below the passing "cut" will be failed. This is true with proficiency classifications on state tests as well. A test-taker below passing fails, no matter by how small a margin, while a test-taker just one point above may "squeak through." The decisions are made on the assumption that the effect of random measurement error is very low. This is why it is so important for reliability to be as high as possible in high-stakes tests, and to minimize day-to-day fluctuations by reminding students, for instance, to get a good night's sleep and eat breakfast.

Item and Task Characteristics as a Source of Random Error

Explanation

Whenever we assess something like achievement in a content area, we do so by observing behavior. We ask or expect students to perform: answer a question, display a skill, and so on. Even simple individual assessment items that we offer have little idiosyncrasies of wording that affect student behavior in unpredictable ways. Groups of items that compose larger tasks also have characteristics that are not essential to the learning objective, but we need them to prompt students to respond. For instance, student ability to read directions is not typically an educational objective. However, if directions are unclear, students' scores will be influenced in ways that have nothing to do with their achievement on the objective. The number of items on an assessment task is another task characteristic that influences scores, although it is not part of the measured construct.

More complex essay and performance assessments results can also be affected by seemingly random influences. Many studies have shown that when students perform multiple complex tasks within a single domain, their scores can vary considerably from task to task (e.g., Brennan & Johnson, 1995). Say, for instance, that students are asked to interpret, analyze, and make predictions from data about different but similar topics in biology. Researchers have found that their scores vary even more than would be predicted due to day-to-day fluctuations alone. This has been found to be true in the domain of writing as well. This phenomenon has become known as the *person x task interaction*, meaning that people's performances are different depending on the task they're given, even when tasks are very similar. This is one of the reasons large-scale testing programs do not often include essay tasks or performance assessments: they do not provide reliable samples because their results are affected by item-specific factors, and it isn't feasible to include enough of these complicated tasks to improve reliability to a satisfactory degree.

Evaluating Error From Item and Task Characteristics in Classroom Assessment

The *person x task interaction* has implications for your CA practice. When you need to be highly confident in an assessment-based decision, for instance when you are submitting your grades, a few essays or labs per semester probably do not provide enough information. In general, problems crop up when we gather too little information to form a precise estimate of student knowledge or skill. As you read the scenario below, ask yourself, "How many questions is enough?" Figure 6.3 shows a middle school social studies teacher's quizlet of three selected-response items, each constituting a mini-task. The items are intended to assess learning objectives related to the Common Core literacy standard in eighth-grade social studies CCSS.ELA-Literacy.RH.6–8.8: "Distinguish among fact, opinion, and reasoned judgment in a text."

Directions: Each of the statements below is a different kind of statement. Label each of the statements according to which kind by writing if it is: fact (F), opinion (O), or reasoned judgment (RJ). Each kind of writing is used only once. (CCSS.ELA-LITERACY.RH.6–8.8)	
Statement	**F — O — RJ**
The influenza pandemic that began in 1918 was first identified among soldiers fighting in Europe in World War I.	
The disease was hard to track because some countries in Europe minimized reports of fatalities to boost wartime morale.	
Modern transportation posed the greatest threat to public health safety during the pandemic.	

Figure 6.3 Example Quizlet in Social Studies

Think about this example as an overall task. Does it provide sufficient information for you to feel confident interpreting a student's score? Note that the chance of earning a score of 100%, or three out of three, by randomly guessing is 50%, if a student has the partial knowledge to answer one question correctly. The student can use the process of elimination. Random chance and the day-to-day fluctuations of luck described in the previous section have a large influence on scores where the scores are based on a very small number of tasks. You could improve this quizlet by changing the directions and sentences so that some types of statement appeared more than once or not at all. This would reduce the probability of guessing correctly by chance.

However, we want to bring your attention here to another challenge for reliability with this quizlet and many short tasks of this sort. When the teacher who designed this quizlet made these three items, they essentially took a tiny *sample* of statements from the universe of possible statements of fact, opinion, and reasoned judgment. If you took an undergraduate psychology class, you may know that most psychology experiments use samples of people to make inferences about a population. An educational psychologist who wants to study high school teacher beliefs about grading selects a sample of 200 high school teachers to survey, but she draws her inferences from assumptions about the population of high school teachers nationwide. Researchers in the behavioral sciences use samples because it is frankly not feasible to survey all the teachers in the population, and also because large samples usually do a pretty good job of representing the population.

The same concept of sampling holds true in asking questions to assess student knowledge, and this is where the *person x task interaction* comes into play. When there are a large number of possible items or questions that you could find or create, each statement you actually use in an assessment is but one sample of all the possible statements. In the domain of mathematics, you can imagine this fairly easily. The Common Core standards state that by the end of third grade, students should know from memory the multiplication tables through 100. How many possible questions could you pose on this content? The answer is exactly 100. How many questions should you ask at one time to get a reliable estimate of student skill in this area? Certainly more than three, which is a very small sample of all the possible items.

The easiest way to solve the problem of low reliability due to having only a few questions is to increase the number of questions on an assessment task. There is a formula that allows us to predict how much reliability will increase as the number of questions increases, the Spearman-Brown Prophecy formula. While we think that it's wonderful to be in a field that makes prophecies, to go into full detail on the formula is beyond the scope of this book. Suffice it to say that, doubling the length of a test by adding items of the same quality as the original items increases the test's reliability considerably. Random inconsistencies from one item to the next make less difference overall when there are many items on the same topic. However, increases in reliability taper off as you add more and more items.

The direct relationship between reliability and test length explains why most high-stakes examinations like the SAT and professional licensure tests are quite long. Tests of such length are not realistic for classroom use for many reasons; for example, they use up valuable instructional time, are hard to develop, and fatigue students.

How many questions is sufficient for CA? There is no real answer. The issue of how reliable or sufficient your information has to be relates in part to what you intend to do with the information (see also Smith, 2003). For Stage 1 pre-assessment, information does not always need to be highly reliable, because you will have multiple opportunities to readjust your planning as you learn more about students' skills. If the teacher provides 10 items, the influence of chance will be much lower, and the reliability of the task will be higher. A 10-item task might

104   Section 2 Chapter 6

be sufficient to use as a pre-assessment to find out whether students know the general concept of the standard, isolated out of the context of the social studies content.

Evaluating and Reducing Error in Complex Tasks and Performance Assessments

Continuing to use the CCSS.ELA-Literacy.RH.6–8.8 standard, another approach to assessment would be to ask the students to identify parts of an actual non-fiction writing sample according to the three categories. You might ask your students to read a passage on the influenza pandemic and use different ways to mark statements of fact, opinion, or reasoned judgment. To provide scaffolding and support self-regulation, you could ask students to identify a statement in the passage that they were not sure how to categorize or to ask themselves (or their peers) about their choices before making their final decisions. After reviewing their work and providing feedback and additional instruction as needed, they could do the exercise again with a different reading passage on the same topic, in the second iteration.

This is consistent with our concept of multiple iterations of assessment and instruction in Stage 2. Continuing with the example, classifying the sentences in the context of a non-fiction reading passage is what we call an authentic task, discussed in Chapter 4. However, with authenticity we may pay a price in reliability. Is the context-embedded approach reliable? Can you be confident in the results? It's hard to say. The evidence you have is from two separate complex tasks. The differences in students' responses to one or the other may be attributable to what they know and what they learned, and that's probably how you'll interpret them. But they may also be due to differences in the two reading passages. A student's ability to classify each statement is not isolated, but embedded in the context of their overall reading comprehension. Their reading comprehension may be influenced not only by random qualities like attention, but by interest in the passage and prior knowledge, the *person x task interaction*. However, despite these issues that affect your confidence in results on the specific task performances, we take the stance that some sacrifice of reliability is justifiable in CA if multiple pieces of evidence are collected before you as a teacher make evaluative decisions.

Large-Scale Testing Approaches: Parallel Tests, Generalizability, Internal Consistency

Test developers estimate error due to tasks in multiple ways. The classic way, and the one easiest to understand, is by creating two tests that are *parallel forms* in all respects, except in incidental features of item content. Parallel forms follow the same test content specifications: number of items, format, standards addressed, range of cognitive complexity, and so on. Distributions of scores on the two tests should have the same mean and standard deviation (measures of central tendency and variability, respectively). The parallel tests are administered to a group of students, and the two sets of scores are examined to evaluate the consistency between one form and the other.

At this point, we introduce a basic descriptive statistic: the *correlation coefficient*. The correlation coefficient describes a bivariate relationship, or the association between two variables. Correlation is usually abbreviated with a lowercase, italicized r. The possible range for the value of r is –1.00 to +1.00. The absolute value of the correlation indicates the strength of the relationship. The sign of a correlation indicates whether the two variables tend to rank students in the same way or different ways.

The *reliability coefficient* is a specific application of correlation to measure the strength of a test's consistency. Conceptually, the reliability coefficient measures the association of a test with another version of itself. Therefore, its numerical value should always be positive and quite high. The rule of thumb for evaluating a reliability coefficient is that .70 indicates an adequate level for research purposes, .80 for comparing group performance, and .90 for making strong decisions about individuals (Nunnally & Bernstein, 1994).

Parallel forms reliability has its uses in the classroom. Sometimes, a teacher needs two different versions of equivalent tests. For instance, you might want to reduce the possibility of cheating on a major test in social studies by creating an A form and a B form and distributing them alternately in the classroom. But how would you know in advance that the two forms were equivalent?

As a matter of fact, teachers Chen and Bonner were once in this situation. Here's what we did: first, we co-created a test plan by deciding the number of questions on each point of content, the question type, and the kind of thinking skill (using DOK). We each created a set of items, and then reviewed them together. After some editing and revisions, we told our students—167 of them, in several sections of a course—that they would be taking two tests on the same content on two separate days. We set the days one week apart, hoping that students wouldn't remember too well what was on the first test and go home and study it extra hard.

When we had all the students' scores from the two test administrations, we checked the basic statistics for each form. We found that the average score on Form A was 46.8 and the average on Form B was 46.2. The standard deviation values were the same to two decimal places, 6.37. This was all evidence that the forms were parallel. We then calculated the correlation and found the reliability coefficient, $r = .81$, which is reasonably strong, given that this single test was not going to be used for a major decision about students. The scatterplot showing the relationship of the forms is shown in Figure 6.4. We felt reasonably confident administering either one of these tests as an alternate.

While parallel forms are an excellent method for estimating reliability, it is expensive for large-scale test developers to create them. Because of the difficulty in constructing two such

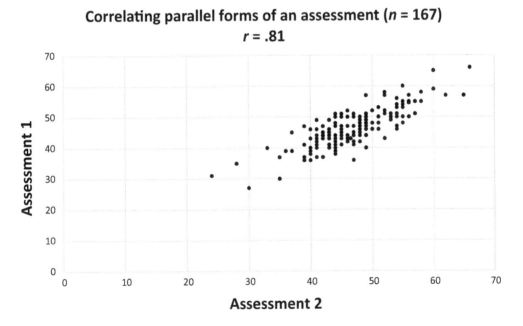

Figure 6.4 Correlating Parallel Forms of an Assessment

106 Section 2 Chapter 6

exactly parallel tests, this method is mostly used when a test developer wants two test forms anyway, perhaps for reasons of test security.

When there is only one form of a test, one can use other methods. One can mathematically compare distributions of one-half the items on a test to the other half, a technique known, appropriately enough, as *split-half reliability*. The more common technique for estimating reliability when there is only one test is to correlate or mathematically associate the distribution of each item's score with each other item's scores. This measures what is known as the *internal consistency* of a test, or how well, overall, the items on the test cohere to achieve a single stable estimate. Although the computation of the internal consistency estimate is beyond the scope of this book, it is a very commonly reported statistic for tests and psychological scales, sometimes also referred to as Cronbach's alpha or KR-21, which you can learn about in other texts (e.g., Nunnally & Bernstein, 1994).

An important thing to remember about the internal consistency estimate is that it is only based on information within a single test, administered one time. Also important: the number of items on a test strongly influences the internal consistency estimate. As we said previously, all else being equal, the more items on a test, the more reliable it is. You may want to consider the implications of the relationship between reliability and test length if you are asked to interpret scores on state tests or similar instruments. Most state tests report an individual total score. It is likely, based on the test development process, that this score is reasonably reliable. Many times, teachers, researchers, and school administrators want to break down information from these tests at the level of learning standards. We caution against this practice. Unless you know that the test developers have stated that sub-scores on separate standards can be reliably interpreted, you have no basis for treating a group of items as a mini-scale on a standard. Most large-scale achievement tests only include a few items focused on each standard; therefore, information at the level of the standard is not measured with strong internal consistency. For that reason, the test company only reports total scores. Test users, including researchers, should be wary of creating their own subscales without verifying reliability first.

Raters as a Source of Random Error

Explanation

It is well known that if two raters, let's say teachers, score the same set of student work samples, the scores will not all be the same from one teacher to the other, even though the work they are

Explanation	Techniques	In large-scale testing
• Aspects of assessment tasks affect how students respond. • Examples are unclear directions or unusual vocabulary. • This is the *person x task interaction* where a student's performance differs by task.	• Consider your sample size: more questions improve reliability. • Increase complexity of assessment, use performance tasks, or use two iterations. • Consider the authenticity of the assessment.	• To estimate error based on item characteristics, create two parallel forms of test. • Calculate correlation coefficient for comparison of score distributions. • Calculate reliability coefficient to examine strength of test association with itself or a parallel form.

Figure 6.5 Source of Random Error: Items or Task Characteristics

rating is exactly the same. This is true even when both teachers are using the same rubric. As a student's behavior will fluctuate a little from time to time, so will the behavior of the person who assesses them, due to all kinds of unforeseeable circumstances, such as attention and the context in which the interpretations are made.

This lack of consistency in scoring is improved if the teachers have been trained in the use of the rubric and if they have benchmark work to refer to. Benchmark work samples are examples of student work that highlight and explain the particular qualities in the work that align with particular rubric levels (e.g., 1 = unsatisfactory, 2 = marginal, 3 = proficient, 4 = excellent). In terms of rubric design, the use of very generic rubrics has been found to result in less reliable scoring than task-specific rubrics, because they require more subjective and unguided interpretations on the part of the teachers who are making the ratings. Analytic rubrics that are specific to an individual assessment result in more reliable scores. However, generic rubrics are more useful than task-specific rubrics for comparing performance over a range of tasks intended to assess the same broad learning goal.

Evaluating and Reducing Error From Subjective Interpretations in Classroom Assessment

Let us look at Figure 6.6, with a sample of student work on a task covering the same Common Core standard as previously discussed in Figure 6.3. This time the student is asked to identify a fact, an opinion, and a reasoned judgment from an authentic primary source. Think about how you as a teacher would score this work.

The example in Figure 6.6 shows an excerpt of an oral history about the Spanish flu (DeBoice, 1979). Students are supposed to circle a fact, underline an opinion, and draw a box around a reasoned judgment. Imagine that you have a scoring sheet that awards three total points, one for each correctly identified type of statement. A student has placed a box around the speaker's statement that begins "We knew what we were up against because." The student has also drawn a box around a second statement, "And he kind of pooh-poohed the idea which

---

The flu struck Camp Grant along in the early fall of 1918. We knew what we were up against because it had hit the Great Lakes Naval Training Station in Waukegan, Illinois before it hit Camp Grant. And they died like flies at Great Lakes. When it hit Camp Grant we knew what we were in for. [...] I was ordered to take a troop train to Camp Hancock, Georgia, a troop movement that involved two thousand troops to Camp Hancock, Georgia and two thousand troops to Camp McArthur, Texas. When I went up to the headquarters to get my orders, travel orders, I met for the first time the medic officer who-- the captain of the medical corps who was to accompany our train, and I told him "You know if this train moves we're going to have a flu epidemic on that train." And he kind of pooh-poohed the idea which touched me off [...]When he showed up afterwards he showed me a pint bottle about three fourths full of compound cathartics, a physic that they used in the Army at that time, and a box about three inches square and six inches tall half full of aspirin tablets [...]

As we progressed towards Chicago on the train they began showing up and I was-- found myself walking up and down the aisles and spotting fellows that were beginning to show fever and isolating them in the back coach. I followed that procedure until we got to Evansville, Indiana along about midnight that night. I was just completely worn out, I had a soldier trailing me with a bucket of water and I was feeding them compound cathartics, aspirins, and water. Well, I went to bed around midnight and the next day it continued again, but they got to the point where I couldn't isolate them. There were just too many [...] I telegraphed ahead to Camp Hancock that I'd be in the next morning at seven o'clock with two hundred cases of flu on board, and I had somewhere between five hundred and six hundred men on my train. Well, no commanding general ever got the reception that [we] got when I showed up there.

DeBoise, B. S. (1979)

Fact, Opinion, and Reasoned Judgment Activity

Directions: Above is an excerpt of an oral history of the Spanish flu. Identify an example of a fact by circling it. Identify an example of an opinion by underlining it. Identify an example of a reasoned judgment by drawing a box around it.

Figure 6.6 Social Studies Assessment With Primary Source Document

touched me off." The student has circled the definition of "cathartics" as a statement of fact. Finally, the student identified the statement "I have somewhere between 500 and 600 men on my train" as an opinion.

How will you score this work? You very likely agree that the first statement is a reasoned judgment. But you think the second boxed statement is an emotional reaction to a personal perception, not a reasoned judgment. Does the student know what a reasoned judgment is? Does he not know? Does he partially know? This is a subjective decision. Consider further the underlined statement. Is it an opinion or an estimation? Are opinions and estimations the same thing or "close enough"? Your decision here must draw on your pre-assessments of student learning and your subsequent decisions about the level of difficulty of your teaching and expectations. Scores for this task might vary from one to three, according to a teacher's subjective judgments. Subjectivity in scoring is not unacceptable in and of itself—after all, you are the expert. The problem is that you can be inconsistent in your subjective decisions. If the inconsistencies are more or less random, they reduce reliability. If they are non-random, they may relate to your own unconscious biases, a topic we will discuss in the next chapter.

Scoring guidelines or rubrics help to minimize subjectivity in scoring. Analytic scoring rubrics assess multiple dimensions of achievement and distinguish multiple levels of proficiency, usually with descriptors for each level. Figure 6.7 shows an excerpt of a rubric designed to assess student knowledge of the fact/opinion/reasoned judgment distinction, based on a writing sample. The directions for this task have two additional requirements, which the teacher incorporated after piloting the task and finding ambiguities in scoring it. The students

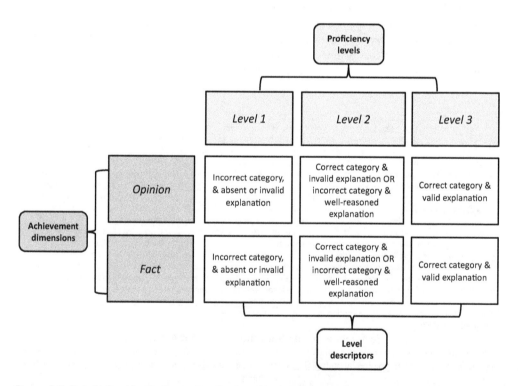

Figure 6.7 Rubric for Use in Assessing Student Knowledge

are directed to mark only ONE statement for each category and to write an explanation for each identification. Two achievement dimensions, three proficiency levels, and a descriptor for each proficiency level are shown.

As you gain practice with rubrics, it should be part of your professional practice to improve them. If you think that a dimension is poorly defined, add notes in the margin to better guide yourself. Annotations to your rubric will not only help you interpret each level of scoring, they may help you improve the task or even guide instruction in the future. To improve reliability in scoring, you might also collect benchmark work samples that you can refer to as you interpret. Let us imagine that the student whose work is shown in Figure 6.6 provided the following explanation for their identification of a statement: "The statement is an opinion because the author doesn't know it for a fact, he just believes it." That could become a benchmark to illustrate a proficiency level 2 score on the opinion dimension of the rubric.

Some rubrics are professionally developed and widely disseminated in K–12 education. An example is the 6 + 1 Traits Writing Rubric, developed by Education Northwest (2017). This rubric is used by teachers and school districts across the country to assess six dimensions of proficiency in writing across the curriculum: ideas, organization, sentence fluency, word choice, voice, and conventions. The + 1 dimension is used to assess presentation of a final written product. Teachers or school district representatives can attend training institutes for this rubric, which has been studied and used in teaching and assessment for many years.

There are other tips to improve reliability in scoring based on rubrics. The most important thing is to refer to the rubric and benchmark papers frequently to keep your rating standards consistent across a class and over time. Rater drift occurs when raters tend to pay different levels of attention to criteria over time or interpret the criteria differently as time goes on. Thus, you need to periodically review your scoring rubrics and the descriptions of the criteria at various levels of mastery.

Finally, remember that you are not alone in making these judgments. Many times, it is perfectly appropriate to ask the student to clarify their own work, especially for assessments during Stage 2. If you are truly in doubt about how to score a performance assessment, you should solicit the opinion of another professional. With contemporary technology, is easy enough to take an image of a student's (anonymous) work and your rubric. You can send the material to a colleague for input. Technology gives teachers a broad community of practice to draw on to improve methods of assessment.

Large-Scale Testing Approaches: Inter-rater Reliability

The way individual differences among raters affects the reliability of scores is not very different in large-scale assessment than it is in the classroom. You want to estimate this kind of error when subjective scoring is a necessary part of the assessment design, for instance, in the writing section of a state accountability test. In large-scale testing, the conditions for subjective scoring are quite standardized. All raters are trained using official rating experts and benchmark examples. Scoring rules are well-established; there will often be a scoring handbook that raters use as a constant reference. During rating sessions, raters may occasionally be given the same student work to score that they have reviewed before, to estimate their self-consistency. If a single rater is not consistent in the scores they give to an identical essay seen on two occasions, they may need further training. For most scoring purposes for important tests, two raters score each student work sample independently. If they have more than a slight difference in scores, an expert rater will intervene to resolve the difference. In some testing situations, automated scoring (see Chapter 9) is used as a second or third rater.

Summary and Conclusion

Time, task, and rater: these are not the only sources of measurement error that affect reliability, but they are some of the main ones for classroom assessment. These sources of error also occur in combination. For instance, one part of a student's performance on an essay task may be due to random fluctuations in their mood that day. Another part of their performance may relate to particular facets of the essay prompt that were idiosyncratic to that student—differences in motivation about the topic or familiarity. Still another matter influencing a student's score is the teacher's own mood, motivation, and thoughts as they rate student work. There is, in short, a whole lot of "noise" combining between the signal of what a student really knows, and the information you perceive.

We have shown many characteristics in classroom assessment that lead to low reliability and high measurement error: chance occurrences, too few item samples, the *person x task interaction*, and subjectivity in scoring. We have seen methods that classroom teachers can use to improve the reliability of their assessments. We review a few of these in Figure 6.9.

Even with all these methods, can we ever be confident that an estimate of student classroom learning is precise? The answer is "no." No single estimate of student skill is enough to form a precise judgment. At this point, you may be discouraged from even trying to assess your students, and rather annoyed by the topic of reliability. Do not be discouraged. Remember that many times our judgments do not need to be based on highly precise information. Think about the CA:SRL framework and its four stages, with all the different kinds of interpretations and feedback you give yourself and your students.

Explanation	Techniques	In large-scale testing
• Rating or scoring work is always subjective. • Different raters (like teachers) will rate or score work differently. • Rater attention, the context of rating, and poor scoring guidelines can contribute to poor reliability.	• Use analytic scoring rubrics, including multiple dimensions of achievement and distinguishing levels of proficiency. • Include a descriptor or example for each level. • Avoid rater fatigue and check your rating against others' judgments.	• Standardize conditions for scoring with certified expert raters. • Provide raters with benchmark examples and a scoring handbook. • Calculate inter-rater reliability to compare raters' scoring choices.

Figure 6.8 Source of Random Error: Raters

- Minimize guessing by using supply-type items.
- Ask more questions when using selected-response formats.
- Provide multiple opportunities for assessment on complex tasks.
- Use and refine rubrics and benchmark papers.
- Gather more information before making decisions you aren't confident about, and remember that the students themselves, as well as peer teachers, can be a source of information.
- Try multiple short assessments when you need high precision.

Figure 6.9 Guidelines for Improving Reliability of Assessments

At Stage 1, you may think that your students need more basic skill practice. If you find out over the next day or so that they were just sluggish on the first day of class, you can readjust your plans. Pre-assessment is a very low-stakes assessment, and so we say that at this stage, your tolerance for measurement error is high. You can easily reverse decisions you make from pre-assessment.

At Stage 2 when assessment and instruction go hand-in-hand, you can continue refining information until you are satisfied that your evidence about student learning is reliable. You can also update your informal notes about achievement as the term progresses. Revisiting prior assessments of learning is consistent with standards-based grading, discussed in Chapter 5. At this point, you should be interacting with students so frequently that it is unlikely your day-to-day inferences will be in serious error.

At Stage 3 you will take extra pains to design an assessment with a sufficient number of questions, to prepare students to be assessed, and to score student work consistently. Then, when it comes to Stage 4, and you make your reports of performance, you should have many points of information. No single point of information is completely reliable in CA or any other educational assessment, but if you use many sources and iterations of assessments to guide your decisions, you can be confident that your decisions will support student learning and reflect their achievement.

References

Brennan, R. L., & Johnson, E. G. (1995). Generalizability of performance assessments. *Educational Measurement: Issues and Practice, 14*(4), 9–12.

College Board. (2015). *Test characteristics of the SAT: Reliability, difficulty levels, completion rates.* Retrieved from https://secure-media.collegeboard.org/digitalServices/pdf/sat/sat-characteristics-reliability-difficulty-completion-rates-2015.pdf

DeBoice, B. S. (1979). Interview by C. Ruge & C. Davis [Tape recording]. *The oral history collection of the University of Illinois at Springfield.* Springfield, IL: Illinois Digital Archives. Retrieved from www.idaillinois.org/digital/collection/uis/id/5454/rec/1Inboxx

Education Northwest. (2017). *6 + 1 traits rubric.* Retrieved from https://educationnorthwest.org/traits/traits-rubrics

Nunnally, J. C., & Bernstein, I. H. (1994). *Psychometric theory (McGraw-Hill Series in Psychology)* (Vol. 3). New York, NY: McGraw-Hill.

Smith, J. K. (2003). Reconsidering reliability in classroom assessment and grading. *Educational Measurement: Issues and Practice, 22*(4), 26–33.

Chapter 7

Validity in Classroom Assessment
Purposes, Properties, and Principles

Like reliability, *validity* is one of the big concepts in educational assessment. When we ask about validity, we are asking, "Are we measuring what we think we're measuring?" Remember that reliability had to do with consistency, whether the scores or ratings we give students yield dependable information. Validity relates to the *interpretation* of the scores or results, and the strength of the relationship between what you intend to measure and what you have actually measured. Interpretations can be consistent or reliable without being valid. For instance, you might interpret a student's repeatedly poor performance on a math task as evidence of poor problem-solving skills. But if you could see into the student's thinking, you might find out that the results, though consistent, really derive from a language problem. Your interpretation in such a case is not valid.

Validity also relates to the *usefulness* of the assessment information for its given purpose. If you intend to use assessment information to promote learning as in Stage 2, but fail to give feedback that helps students make progress, your use of the assessment is not valid. Validity in educational assessment is a core value, whether we speak about assessments that take place in the context of the classroom instructional cycle or large-scale tests.

Unfortunately, methods for validation of assessments that teachers use in their classrooms are not well defined. This is probably because the traditional arsenal of validation approaches was developed for large-scale testing contexts. The conditions that characterize large-scale assessment are not the same as classroom conditions. Large-scale test developers rely on standardization so that many people can be measured on the same scale; in classrooms, we take learner differences and context into account. Large-scale test validation techniques often require large sample sizes, which we do not find in classrooms. Most importantly, perhaps, the focus of large-scale assessment is to take a snapshot of the outcomes *of* learning—not to promote learning, which is a more typical goal in CA. In fundamental ways, classroom assessments differ from large-scale assessment. From some perspectives, classroom assessment differs from other educational assessments so radically in its purposes and its qualities that it requires a whole new approach to thinking about validity.

In this chapter, we put forth a set of principles for validation in classroom assessment. These principles are drawn from traditional frameworks of measurement, but are re-conceived for the classroom. This list of principles for validity in classroom assessment is not intended to be exhaustive, but is offered as a step in the development of a classroom-based theory of assessment or "classroometric" theory (Brookhart, 2003).

As we did in the chapter on reliability, we state each big idea, describe techniques you can use to assess the quality of the inferences you draw from student assessment work, and provide summaries (Figures 7.3, 7.4, 7.5, 7.8, and 7.11). Remember that inferences are your mental step that you make between student evidence and your interpretations (see Chapter 1). Our five validity principles are critical to the process of making claims about the validity of an educational interpretation based on classroom assessments. We believe the techniques are within the resources available to those working in classroom assessment and also reflect the sensitivity to individual learners and learning outcomes that are important for most classroom assessment purposes. The principles strongly relate to core values about the technical quality of validity in educational measurement that have been developed over more than a century by researchers and theorists in psychology and educational psychology. After each validity principle, we therefore provide a table that includes analogous approaches in traditional validation frameworks.

Our suggested principles of validity in assessment are relevant whether the validity claim is made by researchers, teachers, students, or other stakeholders; whether the assessment yields qualitative or quantitative data; and whether the purpose is one of measurement, learning, or both. They are intended to distill elements of existing theory into a framework that supports school-based stakeholders in reflecting on and improving the validity of classroom assessments.

Validity Principle I: Assessment Should Be Aligned With Standards, Objectives, and Instruction

Explanation

To make valid inferences about learning in the classroom, your assessment tasks should be aligned with standards and classroom instruction. Schools expect teachers to enact a curriculum that promotes learning according to educational standards. If you teach the standards-based curriculum but your assessments don't match what you teach, your assessment and instruction are not aligned. If you do not teach the curriculum, and your students have to be tested on the standards, your instruction and the assessment are also not aligned. Alignment from the student point of view is also important. Students appropriately expect that they will be assessed on what they were taught; to assess differently risks loss of trust in the student-teacher relationship.

The alignment of standards, instruction or enacted curriculum, and assessment is known as *curricular alignment* (Anderson, 2002). In classroom practice, alignment is not always simple. Through pre-assessment, we often find that students are not ready to learn at the level of expectations according to the standards. We therefore take instructional time for remediation. If instruction differs from the standards, do we align assessment with the standards or with instruction? Can you use a textbook test if your instruction has enhanced or omitted part of the curriculum? If there is differentiation in instruction, should there be differentiation in assessment? Sometimes, there may be a trade-off between validity in terms of matching assessment to standards-based content and matching assessment to instruction.

Techniques to Evaluate and Improve Validity of Assessment of Objectives and Instruction

We start at the planning stage to ensure that classroom assessment tasks relate well to standards and instruction. The first thing you should consider when you plan a classroom assessment is its purpose: What standards and specific learning objectives do you intend to assess? When you consider the "what" of your assessments, you steer your task design toward the right goal. As a professional, you will already be in the habit of using standards to plan specific learning objectives for each unit or cycle of instruction. It is essential that you refer back to the standards and SLOs when you think about assessment.

Guidance to help classroom teachers review the relevance of their assessment tasks to standards dates far back. According to Robert Mager (1973), "The task at hand is to determine whether a test item (or task) is suitable for assessing the achievement of an objective. What is a suitable item? It is one that asks the student to do that which the objective expects him to be able to do, one that asks him to do it under the conditions described by the objective. A suitable item, in other words, matches the objective in performance and conditions" (p. 16).

To judge the suitability of a task for a SLO and its corresponding standard, we must return to the SLO itself. For the purpose of simplicity, we will assume that your SLOs are already well matched to your state standards for student achievement.

Let us begin by looking at a teacher's specific learning objective for a twelfth-grade English Language Arts class. Referring to the Common Core standards for writing, the teacher, Ms. Q, sets the following learning objective for a short cycle of instruction that is part of a larger unit on the novel *The Martian Chronicles* by Ray Bradbury:

- W.9–12.9: Draw evidence from literary or informational texts to support analysis, reflection, and research.

  - SLO: Given an articulated argument, students will cite evidence in support of the argument. (DOK Level 3)

The first thing we come to when reading this specific learning objective is the phrase "given an articulated argument." In an SLO, this phrase is an example of what we call a *condition*, which was introduced in Chapter 2. The condition describes the circumstances under which the student is expected to perform the task and is important when evaluating the alignment between an assessment task and an SLO. Note this condition tells us that the students are not expected to create their own arguments for this specific task. Instead, Ms. Q will provide the argument, and it will be the student's job to refer to the text for evidence. This SLO is part of a set that together build progressively toward the analysis and synthesis that are expected for writing about literary texts under Common Core.

The next thing we see in this SLO is the main verb of the sentence, "cite." "Cite" is what we call a measurable performance. It corresponds to a skill that can be shown through a behavior. For assessment purposes, it is essential that we state achievement expectations in terms of behaviors that we can observe. Based on the condition and the performance stated in this SLO, Ms. Q should assess students by giving them an interpretive statement about the book and asking them to provide specific evidence for the interpretation from the text.

Let us now look at one assessment task that Ms. Q designs for her students in Figure 7.1. As you consider the task, ask yourself whether it meets the condition for assessment and the performance or behavioral expectations for students. A sample of student work is included in Figure 7.2.

Do you think this task assesses the objective? It requires students to provide evidence based on a statement about a text that is provided for them. Will that ensure that the task yields valid scores on learning aligned with objectives? We do not yet have enough information to answer that question, because we don't know how Ms. Q will score and interpret student work. Validity is about interpretations, not the task itself.

As it turns out, Ms. Q teaches the skill of citing evidence in a very particular way. She teaches students to use three types of evidence: stretched, spanned, and chopped. Stretched evidence makes novel and creative connections between the text and the argument. Spanned

CCSS W.9–12.9: Draw evidence from literary or informational texts to support analysis, reflection, and research.
DOK level 3: Given an articulated argument, students will cite evidence in support of the argument.
Student name:
Date:
Directions: Below are three topic sentences that a writer uses to describe themes in *The Martian Chronicles*. For each topic sentence, cite at least three pieces of specific evidence from the text that support or counter the "provable" point of the topic sentence. If you choose to cite additional evidence, you can add lines to the page. If the evidence counters the claim, be sure to make that clear by labeling the evidence as "Counter." Turn in your work by Tuesday.
1. Mankind continues to destroy itself because our ability to remember the past hinders progress.
2. The only way for individuals or groups to satisfy their need for a sense of self-worth is to assert dominance over other individuals, groups, spaces, or ideas.
3. Humans want their accomplishments to measure what their lives are worth.

Figure 7.1 Assessment Conditions and Performance Expectations

1) "The third Expedition": Captain Jack and his crew started to see dead family members. They all let their guard down and died.

2) "...And the Moon Be Still as Bright": Jeff Spender resides on past situations when humans have destroyed beautiful things. This eventually leads to his death, because he loses sanity and kills many of his members.

3) "The Settlers": Benjamin Driscoll holds on to the past because he wants Earths oxygen. He becomes weak because of the lack of oxygen and pass out.

Figure 7.2 Student-Provided Evidence for Topic Sentence One

evidence is gathered from throughout a text, rather than a narrow area like a single chapter. Chopped evidence uses succinct, relevant, and direct quotations. Ms. Q intends to analyze student work on this task according to this typology. She creates an analytic rubric with a row for each type of evidence and an analytic scoring rubric for each with four levels of quality.

Ms. Q administers this task to her students and analyzes their work. She finds that very few students use chopped evidence. However, she is unable to tell from their work whether students are failing to use chopped evidence because they don't understand that citing evidence includes use of direct quotes, or because they don't understand the expectations of this particular task. She therefore realizes that her assessment task does not allow her to make valid interpretations of the full range of student ability to cite evidence, as she has instructionally defined it.

This is where the CA:SRL framework could have helped her. Here is Ms. Q's problem: she could not derive valid inferences from her assessment task, because she couldn't distinguish the difference between students not knowing the three types of evidence and not knowing that she wanted them to show her that they knew. How can she improve her task, while promoting SRL?

We have a few suggestions for Ms. Q. She can include her rubric with the task or provide more explicit directions informing students of the types of evidence they are expected to include, to help them self-monitor. At the beginning of the task, she can provide a space for students to freely generate the three dimensions of evidence they had studied to help them mentally plan how best to accomplish the task. She can simultaneously build student SRL and obtain validity evidence by asking students to complete a short anonymous survey about their perception of the relevance of the task to what they studied.

Be aware that instructional validity does not only include making sure that teaching and assessment both relate to the same learning goals. Feedback is an essential part of CA; therefore, for CA to be valid, feedback should also be aligned with objectives and instruction. We discussed in Section 1 that your feedback to students should help them keep the learning goal front and center in their minds and point them to next steps toward reaching the goal (Hattie & Timperley, 2007). This technique not only serves a learning purpose; it improves validity. Referencing the objective in your feedback prompts you to mentally verify that the task is indeed relevant to the objective. When you suggest or prod students with questions about next steps, you continue to emphasize validity and a coherent relationship between learning objectives, instruction, and assessment.

The example of Ms. Q's writing tasks shows strengths and weaknesses of a single task in terms of content and instructional validity. You should not only consider these qualities in individual tasks, but over the course of your instruction and assessment as a whole. Do your assessments cover the breadth of your instruction? Are you using too few resources (especially time) on quality assessments of complex learning objectives, and too much time on basic knowledge assessment? Do your tasks represent the same depth of knowledge and the same kinds of thinking skills that students have practiced in your course and that are the goals of instruction? Historically, content analyses of classroom assessments have shown that teacher-made tests predominantly favored objectively scored, selected-response formats and tended to emphasize lower-level aspects of learning (Marso & Pigge, 1991). This emphasis on lower-level aspects of learning does not necessarily mean that teacher-made tests lack validity as measures of instruction and learning goals for students. The question for validity is one of alignment between intended instructional targets and assessment content. Thus, if the expected curricular objectives are at a low level, teacher-made tests at that level may be

Explanation	• You want to make valid inferences about student learning and understanding. • Aligning assessment tasks with your classroom instruction, your curriculum, your learning objectives and the standards they are based on.
Techniques	• Identify the conditions for performance. • Create a rubric to interpret student work with relevant standards and SLOs. • Consider the qualities of assessments in relation to the breadth of your instruction. • Provide explicit directions to students about the kinds of thinking they are expected to perform (e.g., analysis, recall). • Use assessment to elicit critical thinking.
Supporting SRL	• Share goal-aligned rubrics with students to encourage planning and reflection. • Survey students about the relevance of tasks to what they have studied. • Align your feedback with objectives and instruction.
Traditional validation approaches	• Use expert judgment to analyze item relatedness and test representativeness, in comparison to curricular or other standards.

Figure 7.3 Principle I: Assessment Should Be Consistent With Objectives, Curriculum, and Instruction

valid. However, educational policy today promotes critical thinking as a goal of instruction, and state standards and the Common Core reflect this emphasis on critical thinking.

Validity Principle II: Assessment Processes Should Elicit Construct-Relevant Thinking Processes

Explanation

Classroom assessments should involve the kinds of thinking we want to assess. This may seem obvious, but when students get bogged down by extraneous details or confusion about the task, they are not doing *construct-relevant* thinking. Your students should be able to focus on the substance of the task. During test-taking, students can run into various obstacles that interfere with their ability to focus on the goals at hand. During basic written assessments, they may be confused by language in the problems or the directions. If you set up assessment conditions that make them anxious, they may be worrying instead of thinking of the task at hand. They may be drawing on test-taking strategies to answer questions, rather than using what they have learned about the concepts or skills.

Throughout the processes you use in assessment, you should try to understand the thinking processes your tasks assessments elicit and reinforce. This will help you to create tasks that provide sound information about gaps in learners problem-solving, to develop scoring rubrics that are sensitive to gradations of student skill and understanding, and to develop tests that stimulate fluency, effective study habits, and motivation.

Techniques to Improve Construct-Relevant Thinking Processes

When you are preparing your assessment tasks, be mindful of ways that the content of tasks can introduce irrelevant thinking processes for individuals or groups. For instance, grade-inappropriate language, excessive wordiness, or logical conundrums like double negatives interfere with the ability of all students to focus on demonstrating their learning. Students get tangled up trying to understand the meaning of the question, and may either run out of time to answer it or misinterpret it completely. This is very much a problem for English language learners when presented with wordy items in science, social studies, or math that rely on general knowledge of English. It is perfectly appropriate to assess domain-specific technical vocabulary, but the ability to demonstrate that knowledge shouldn't be contingent on having a sophisticated general vocabulary.

To check for grade-appropriate language, we recommend two methods. First, pilot your assessments. Try them out before using them for decision-making. You may use a task for informal Stage 2 assessment one year, without recording scores. Allow students to make marks beside directions or on questions where they think the wording is unclear. If the pilot information indicates that the students understand the assessment appropriately and can answer in relevant ways, you can use or adapt that assessment for formal Stage 4 purposes in the following year. Second, if you have a passage that students need to read to respond to your assessment, analyze the passage with a Lexile analyzer tool (or something similar), which can be found at no cost online, or check with a reading specialist in your school. Your reading passage should be grade-appropriate or slightly lower.

More In-Depth Methods

To see whether assessments engage students' thinking processes, you can also ask students to think aloud, annotate their work with questions or comments, or reflect orally on the work they have done. This approach is consistent with the kinds of cognitive and metacognitive approaches we discussed in Section 1, and with the concept that an assessment task is an opportunity for students to self-regulate and engage in peer assessment and discourse.

Explanation	• Assessments should ask students to do the kind of thinking you want to assess. • When an assessment requires construct-relevant thinking, students can perform regardless of irrelevant traits like shyness or lack of exposure to specialized vocabulary.
Techniques	• In creating tasks or items, don't use unfamiliar or excessively wordy vocabulary. • Check for grade-appropriate language by piloting your assessments. • Ask students to think aloud or annotate their work, to check and understand how they are thinking.
Supporting SRL	• Use tasks that elicit deep mental processes (think-aloud, annotation, oral reflection, peer discourse, discourse with you).
Traditional validation approaches	• Gather evidence of test-taker cognition through think-alouds or cognitive labs in the test development phase, particularly in diagnostic testing.

Figure 7.4 Principle II: Assessment Processes Should Elicit Construct-Relevant Thinking Processes in Performance

Some of these techniques can usually only be administered to one or two students in a class, but over the course of the semester, you can involve all your students at least once. Very short on-the-spot interviewing is feasible when a task is highly focused. For instance, if you have a multiple-choice test and want to know whether students find the distractors plausible, in addition to conducting item analysis (Chapter 4), you can ask a student to "think-aloud" while he or she answers the items. This will give you information about how the students consider all the options. Note that this example is very similar to the kind of informal interactive assessment we described in Stage 2. What is different here is the purpose: in this chapter, we are asking you to focus not only on what you can learn about student learning, but what you notice about your assessment method.

Validity Principle III: Assessment Processes Should Have Minimal Bias in Interpretation and Scoring

Explanation

Principle II said that our assessments should involve the kinds of student thinking we want to assess. Eliciting relevant thinking from the test-taker is not the only place where the "right" mental processes are important. When you as a teacher get distracted by characteristics of persons or groups in interpreting student work, you are not using construct-relevant thinking. You, like your students, should focus on the substance of the task objective. Above all, your interpretations of students' work should be free of bias, which leads to the discussion of Principle III.

Problems that interfere with your ability as a teacher to focus on the construct you are assessing can crop up especially during scoring and feedback. You can be influenced by unconscious biases when scoring assessments and when providing students with feedback about assessment results. A number of historical experimental studies have found biases in teacher subjective rating of student work, including effects of extraneous variables such as prior knowledge of students, pre-conceptions about student personality, and handwriting (Chase, 1986; Clifton, Perry, Parsonson, & Hryniuk, 1986; Powers, Fowles, Farnum, & Ramsey, 1994). Use of rubrics is intended to reduce such bias, but studies have still found considerable variability among trained teachers in rating student essays with rubrics (Llosa, 2008; Rezaei & Lovorn, 2010). Another consideration is bias about the content of student responses, particularly in argumentative speaking or writing. Are you as a teacher equally open to diverse points of view on topics of debate, such as restrictions on violence in video games, food choice in schools, or community service requirements? Does this show not only in your scoring, but also in the feedback you give your students? Don't try, through your feedback, to personally judge students according to their beliefs, opinions, or culture.

Techniques to Reduce Bias

Methods to reduce bias during scoring and feedback include careful use of rubrics, of course, but as we stated above, rubrics are only good when used in an unbiased way. As discussed in Chapter 6, we advise you to refer frequently to benchmark papers (i.e., exemplars for each quality level of student work). You should routinely check your rubric-based scoring procedures by asking a colleague to co-score one or two tasks independently, and when you are particularly concerned that your judgment is being swayed by subjectivity, you should definitely ask another teacher how they would evaluate the work. There are many other techniques to

Explanation	• When interpreting student work, avoid bias. • Sources of bias include student characteristics like personality or previous achievement, student group characteristics, or student handwriting. • Focus on student achievement on the task at hand.
Techniques	• Ask colleagues to support you in developing tasks or to check your scoring and evaluations. • Ask students to provide feedback on quality of your assessments. • Use rubrics and compare against benchmarks. • Remove student name or cover it while evaluating their work.
Traditional validation approaches	• Test developers train raters extensively and create objective scoring rubrics. • They hold cognitive labs examining how test-takers verbalize their thinking processes when approaching a task.

Figure 7.5 Principle III: Assessment Processes Should Have Minimal Bias in Interpretation and Scoring

minimize sources of bias in scoring. To avoid being influenced by your own pre-conceptions about students as individuals, a phenomenon known as the "halo effect," you can evaluate students' work anonymously. Some teachers tell students to put their names on the back rather than the front of their work; some cover names with Post-it notes; some even assign special ID codes for assessments. Scoring anonymously helps reduce the influence of your unconscious preferences and prejudices on student assessment results. Also, a carryover effect can occur when a rater's judgment of a student's response to one prompt affects that rater's judgment of the student's response to the next prompt. To avoid this phenomenon, score work with multiple short essay responses by prompt, rather than by student and shuffle students' papers between prompts so that the order of students' work changes between your evaluations of each prompt.

Validity Principle IV: Base Assessment Interpretations on Evidence From Multiple Sources

Explanation

As a rule, assessment-based decisions in the classroom should never be based on a single source of information. Whenever possible you should not make your plans for instruction or record your interpretations about student achievement in the gradebook without multiple pieces of assessment information. We already discussed in the previous chapter many sources of random error that affect our confidence in our assessment-based interpretations. With reliability in mind, it is obvious that no single piece of information can suffice for you to make an evaluative judgment.

Multiple sources do not only mean multiple pieces of evidence about each student, but evidence from the whole class, as we will discuss next. Equally strongly, we recommend bringing multiple viewpoints into your reflections on the validity of your assessment practice. Responsibility for assessment validation should not depend upon your sole judgment as an individual.

Seeking multiple sources of information should be the rule, not the exception. Many individuals have stakes in classroom assessment processes, interpretations, and decisions, including your students, parents, principals, and other teachers. You should realize that the validity of your assessment-based interpretations and decisions may be questioned by other stakeholders; you will need to be prepared to defend your claims and revise them if needed. Because you are closest to the assessment development process, you have primary responsibility for evaluating your assessment-based interpretations and decisions. But you should understand that potentially important validity issues in those processes, interpretations and decisions can only be detected if the perspectives of others are considered.

Techniques to Improve Validity Through Multiple Sources

Obtain Information About All Students, Not a Few

In whole-class questioning and discussion, you should not make even in-the-moment decisions about next steps based on the response to a question of a single student who raised their hand. It is all too easy for us to interpret a single raised hand and a single verbal response that is correct, along with many nodding heads, as general understanding. We know some wonderful teachers who take the responses of one or two individuals in their class as a sign to "move the class forward." This may be a fair pedagogical technique, but it is not an effective method of assessment.

For whole-class questioning to be useful for assessment purposes, you are better off using a method to poll the whole class. There are numerous ways to get the whole class to check in: asking students to hold their thumbs up or down (in front of their bodies to reduce peer influence), using colored sheets (green for full understanding, red for please stop and go back, yellow for in the middle), individual white boards, or technology-facilitated polling methods, which may or may not require students to have access to devices (see Chapter 8). When asking more analytic questions or for problem-solving in a domain like math, you can use a method to randomly rotate through the whole class when calling on students. Some teachers simply keep a jar of sticks with student names on them. They pull a stick at random and ask that student the question. They can either replace the stick so that student has a chance of being called on again during the class session, or not. We do not advocate "cold-calling" when students are unprepared, but if you communicate that all voices in the classroom are heard equally, your interpretations about whole-class learning will be less biased by individuals with strong voices.

If you administer surveys or quizzes as pre-assessment that generate scores, be sure to look at the distribution of the results of the whole class. Online survey and quizzing tools will almost always show you the shape of the distribution of your students' scores in the form of a *histogram*. A histogram plots scores from low to high along the x-axis, and shows bars that indicate how frequently they occur by height along the y-axis. If you are hand-calculating scores, is not too difficult to enter them in a spreadsheet and generate a histogram, or even hand-draw one. Histograms can be very useful for thinking about how the whole class, not just a few memorable students, are engaging with learning.

Take a look at the score distribution in Figure 7.6. For our present purpose, let's assume that scores above 70 are passing. The histogram shows a large group of scores at the high end of the scale and a small number at the bottom. We call this *a left-skewed distribution*. The histogram helps you readily see that four of your students are well below your passing standards, while all the rest are doing well. This information can help you decide where and how to go next; for instance, you may choose to place the upper-performing students in small groups for some

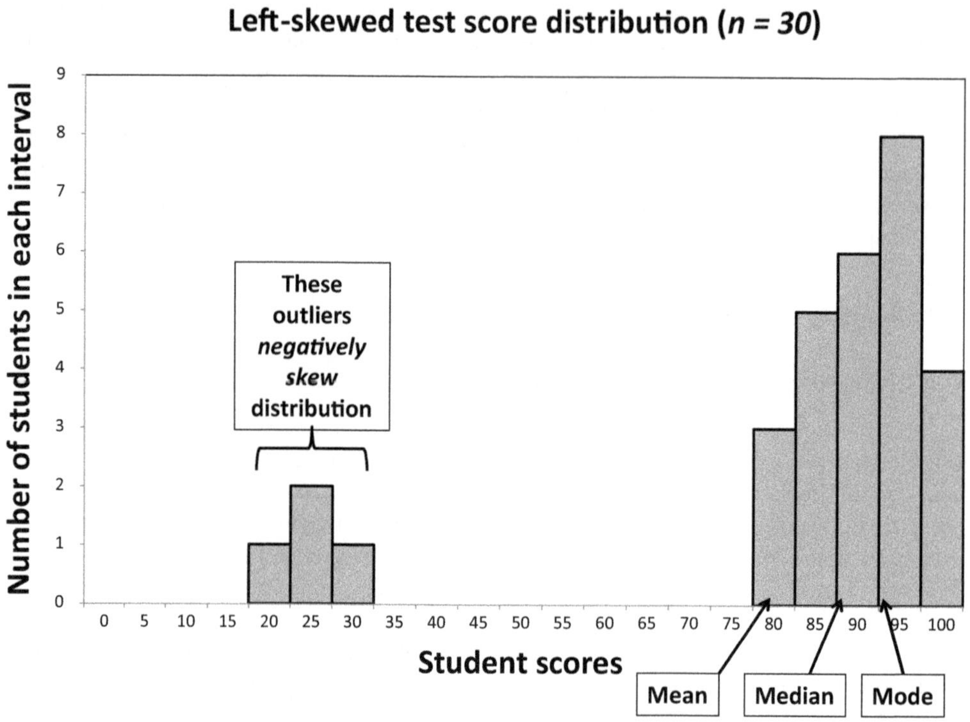

Left-skewed test score distribution (*n = 30*)

Figure 7.6 Example of a Left-Skewed Test Score Distribution

kinds of work they can do more independently, while you temporarily concentrate on the small group of students who are struggling with content.

Looking at the distribution in Figure 7.7, we see quite a different pattern. There are two distinct groups of students, in terms of scores or assessment performance (we call this a bimodal distribution). Perhaps this pattern suggests that you should try a more highly differentiated instructional approach, until you have evidence that the gap between the two student groups is reduced.

Allow Multiple Opportunities to Be Assessed in Multiple Ways

This principle has been one of the main emphases of the first section of this text. It also relates strongly to the idea of reliability. As we have stated before, any single piece of evidence about student learning is not likely to be reliable enough for decision-making. When interpreting student work, you not only have to think about what the work itself shows you, but the social and personal context in which the student performed the work. Allowing multiple attempts helps override contextual factors that may have randomly affected results on a single occasion. We recommend multiple iterations of assessment on the same or overlapping learning objectives, as a way for you as a teacher to confirm or modify your interpretations. Further, multiple iterations of assessment give students a running record, as it were, to monitor their own progress, supporting their SRL through reflectivity and further goal setting as they proceed along the learning progression.

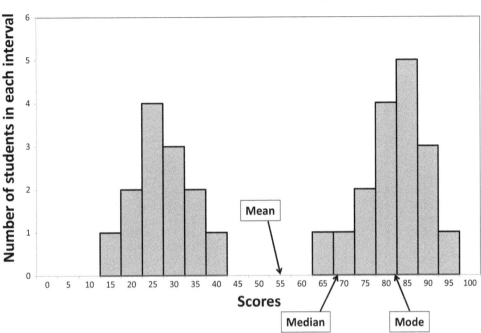

Figure 7.7 Example of a Bimodal Distribution

You also should use multiple methods in assessment. Students who understand the scientific method well might have a hard time showing their knowledge when bits of information are presented in a multiple-choice format, but will clearly demonstrate a sound understanding of the method when given the opportunity to write more freely. Some will be more able than others to logically discriminate between correct answers and distractors in multiple-choice items. Others will show their knowledge best during an actual lab performance. You should remember in your assessment design that there are multiple ways students can express learning, and each method taps into slightly different, legitimate mental processes of knowledge. The use of multiple methods of assessment is particularly important for grading decisions, when you combine information for an overall score or rating. For instance, basing an entire grade in an English Language Arts class on essays alone can lead to inaccurate representation of the content learning that a student has acquired or their ability to engage in oral arguments.

Involve Other People in Your Assessment-Based Decisions

In the "big field" of validity theory in educational measurement, argumentation has become a core value (Kane, 2006). In the light of social-constructivist views of learning, we know that when people interact over ideas, they bring more diverse kinds of knowledge to bear on problems, which may in turn help their solutions fit better to their context. People in many roles participate in CA processes, interpretations, and decisions, including classroom teachers, students, parents, and principals. All these people can be sources of information for your decisions.

Explanation	• Inferences are more valid when based on multiple assessment tasks. • Classroom decision-making is more valid when you base it on all students' performance, not the achievement of a few.
Techniques	• Use multiple iterations and multiple methods of assessment. • Record grades or plan for instruction only with information from multiple sources. • Be prepared to defend your claims and revise if needed. • Poll the class on their understanding. • Look at score distributions on assessments that are scored.
Supporting SRL	• Multiple iterations of assessment support students' evidence-based monitoring and future goal setting. • Including students as a source of evidence is co-regulation and co-monitoring of assessment interpretations.
Traditional validation approaches	• Use correlational statistics to evaluate convergence of test scores with other measures of similar things. • Offer multiple opportunities to take high-stakes tests. • Use "dialogue-based warrants" to argue for a given inference.

Figure 7.8 Principle IV: Base Assessment Interpretations on Evidence From Multiple Sources

From our perspective, the most important sources of information about the validity of assessment practices are you and your students. We are not alone in advocating for teachers to involve their students in co-inquiry into the quality and value of interpretations about their performance. Moss (2003) narrated the types of critically inquiring processes she used as teacher to make inferences based on her assessments and interact with students to interrogate the validity of those inferences. Andrade and Du (2005) gathered information through focus groups about undergraduate perspectives on rubric use to provide evidence to support the validity of sharing rubrics with students when the purpose is to foster learning effort. We consider that when you elicit student views on the quality of your interpretations, you and your students co-regulate your collective learning about validity.

Of course, not all interpretations and decisions require or are expected to be made with input from teachers. Teachers, those closest to the assessment development process, have primary responsibility for evaluating their assessment processes and assessment-based interpretations and decisions. However, teachers should realize that the validity of their assessment-based interpretations and decisions may be questioned by other stakeholders, and they must be prepared to argue their claims and revise them if needed. Kane (2006) refers to this as the use of "dialogue-based warrants" for inferences based on assessment results (p. 49). Teachers should understand that potentially important validity issues in those processes, interpretations, and decisions can only be detected if the perspectives of others, including learners, are considered.

Validity Principle V: Evaluate Whether Your Tests Are Useful for Their Purpose

Explanation

Most classroom assessment has the goal of promoting learning, as well as obtaining valid information. The first goal extends at least one step beyond the measurement purpose of most educational measurement; it extends into the area of intervention, where the validity of inferences from cause to effect is paramount. Assessment for learning also emphasizes the feedback element of assessment. If the feedback has certain qualities—for example, if it is prompt, goal-oriented, and directs students to specific actions within their capabilities to improve—and if instructional opportunities are offered for improvement, the entire assessment process can result in improved learning outcomes.

Another type of impact is generated almost inadvertently through the assessment process. Humans generate knowledge through all their experiences, including the experience of being assessed (Fulcher, 1999; Wolf, 1993). Impacts of assessment *as* learning include a range of motivational and attitudinal adjustments that occur among teachers and students daily, as well as learning one another's expectations and boundaries. McMorris and Boothroyd (1993) describe the reactive quality in classroom measurement and the often-unintended but unavoidable impacts of teacher assessment practices on student attitudes: "The impacts of a test's characteristics and quality . . . include student attitudes and perceptions that affect what students bring to the next encounter" (p. 324).

Understanding the subtle effects of assessment practices on student attitudes and perceptions can help teachers develop and use tests that take educational advantage of such effects and therefore have greater validity as assessments for learning. Performance assessment is an instance of an assessment method that is believed to capitalize on method effects to improve student motivation and learning. Assessment formats other than performance assessment have also been shown to have predictable relationships to variables other than performance. Researchers have examined the effect of assessment format (constructed-response versus multiple-choice) on student metacognition (strategy use and self-checking) and affective variables (worry and effort) (O'Neil Jr. & Brown, 1998). They have found significantly greater strategy use and also worry in the constructed-response format, and greater self-checking in the multiple-choice format.

Techniques to Evaluate the Effects of Assessment

Within the fluid context of the classroom, you should continually monitor student learning with formal and informal assessments. You can also directly investigate the effects of your assessment practices by questioning students about their perceptions about whether they have used your feedback and whether they perceive they have benefited from your instructional adjustments. You should attempt to provide opportunities for students to be reassessed when assessment-based decisions appear to be ineffective or inappropriate, and revise your instructional decisions in light of this reassessment, as needed.

Another kind of evidence is derived from looking at the relationship between two assessments on similar content, before and after instruction. If your initial formative assessment results are very similar to the results from your final assessment of that content, it would appear that your overall goal of improving learning has not been met. Comparing the average score of students before and after instruction will only be useful, however, if the students have been graded on the same scale. If they have—if, for instance, you have a single rubric for all your formative assessments in essay writing—then you can just see if the overall class average is higher.

You may be interested in whether your instructional method is narrowing the gap between under-achievers and average students. For this, comparing averages will not help. What you will want to know is whether the average spread of scores over the class as a whole is lower on the second assessment—if there is less "distance" between the higher and lower levels of achievement. The most common single statistic to describe spread among scores is the *standard deviation.* Conceptually, the standard deviation describes how much on average individual scores deviate from the mean score.

It's fairly easy to calculate the standard deviation of a distribution of scores using any spreadsheet software. If the scales for your first and second assessments are the same, and you find that the standard deviation is smaller for the second assessment and the mean is higher, that is a good indication that the lower-performing students had the strongest improvement in performance.

Graphical displays can help you visualize changes in your students' performance. To compare the spread of scores across two assessments, you can make box-and-whisker plots of the two sets of scores. In a box-and-whisker plot, the boxes represent the *interquartile range*. The middle line represents the median, which is the midpoint of the distribution. The ends of the "whiskers" represent the minimum and maximum scores.

In Figure 7.9, we show the box-and-whisker plots for a set of sample scores from the first and second assessments of 25 students, and in Figure 7.10, we show the scatterplot of the association of scores. The scale for the scores ranges from 1 to 24. From the box-and-whisker plot, you can see that the median score is higher for the second assessment, representing an overall increase for the whole class on the second assessment. You will see that the main range of scores for the second assessment—represented by the box—is lower. From the scatterplot, you can see that the students who started out at the lowest end of the distribution with only two to four points earned, generally earned much higher scores, while the students at the top end also increased their scores, but not to the same extent.

If you wish to learn more about these statistics and how to calculate them, there are many free resources online, including videos that will take you through the process step-by-step.

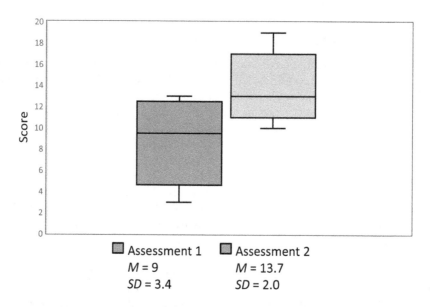

Figure 7.9 Two Iterations of Formative Assessment: Box-and-Whisker Plot

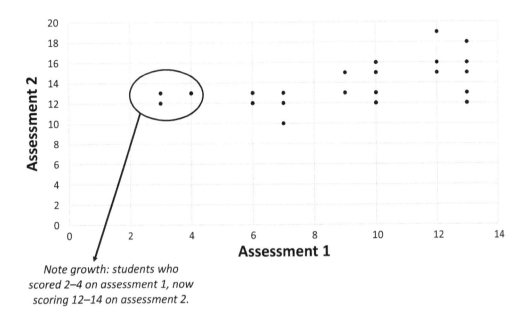

Figure 7.10 Two Iterations of Formative Assessment: Scatterplot

Explanation	• Classroom assessment may be used for promoting learning. • It may also be used to support inferences about student achievement. • Finally, assessments impact student attitudes, perceptions, and beliefs that shape their future performance.
Techniques	• Continually monitor student learning (formal and informal). • Ask students for their perceptions about their perceptions of improvement through assessment feedback. • Provide opportunities for reassessment. • Plot your students' scores and examine the standard deviation.
Supporting SRL	• Be aware that different types of assessment formats are associated with different metacognitive strategies. • Select formats that elicit desired responses (for example, constructed-response may support student strategizing).
Traditional validation approaches	• The purpose of large-scale testing is often to predict future performance (say, in college); such prediction can be checked with statistical procedures, like regression. • Many tests are used for accountability purposes, and the validity of that use is a question of policy.

Figure 7.11 Principle V: Evaluate Whether Tests Are Useful for Their Purpose

128 Section 2 Chapter 7

Validation in CA Practice: A Mini-Case Study

The purpose of this mini-case study is to demonstrate how high validity can be achieved in a classroom. Imagine you are part of a group of three ninth-grade algebra teachers in a culturally and linguistically diverse school. You are developing a unit test and have a textbook that has test items with the related Common Core standards noted, an electronic item bank that provides the same sort of information (see Chapter 9 to learn about electronic item banks), and a test you constructed the previous year. You begin by picking items, discussing as you go whether each item matches your instruction, whether you agree with the way the source matches the item to the Common Core, whether the difficulty of the item is appropriate for your students, etc. One teacher has an "honors" class and collects some of the items that are more difficult, according to information in the source or their judgment. Over an hour or two, you and the other teachers build a core test, with customizations for multiple forms according to each classroom's needs. You also gather some "extra" test tasks that are like the ones you plan to administer.

The following day, you and your colleagues pilot the extra, similar test tasks in your classes. You tell the students that the tasks will not be scored but will be good practice for the upcoming assessment. You urge the students to circle terms they find confusing and write questions in the margins of their page. While students are working, you observe and note their behavior. After students complete the task, you question students about their understanding of each problem and their reasoning when trying to solve the tasks, then collect their work.

You and your colleagues reconvene and revise the CA in light of this practice test. Then you administer the core test. Afterward, you all meet again to score the tests, using previously agreed-upon decision rules for partial scoring and so on. Each teacher passes his or her pile of tests to another teacher to score. Although you don't double-score all tests, when you are uncertain about a score, you cover your tentative score with a Post-it note and pass the test to another teacher, for an independent judgment. Because there are a number of common items among the test forms, you can all pool some of your results. You record the total scores (even, possibly, item-level information) using simple spreadsheet software. If there are three teachers, each of whom teaches four sections of algebra, you will have over 400 total scores. It is easy for you to check the relative difficulty of the test for English language learners compared to native speakers, or make comparisons between other groups.

After analyzing results and discussing your interpretations about student achievement based on the assessment, you and your colleagues return to your classrooms to discuss the results with your students. You return the tests (which you scored but did not write on) to the students, give students a model answer for a challenging open-ended item, and ask each student to compare their own response to the model. Starting there, you lead a dialogue with students about how to interpret an individual's performance on a mathematics task as it compares to an expected performance and how to represent that numerically. You and your colleagues show students the Common Core standard (or a simplified version) to which the item is purportedly linked, and solicit their opinions about how relevant the item is to the standard. Students' opinions are not sought merely as a classroom exercise—if students make a strong rebuttal to the interpretation, scores can be changed.

Later, students who struggled to perform well on the assessment are asked to participate in supplemental learning activities, perhaps through online modules. In one of your classrooms, many students were unable to respond well to many items, and you decide that the test was not a good "fit" to the students. You plan different instruction on the same content for the whole class. For all students who struggled with the content and cognitive demands, you and your colleagues re-assess students after additional instruction so the students can demonstrate that they have used the feedback they received from the test to improve learning. All students have opportunities to show not only where they are in terms of learning but how they develop.

Finally, you and your colleagues bank your assessments and document how and under what conditions the tasks were used, as well as the quality of the results. You refer to your experience with this assessment in subsequent years and share your experience and materials with peers in your professional networks who teach the same content. You also refer to information from this assessment to plan assessments of new content in subsequent instructional cycles; for instance, you may re-use or modify test directions to improve clarity, or use this experience to make decisions about test. However, whenever you think of using the assessment or the assessment method with different students, you plan to make modifications to meet the needs of that particular group. For instance, in a co-teaching classroom you would include more opportunities for differentiation, or you would add more difficult items and omit easier items in a class with a larger number of high-achieving students.

Systemic Validity: A Validation Principle for Teachers?

In addition to the principles described previously, teachers should be encouraged through their professional development, professional organizations, and school-based leadership to consider the systemic validity of the assessments they use in their classrooms. The concept of systemic validity was proposed by Frederiksen and Collins (1989). The idea is that educational tests are components of dynamic systems, and thus, decisions about assessment methods provide feedback that determines the future of the system. Teachers may adopt classroom-based assessment practices that support the most educationally valid purposes of the system, or may adopt practices, such as intensive high-stakes test preparation through drill and practice, that do not support the larger aims intended by the system. The principle that teachers should be responsible for systemically valid assessments is not included under the above key principles, due to recognition that to some extent, teachers are not the decision-making authorities in schools about how instruction should be tested. It is likely that teachers are often pressured in their schools to adopt classroom assessment practices that focus on test-taking strategies or rote memorization. However, teachers should be at all points encouraged to bear in mind the most important educational outcomes of students, rather than a test-as-end-in-itself mentality.

References

Anderson, L. W. (2002). Curricular alignment: A re-examination. *Theory into Practice*, *41*(4), 255–260.

Andrade, H., & Du, Y. (2005). Student perspectives on rubric-referenced assessment. *Practical Assessment, Research and Evaluation*, *10*(3). Retrieved from http://pareonline.net/pdf/v10n3. pdf

Brookhart, S. M. (2003). Developing measurement theory for classroom assessment purposes and uses. *Educational Measurement: Issues and Practice*, *22*(4), 5–12.

Chase, C. I. (1986). Essay test scoring: Interaction of relevant variables. *Journal of Educational Measurement*, *23*, 33–41.

Clifton, R., Perry, R. P., Parsonson, K., & Hryniuk, S. (1986). Effects of ethnicity and sec on teachers' expectations of junior high school students. *Sociology of Education*, *59*, 58–67.

Common Core State Standards. (2018). *Research to build and present knowledge: CCSS.ELA-literacy: WHST.11–12.9*. Retrieved from www.corestandards.org/ELA-Literacy/WHST/11-12/#CCSS. ELA-Literacy.WHST.11-12.10

Frederiksen, J. R., & Collins, A. (1989). A systems approach to educational testing. *Educational Researcher, 18*(9), 27–32.

Fulcher, G. (1999). Assessment in English for academic purposes: Putting content validity in its place. *Applied Linguistics, 20*(2), 221–236.

Hattie, J., & Timperley, H. (2007). The power of feedback. *Review of Educational Research, 77*(1), 81–112.

Kane, M. T. (2006). Validation. *Educational Measurement, 4*(2), 14–64.

Llosa, L. (2008). Building and supporting a validity argument for a standards-based classroom assessment of English proficiency based on teacher judgements. *Educational Measurement: Issues and Practice, 27*(3), 32–42.

Mager, R. F. (1973). *Measuring instructional intent: Or, got a match?* Atlanta, GA: The Center of Effective Performance Inc.

Marso, R. N., & Pigge, F. L. (1991). An analysis of teacher-made tests: Item types, cognitive demands, and item construction errors. *Contemporary Educational Psychology, 16*(3), 279–286.

McMorris, R. F., & Boothroyd, R. A. (1993). Tests that teachers build: An analysis of classroom tests in science and mathematics. *Applied Measurement in Education, 6*(4), 321–342.

Moss, P. A. (2003). Reconceptualizing validity for classroom assessment. *Educational Measurement: Issues and Practice, 22*(4), 13–25.

O'Neil, H. F., Jr., & Brown, R. S. (1998). Differential effects of question formats in math assessment on metacognition and affect. *Applied Measurement in Education, 11*, 331–351.

Powers, D. E., Fowles, M. E., Farnum, M., & Ramsey, P. (1994). Will they think less of my handwritten essay if others word process theirs? Effects on essay scores of intermingling handwritten and word processed essays. *Journal of Educational Measurement, 31*(3), 220–233.

Rezaei, A. R., & Lovorn, M. (2010). Reliability and validity of rubrics for assessment through writing. *Assessing Writing, 15*(1), 18–39.

Wolf, D. F. (1993). Issues in reading comprehension assessment: Implications for the development of research instruments and classroom tests. *Foreign Language Annals, 26*(3), 322–331.

Chapter 8

Fairness in Assessment
Classrooms and Beyond

It goes without saying that we want our assessment practices to be fair. But what does *fairness* mean? And how does fairness differ from validity and reliability? To answer the second question first, validity refers to the strength of the relationship between what you intend to measure and what you have actually measured. Reliability is about consistency of assessment results or scores. Fairness is more about the practice of assessment and how it influences decision-making about individuals, groups, and society. Educational professionals are still grappling with issues around fairness, not just in assessment but in the field as a whole. Fairness is not a simple concept, as it means something unique to each individual who craves it. Furthermore, the literature on fairness in assessment comes out of very different fields of study, whose scholars operate from different paradigms.

In this chapter we will present three major ways that assessment fairness is currently conceived. While sharing fairness as a core value, they have different emphases and derive from different technical—and sometimes philosophical—orientations. Bear in mind that the three perspectives we describe on fairness are neither exhaustive nor mutually exclusive.

First, specialists in test development often write about fairness as a property of tests and scores: tests are fair if they are structured to accommodate individual learning needs (Scott, Webber, Lupart, Aitken, & Scott, 2014) and yield unbiased scores (e.g., Xi, 2010; Liu & Dorans, 2016; Warne, Yoon, & Price, 2014). When we advocate for fair assessment, we seek to support the ability and opportunity of all students to demonstrate what they have learned (Kurz, Talapatra, & Roach, 2012; Elliott, 2015).

Second, experts in test administration, scoring, and reporting think about fairness as the product of a set of practices: an assessment is fair if reasonable procedures have been adhered to (e.g., Camilli, 2013; Gipps & Stobart, 2009; Karami, 2013) and if outcomes are communicated with transparency (Educational Testing Service, 2016; Zenisky & Hambleton, 2012). We seek for all those affected by assessments to understand and feel included, as appropriate, in the process.

Yet a third way of thinking about fairness in assessment is to consider it as a social goal: assessments are fair when they are used to promote supportive environments for learning for all students (e.g., Rasooli, Zandi, & DeLuca, 2018; Tierney, 2014). We therefore seek to use tests in such a way that our assessment-based decisions do not perpetuate social inequities (McNamara & Ryan, 2011; Dorans, 2013).

As in Chapters 6 and 7, we begin by explaining each view, and give summaries of our main points in Figures 8.1, 8.2, and 8.3. Because many of the concerns about fairness in assessment relate to fairness of testing for high-stakes social purposes, we give more attention than usual in this chapter to large-scale testing. Empirical accounts of fair (and unfair) practices are mostly found in the large-scale testing context. Therefore, we take those accounts as one cue to suggest techniques you can use to assess and improve fairness in your own assessment practice.

132 Section 2 Chapter 8

We also draw on recent conceptual work on fairness as a quality of CA (DeLuca, LaPointe-McEwan, & Luhanga, 2016; Rasooli, Zandy, & DeLuca, 2018; Tierney, 2014). Whenever we focus on applications of fair assessment principles for CA, we relate them to the stages in the four-stage CA:SRL framework in which they are particularly important; however, be aware that fairness is essential for any assessment procedure. Demonstrating fairness sets a classroom climate where all students perceive themselves to be treated equitably.

Fairness Principle I: Assessments Should Be Developed With Fairness in Mind

Explanation

One definition of fairness is that it is a *quality* of a particular assessment instrument. This is the technical aspect of fairness, similar to reliability and validity. In fact, this way of looking at fairness puts fairness as a foundational technical quality of good measurement (American Educational Research Association, 2014). Like reliability and validity, fairness cannot be proven to exist, but evidence can be compiled that a test use or interpretation is more or less fair.

Because the view of fairness as a technical quality of assessment is closely related to validity, some of the methods used for evaluating the fairness of tests from this perspective will be familiar to you from Chapter 7. However, fairness most often comes into play when decisions based on tests are applied broadly to groups within a population and when those decisions appear to be discriminatory against specific groups. Validity is a very broad principle that encompasses the quality of interpretations made at many levels: interpreting mental processes based on behavior, interpreting behaviors to create scores, using scores to rate students or make statements about proficiency, and so on. Fairness issues may arise at each of these interpretive junctures, when there is a possibility that the interpretation may be discriminatory. Therefore, fairness from the technical perspective is mainly associated with bias and with testing procedures and interpretations that may result in bias against special population groups like students with disabilities and English language learners or biases related to gender, racial, or cultural differences.

Large-Scale Assessment Approaches to Developing Fair Tests: Technical Quality

Large-scale testing experts start during the test development process to ensure fairness as a technical quality in testing. Vocabulary in test items should be selected in a way that does not allow students from different regions of the country or backgrounds an unfair advantage. An example is found in the SAT, formerly known as the Scholastic Aptitude Test. Up until 2005, the SAT included analogy items, where test-takers compared relationships between pairs of words or pairs of mathematical concepts. For instance, older versions of the SAT had a verbal reasoning section that has now been replaced by critical reading. The verbal reasoning section included analogies. Many critics of the analogy items pointed out that these analogies related unnecessarily to logical reasoning versus verbal or reading skill, that they were coachable through memorizing lists of vocabulary words, and that they privileged affluent students. For instance, one item required students to understand that the term *regatta* had the same relationship to *oarsman* as *marathon* had to *runner*. Critics considered it unreasonable to use a term like *regatta*, which privileged affluent students living in environments where boat-racing was a familiar sport. You may wonder why on large-scale tests reading comprehension passages are often about obscure events or people outside the general population of the country. Test developers try to construct reading passages that will deal with topics that all students can understand, but with which no groups will have special familiarity.

Also, test developers take steps to ensure that the test can be administered in ways that provide reasonable accommodations for students with specific disabilities, which are funded under the U.S. Department of Education's Individuals with Disabilities Education Act (IDEA), and also covered for a broader range of disabilities under Section 504 of the Rehabilitation Act of 1973. The Rehabilitation Act is a federal civil rights law to stop discrimination against people with disabilities. These laws require schools to create Individualized Education Programs (IEPs) or Individualized Family Service Plans (IFSPs) for each student with disabilities, tailored to the student's needs. The U.S. government also requires that all students whose primary or home language is other than English be tested to determine their English proficiency. If the student is identified as having limited English proficiency, schools are required to create a Limited English Proficient (LEP) Accommodation Plan that includes testing accommodations.

When all learners, including students with limited English proficiency and those with IEPs or accommodations under Section 504, are required to take tests of the same content that yield comparable scores, tests must be developed so that all students can respond. Generally speaking, we want to accommodate learners with special needs in ways that put them on a level playing field with students from the general education population. A testing accommodation is considered a fair test accommodation if it allows the learner with the disability or LEP to perform to their level of achievement, but is not a change in testing that would generally boost the scores of students without disabilities. In other words, the accommodation levels the field for students with disabilities, without advantaging them in test-taking. For instance, it is appropriate to accommodate a visually-impaired student by providing the test in an enlarged format or in Braille. This accommodation would not advantage students who did not need it based on a disability, so it is considered fair. Test developers must pilot test forms with different accommodations to ensure that the changes in form meet the needs of the students for which they are intended, without altering the test in such a way that the scores of students with special needs cannot be placed on the same scale and related to the scores of the general education testing population.

There are many types of testing accommodations: method of presentation, method of response, test timing, test setting, and language accommodations. Method of presentation refers to changes in the ways test questions/directions are presented to students. For instance, directions to the test, or the entire test, may be read aloud. Method of response includes changes in the ways that students can respond to test questions. Oral responses may be allowed, or students may be able to give responses using clickers or eye movement. Test timing refers to alternatives to when students take exams. For instance, students may be allowed extended time to take the test, or the test may be administered in multiple short sittings. Test setting includes where and with whom students take exams. Tests can be administered in secluded spaces or at special testing centers.

Some of the possible accommodations recommended for visually impaired students consist of bold-lined writing paper, use of magnifiers, enlarged print materials or Braille for exams and classwork, oral instead of written exams (human readers), pre-recorded exams and instructional materials, screen readers, and tactile maps. Some recommendations for students who are hearing impaired include amplification devices, media with closed captioning, and speech-to-text translation.

For English language learners, tests may be provided in the student's native language, a native language-to-English dictionary may be used, or the person administering the test may be permitted to explain words that are confusing only because of limited English proficiency (not because of incomplete content knowledge).

Assuming reasonable accommodations are provided for testing those with special needs, the next approach to ensuring technical fairness uses statistical analyses of test items based on data gathered during test piloting. Such analyses typically look for what is known as *Differential Item Functioning* (DIF). DIF analysis allows us to estimate whether groups within the overall population, like African Americans or women, score systematically higher or lower on individual test items than do other population groups, even when estimates of their overall ability in the content area is the same as that of other groups. For instance, let's imagine an eighth-grade state test in mathematics. The test has 100 problem-solving items. The test developers use data from a pilot test administered to a large sample of eighth graders in the state to place all students on a scale that rates their mathematical problem-solving ability. Using those overall ability estimates, the test developers can compare boys and girls who have the same estimated mathematical ability in terms of their scores on individual items on the test. They may find that girls in the sample score lower than boys on one or two items, even when their overall abilities are similar. Or they may find the opposite trend, boys scoring lower than girls. Whichever way the trend, if this systematic difference at the item level is sufficiently large, the developers will almost certainly remove the item from the test.

Classroom Techniques for Tests That Are Fair in Terms of Technical Quality

All the methods described above have parallels in classroom assessment. For instance, when writing or adapting test items, consider whether all students have reasonable familiarity with the vocabulary in the items. "Window dressing" was discussed in Chapter 2, as part of assessment at Stage 2, during instruction, and also applies to design of any tasks administered in Stage 3, formal assessment. Window dressing is a general problem in multiple-choice items because it puts a heavy reading load on students; it poses an additional problem when the words in the window dressing are exotic. If you use homework to assess students (a practice we do not recommend, see Chapter 5 on Stage 4), realize that some of your students have chores, child care, or other duties outside of school, or live in conditions that make homework difficult. When you construct a project that requires out-of-class time, consider whether all students have access to the resources they need to complete it when they are away from school. Other common problems of bias occur during scoring. One is known as the halo effect, which refers to the fact that raters' judgments of a student's response can be influenced by the general impression the student makes. This can also be considered a "demon" effect, if negative impressions of a student taint the judgment of the scorer. In a carryover effect, a teacher develops expectations of student performance on one item or subtask of an assessment, and bases further scoring on those expectations, rather than the evidence in front of them. Some suggestions for reducing both the halo and the carryover effects were provided in Chapter 7.

When you administer assessments at any of Stages 1–3, most of the accommodations that your students may need will be provided by the school, although sometimes, very unfortunately, not all of them. Extended time, secluded or special space, and oral reading of directions should be accommodations any school provides. Classrooms should have native language-to-English dictionaries available for all students. Inexpensive colored overlays improve text readability for some students. For students with ADHD (and many others), noise-canceling headphones or white noise help screen out auditory distractions; stability balls help those with restless bottoms, and stress balls and "fidgets" give students quiet ways to express active hands.

We hope that you as a teacher will not find yourself purchasing any materials yourself to accommodate the needs of your students.

Sad to say, some other kinds of accommodations are only offered in wealthy districts or when highly agentic, often more affluent parents consult experts outside the school system, such as clinical psychologists and even lawyers, who can make compelling demands on the child's behalf. Students may benefit from use of electronic magnifiers, voice recognition software, screen readers, noise-canceling headphones, reading pens, or talking calculators. It is best to not accommodate students by specific disabilities or language needs, but rather accommodate students individually (Salend, 2008).

After you have administered a formal assessment (Stage 3) in your classroom, there are ways you can evaluate whether the results of your assessments are biased against groups, even though you don't have the statistical tools to detect DIF. If you have a fairly balanced number of students with IEPs or ELLs in your classroom, you can use the techniques of item analysis that were introduced in Chapter 4 to compare the relative difficulty of items on your assessments for your general education students and those with IEPs or ELLs. Big differences between groups on individual items, especially when the groups have overall similar scores, may indicate problems of bias with those items that you should attend to by reviewing the item content. Although this quantitative evidence would be far from conclusive due to small sample sizes and the limited statistical procedures that are likely available to you, the results may be suggestive.

You can also compare the overall scores on the various fields that go in your gradebook between groups at Stage 4. For instance, you can look at students' mathematics test scores, averaged over multiple unit tests. If the girls have markedly different scores on average than the boys, this suggests the possibility of bias. Of course, it could also mean that the girls in the class are simply, on average, less proficient in mathematics. Unlike professional test developers,

Explanation	• Fairness is often conceived as a quality of an assessment task or instrument. • A fair test WILL NOT discriminate between groups within a population (be biased) in its form or substance, or in decisions made based on test outcomes. • A fair test WILL provide all students with the opportunity to demonstrate their learning and WILL be adapted when necessary to accommodate students.
Classroom techniques	• Implement appropriate accommodations for students who need them. • Do not put undue burden on students (assessment time, task demands, "fluff" in items). • Use item analysis to check relative item difficulty, and compare overall scores to detect any gaps.
Policy and large-scale testing	• Provide reasonable accommodations consistent with IDEA and Section 504 of the Rehabilitation Act of 1973. • Develop tests with sensitivity toward individual differences (class, race, sex, language, ability). • Examine tests for evidence of DIF and aim to eliminate such systematic biases.

Figure 8.1 Assessments Should Be Developed With Fairness in Mind

you do not have the resources to statistically control for overall mathematical skill. However, such a result definitely gives you a heads-up that you need to consider gender differences in your approach to teaching so that all students can learn.

Fairness Principle II: Fair Processes Should Be Used in Assessment and Reporting

Explanation

One can also approach the goal of fairness by attending to the processes that go into testing. Process-oriented attempts to ensure fairness do not replace the concept of fairness as a technical quality, but are used in tandem. Once tests have been developed to reduce bias against groups and to provide reasonable accommodations, we administer them and report their results in fair ways. The overarching principle for fair procedures at all stages and levels of an assessment system is transparency. Certain actions in assessment are fair if students and other important stakeholders in the assessment process have full access to information about the process. We look at the procedural approach to fairness as an over-arching principle with safeguards in place before, during, and after testing.

Large-Scale Assessment Approaches for Fair Assessment Processes

Well before important tests take place, teachers or external testing bodies should take pains to communicate fully with test-takers. They must let students know why, when, and how they will be assessed, and what are the consequences or uses of the results of their performance. Transparency in communication with parents is also essential, so that parents can support their students in preparation for days when an important test will take place. For state tests, most districts will schedule tests well in advance and send information notices to parents to encourage them to plan travel outside of testing times and to make sure the students have a good night's sleep and breakfast on the day the test will occur.

Large-scale testing systems should provide fair processes during test administration to ensure that any accommodations to which students are legally entitled are actually available and put into use. For students who need test directions to be read aloud or in a student's native language, the school must provide personnel to perform that function. If a test is designed to allow Braille or speech-to-text recognition, the school district must provide equipment that will allow the student to take advantage of these resources. Note that measures to prevent cheating can also be considered part of fairness. If the school allows an atmosphere for testing that is conducive to cheating, for instance by allowing school personnel access to students' completed test forms before they are sent for scoring, that school is playing with loaded dice. Someone at the school has inserted an unfair—indeed, an illegal—practice into the assessment process.

After test administration, procedural views on fairness in testing focus on clarity in communicating results and confidentiality or privacy. To begin with clarity in communication, when individuals are tested, those individuals or their legal guardians should, in all fairness, be able to understand the performance reports. You should not need to be a specialist in psychology to understand test scores. Some types of test scores are notoriously hard to interpret, and it raises issues of fairness when those who report test scores or other summaries of student learning don't use metrics that students or parents can understand.

To elaborate slightly on this point, in most K–12 educational testing, there are two kinds of scores: norm-referenced test scores (NRTs) and criterion-referenced test scores (CRTs).

On an NRT test, individuals' scores are compared to the distribution of scores from a large, representative group of students from the same population, known as the norm group. CRTs report performance in reference to expectations for proficiency, which are derived from expert judgments about what a student at a particular grade level should know and be able to do. In the past, score interpretation has been complicated by the fact that a large number of "scores" can be reported, each of which means something slightly different to the community of testing experts.

There are a number of types of NRT scores: the percentile rank (PR), the Stanine, the Grade Equivalent (GE), the Normal Curve Equivalent (NCE). A layperson would have difficulty interpreting many of these score types. As an example, we consider the GE. The GE score conveys the grade and months of school within the grade out of which a student would be expected to obtain the score they obtained. If a student is average-performing in his or her grade, the student's score will be at the same level of his or her grade attainment. For instance, on a vocabulary test, the average-performing sixth-grade test-taker in his or her fifth month of school would attain a GE of 6.5. On the other hand, a sixth grader with a GE score of 3.2 has performed well below average for his or her grade level. On the sixth-grade vocabulary test, that student's score is closest to the score which would be expected of a third grader in the second month of the school year.

GE scores used to be commonly reported to parents, as did many other score types. However, many people argued against them on the grounds that they did not meet the fairness expectation of clarity in reporting test results. Nowadays, the most frequently reported score—sometimes the only reported score—is the PR. The PR tells you the percent of test-takers in the norming group who scored at or below the rank of any single individual. PR scores are fairly easy for the layperson to learn to interpret, using explanations about their meaning that are also provided in the score report.

For CRTs, like state tests, the most commonly reported interpretation is a statement of whether the student fell far below, below, at, or above the standard for proficiency in the tested domain. Some tests will report both NRT and CRT scores. Large-scale test developers are paying more and more attention in recent years to the interpretability of score reports. Test reports to parents and school administrators have increasingly clear and informative graphics and explanations about how to interpret test results.

To ensure fairness in communication, assessment results should also be reported in a confidential manner, and they should be held private from those who have no legal access to individual results. Federal and state laws govern the privacy and confidentiality of data from testing, and test administrators should follow procedures to safeguard the privacy of individual scores, or scores that can be linked to an individual. For instance, the release of classroom-level data that can be associated with an individual teacher is considered highly confidential.

Classroom Approaches for Fair Assessment Processes

In the classroom, fair assessment processes apply to pre-assessment, assessment during instructional cycles, formal assessment, and compiling assessment results—in other words, all four stages in the CA:SRL framework. We will be mindful of this in our presentation of classroom techniques in the following, even when we emphasize practices that are particularly important at certain stages.

For instance, you should always give your students the information that assessment is taking place, even when it is done quite informally. Before you pre-assess at Stage 1, briefly let your students know that the questions you will ask them are for the purpose of helping you identify their misconceptions or survey their attitudes. Otherwise, they will very likely be confused and think they are taking some kind of a test before they have learned anything at all about the content. Let them know their scores or your interpretations of their performance will not in any way be used to evaluate their learning, only to help you and your students plan and strategize together for learning. As you interact with them at Stage 2, again let them know that you may be administering short quizzes or conducting interviews only to gauge their progress and help them make decisions about setting new learning goals and taking next steps along their learning progressions. However, when you reach Stage 3, you want them to know that it's time to look very carefully at what they have accomplished over the course of Stage 2 and that they should be sure to be prepared to be assessed. We recommend giving students at least one week's notice before a formal assessment will take place. With younger children, their parents and guardians should be notified as well. When possible and practicable, for instance with high school students, you should have a syllabus that shows important assessment dates and due dates further in advance. For Stage 3 assessments that have a long timeframe, you should inform students of any progress benchmarks they are expected to turn in for your feedback, their due dates, and your availability to provide scaffolds when needed. At Stage 4, fair warning still matters. Students who have work they have not yet turned in need to know if you have a final deadline beyond which nothing can be entered in the gradebook.

In terms of accommodating the needs of individual students in assessment, you as a classroom teacher are not being fair if you neglect to find out the accommodations in assessment that your students are entitled to or do not provide appropriate accommodations to your students who need them, whether during Stage 1, Stage 2, or Stage 3 assessment. You should talk to the special education teacher who is responsible for any student's IEP or 504 plan. If that person is hard to find, seek them out assiduously. We strongly recommend that you also talk confidentially with your English language learner students and those who have IEPs or 504 plans, and find out what kinds of supports have worked for them best in the past. Encourage your students to avail themselves of the tools that your school provides, because some students are shy to ask. This is a way of involving students in identifying their own needs and helping them develop skills in help-seeking, being resourceful, and being self-regulated. Another option that can help English language learners is to consider arranging any group assessments at Stage 2 so that students with the same heritage language can work together.

Put fair assessment processes into practice when you formally score the work students have produced in a Stage 3 task and when you compile the results of their formal assessments into any kind of the summary report in Stage 4. We presented techniques for the fair use of rubrics in Chapters 4 and 7. Use these techniques when you interpret Stage 3 work, and re-check your use of them when you accumulate scores at Stage 4. Make sure that you have not entered any scores of "zero" when work was missing, but instead entered either the highest failing score on that assignment or, preferably, tracked that student down and obtained an estimate of their achievement. Review all the scores in your gradebook and all your calculations. You may have made adjustments to student scores after they are first entered. You will have done this either because a student alerted you to an error in the scoring or because you allowed a student to raise their score by demonstrating achievement on that SLO in another way. Sometimes, we forget to update the scores we put in the gradebook. Therefore, at Stage 4, check your notes.

In classroom assessment, confidentiality is important during assessment administration, not only during reporting of results. While we advocate for a classroom culture with explicit learning goals and criteria for success, not every student performance should be "open to the

Explanation	• Fairness is achieved throughout the process of assessing, from developing an instrument to administering it and interpreting outcomes. • Fair testing procedures WILL be transparent in intent and consequence and ensure all stakeholders have access to information about the assessment.
Classroom techniques	• Help students understand purpose of each stage of assessment—for instance, pre-assessments identify gaps. • Score work and report outcomes with attention to detail and accuracy. • Respect students' privacy when giving feedback. • Keep grades confidential.
Policy and large-scale testing	• Communicate the purpose of the test and the consequences or uses of test performance. • Standardize administration and take measures to prevent cheating and ensure confidentiality. • Communicate performance in reports that are clear and accessible (percentile rank, proficiency).

Figure 8.2 Fair Processes Should Be Used in Assessment and Reporting

public." As Stage 1 pre-assessment, if you are using a survey to measure attitudes, students who are nervous in anticipation of new and challenging content may not honestly report their concerns if they feel other students will find out about them. During any Stage 2 one-on-one assessment, you should find a semi-private corner of the classroom in which you can interact with students without them being overheard. You want to communicate to your students that it's okay to make mistakes, because mistakes are opportunities for them to receive feedback, learn from feedback, and try out new strategies. Most Stage 3 formal assessments are completed by students individually, and here you mostly want to be sure that students are not peeking inappropriately at one another's work or comparing their work in reference to one another rather than in reference to the criteria you have set. When your formal assessment requires students to act ensemble, for instance in a band performance, the students cannot help seeing or hearing one another's work. In that case, performance is public, but you can still take steps to ensure that your feedback to individuals is private.

Finally, student grades should always be confidential. We recommend that you do not display students' scores at the front of the classroom, give call-outs to top performers, or otherwise publicly show student outcomes in a way that ranks them in comparison to one another. When you discuss an individual child's progress with a parent or guardian at a school Open House, have that conversation in a part of the room where others are not listening in. Also be sensitive to language issues when you communicate performance to parents. Few parents will understand much of the language of academic standards and the professional vocabulary you use in planning. Therefore, use plain, exact, and respectful words. Sometimes you may need a language interpreter, in which case we hope that the school will provide one. We do not recommend that a student act as an interpreter for his or her own parents in a conversation about learning outcomes. The student should be a participant in their own assessment, but communicating that information to parents puts them in a difficult position.

Fairness Principle III: The Goal of Fairness Is to Support Fair Outcomes for All Learners

Explanation

The historical evolution of work on fairness in the field of educational testing is somewhat interesting. Much of the treatment of fairness in testing has been historically treated under the umbrella of validity, where the writings of Lee Cronbach began to show a concern about fairness not only in terms of measurement quality but in terms of adverse consequences of testing for certain groups (1971). As Cronbach wrote in his title to a paper in 1976, equity is where measurement and political philosophy meet. Building from there, in 1989, Messick wrote that consequences of testing were an essential societal concern, and attention to the social consequences of testing was a responsibility shared by test developers as part of test validity. There was a very mixed reaction to that assertion, because it suggests that when test results are willfully misinterpreted or misused, the developers still have some responsibility. The debate about whether test developers are responsible when tests are used for purposes for which they are not intended—especially when used as part of public policy—continues to this day.

Social concerns about fairness in assessment are largely motivated by evidence or beliefs that assessment processes, interpretations, and outcomes have a ripple effect throughout our society. We hope that the goal of testing in education is to provide information to improve educational practice for the betterment of all sectors of society. Sometimes we clearly miss that goal. In the U.S., many tests have been questioned on the grounds of fairness because their uses have resulted in maintaining social inequities, rather than helping all students achieve success.

Interestingly, some tests that are now questioned on the grounds of fairness were in fact designed to promote fairness. The SAT is a prominent example. Prior to the use of the SAT in college admissions, elite men's schools, particularly Harvard, generally admitted only students from elite private schools in the northeast. In 1933, the president of Harvard started to award scholarships based on intellectual merit as measured by tests and selected the SAT as Harvard's selection method. Soon all schools that belonged to the College Board, at the time a small number of mostly private colleges and universities, adopted the SAT for student selection, at first only for scholarship students, and later for all students. The use of the SAT was perceived to make admissions decisions fairly based on academic aptitude rather than on religion, race, or social standing.

In addition to the concern that test use can perpetuate inequities deeply embedded in American society, many people have concerns about unintended impacts of testing: the way large-scale testing in particular, but also classroom assessment, can shape what is learned and how it is learned. The term *washback* has been used to refer to the effects of testing on instruction (Fulcher, 1999). Washback can be positive, for instance, when instructional quality is improved by attention to student strengths and weaknesses as demonstrated by tests aligned to high-quality standards. Washback also can be negative, for instance, when schools narrow the curriculum they offer to focus on a limited range of readily testable knowledge and skills. Washback has the ripple effect we mentioned above. When institutions like schools, districts, or states drive students to perform well on a specific test or small set of assessments, curriculum developers will create products for the test-driven market. Because no single assessment instrument can measure well the broad scope of the learning goals we hold for students, this kind of washback will limit instructional opportunities. Such limits especially affect students in under-resourced schools that are high in numbers of students with special needs and English language learners.

Supporting Fair Outcomes for All Learners in Large-Scale Testing

Perhaps we can best describe approaches to supporting fair outcomes for all learners from the perspective of equity under the umbrella term *responsiveness*. In response to evidence or perceptions that the use of certain tests have negative social consequences or unfair impacts on sub-groups in the general population, there have evolved over time many changes in the way large-scale assessments are designed, administered, and used in the U.S. We will look at a few specific instances where different levels of stakeholders have shown responsiveness to issues about the fairness of educational testing. These stakeholders include legal experts, advocacy organizations, test developers, individual educational institutions, and policymakers.

The judgment of legal experts has frequently been directed at fairness in educational testing. For example, decisions in court have compelled changes to the practice of "tracking" students based on ability groups. *Tracking* means placing students in particular curricular programs based on a sorting mechanism, usually test scores. Tracks may include vocational, general, and academic programs. The use of tracking is controversial from the fairness perspective, because it deprives students of lower abilities of the educational advantages of some curricula, and in some cases has the effect of segregating students within schools by race, socio-economics, or language. In an early case, *Hobson v. Hansen* (1967), the court ruled that it was unfair to track students into ability groups based on tests that were normed for a different population; in other words, tests in which "normal" meant White and middle class should not be used to make tracking decisions about lower-class or Black students. Numerous cases have also revolved around the use of IQ tests for placement into special education, where non-White students are disproportionally represented. Since the 2004 reauthorization of IDEA, states have the option to use the IQ in decision-making about special education placement, but are not required to do so. Some states have moved to a different model of fortification called Response to Intervention (RTI). In RTI, students are observed and data are collected on their performance starting in their early years. When they do not advance as expected, increasing support is given within the regular classroom. When the student does not respond (through improved performance) to the kinds of scaffolding that can be offered in the general education or combined general and special education classroom, the student may be considered for special education services. This method, which looks at children in context instead of in comparison to a population that may not be representative of them, is considered to be fairer than IQ-based placement alone; however, IQ tests are still considered one useful component of a decision about special needs.

Advocacy organizations, in particular the National Center for Fair and Open Testing (FairTest), attempt to promote "fair, open, valid and educationally beneficial evaluations of students, teachers, and schools" (fairtest.org). Among its initiatives, FairTest has long argued against the SAT on the basis that students from more affluent families have an unfair advantage in college admissions because their parents can afford professional coaching for the exam. Also, FairTest and local advocacy groups work to influence lawmakers to make changes in educational policies that use testing for high-stakes decision-making.

In response to evidence about fairness and/or advocacy, test development companies may change aspects of test design or administration procedures. We have already discussed issues for fairness related to technical item quality on the SAT. Many people perceived that certain SAT questions gave an advantage to students from privileged backgrounds and were not good indicators of college-readiness. Statistically speaking, not all the questions identified by critics as culturally biased showed DIF, described earlier in this chapter. However, rather than defend the content of every item, and in response to criticism about the relevance of SAT content to the college performance it was supposed to predict, in 2005 the College Board dropped analogies from the verbal section of the SAT and quantitative comparison items from the math section. Also, in direct response to public concerns about SAT coaching, since 2016 College Board has partnered with Khan Academy to offer free test preparation services.

Individual educational institutions also respond to questions from the public about fair use of testing. In particular, colleges and universities have options about the use of tests in admissions. In recent years, higher education institutions have become more liberal about testing in admissions. First, many East Coast colleges that previously required the SAT began to accept ACT scores as well. More recently, many institutions have stopped requiring either test as part of a student application, and even more have allowed students to use evidence from other examinations (such as Advanced Placement tests) in lieu of SAT/ACT scores, or require SAT/ACT tests only when core requirements such as high school GPA are not met. "Test-optional" and "test-flexible" institutions set these policies not only based on evidence that measures other than the SAT/ACT predict college success about equally well, but out of concerns about fairness.

Finally, state and federal policymakers may respond to concerns about fairness in educational assessment by passing or amending laws that include testing mandates. In the last few decades in the U.S., federal legislation has heavily influenced public education. Under the 2002 legislation No Child Left Behind (NCLB), the federal funding provisions under Title 1 of the Elementary and Secondary Education Act (ESEA) of 1965, which are awarded to schools with high percentages of low-income students, became tied to the demonstration that students were meeting high, standards-based performance benchmarks. Schools were held accountable for making what was called Adequate Yearly Progress (AYP) toward the goal of having 100% of students score at proficient levels on tests of educational standards in their state. Part of the logic of the test-based accountability system of NCLB was that schools with Title 1 funding would need to show outcomes to prove that they were providing highly effective instructional services to their low-income, high-needs students. One could see this as step toward fairness through testing: students in Title 1-funded schools would benefit from the improved instruction that the schools would have to provide in order for students to score well. However, NCLB had many detractors. Many people came to believe that federally mandated state

Explanation	• Fairness matters because the consequences of testing matter as a societal concern. • Tests should be used to promote equity, not to perpetuate or result in disparities between groups. • Assessment can have unintended effects on the classroom: "washback."
Classroom techniques	• Involve students in the assessment process and support them in setting appropriately challenging and attainable expectations for themselves. • Use differentiation with purpose; utilize a variety of sources of evidence in making inferences about achievement. • Challenge your own biases and ask students about their perceptions of your practices.
Policy and large-scale testing	• Multiple stakeholders respond to charges of unfairness. • Legal experts, advocacy organizations, testing companies, and educational institutions make changes to their use of tests.

Figure 8.3 The Goal of Fairness Is to Support Fair Outcomes for All Learners

Fairness in Assessment 143

testing was heavy-handed, particularly in low-income, educationally disadvantaged communities where the pressure to make AYP was high. Some argued that being held to a single, statewide standard was unfair and insensitive to local contexts. In 2015 Congress passed the Every Student Succeeds Act (ESSA), a reauthorization of ESEA. Among other things, ESSA gives states and local authorities more control over what is tested and how. One can view ESEA, NCLB, and ESSA as part of a long conversation at the national level about how tests can help or hinder society make the goal of fair education.

Classroom Techniques That Support Fair Outcomes for All Learners

If you as an individual teacher want your classroom assessment practices to contribute toward the goal of fair outcomes for all learners, you will start well by implementing the practices described in this book. Here are a few big ideas and general suggestions for how to achieve fair – although not necessarily equal – outcomes for all learners in the CA:SRL framework:

- Involve your students in their own assessment. The results will impact them most, so they should not be passive in the process.
- Do not keep secrets from your students about your plans for assessment and expectations for success. Just like a basketball player can't make a shot if he or she can't see the basket, students are unlikely to meet goals if the goals are not evident to them.
- Give your students opportunities to set expectations for themselves. They will internalize self-made goals and learn to self-monitor against their own standards.
- Be aware of your own biases and potential biases, and take steps to eliminate them from your classroom practice.
- Don't rush to judgment with insufficient evidence. Just as you want your students to experience rich understanding of math, science, reading, history, and content in the arts and languages through a wide array of learning experiences, we encourage you to gain rich knowledge about your students' learning through multiple methods of assessment.
- Use differentiation in assessment purposively. When you want to know "why" or "how" a student is thinking, every individual's assessments can be differentiated, especially if you use supply-type, open-ended questions or student-teacher interactions. When you want to know "how well" a student can demonstrate conceptual knowledge or skill, never fail to give each student any accommodation that will help them show their learning to the best of their ability.
- Ask students for their feedback, especially about your assessment practices. Do your students perceive them to be fair?
- Above all, make sure your students have the opportunity to learn what will be assessed.

References

American Educational Research Association, American Psychological Association, & National Council on Measurement in Education. (2014). *Standards for Educational and Psychological Testing*. Washington, DC: American Educational Research Association.

Camilli, G. (2013). Ongoing issues in test fairness. *Educational Research and Evaluation, 19*(2–3), 104–120.

Cronbach, L. J. (1971). Test validation. In R. L. Thorndike (Ed.), *Educational measurement* (2nd ed., pp. 443–507). Washington, DC: American Council on Education.

Cronbach, L. J. (1976). Equity in selection—Where psychometrics and political philosophy meet. *Journal of Educational Measurement, 13*(1), 31–41.

DeLuca, C., LaPointe-McEwan, D., & Luhanga, U. (2016). Teacher assessment literacy: A review of international standards and measures. *Educational Assessment, Evaluation, and Accountability, 28*(3), 251–272.

Dorans, N. J. (2013). *ETS contributions to the quantitative assessment of item, test, and score fairness*. Princeton, NJ: ETS. Retrieved from www.ets.org/research/policy_research_reports/publications/report/2013/jrmc.

Educational Testing Service. (2016). *ETS guidelines for fair tests and communications*. Princeton, NJ: ETS. Retrieved from www.ets.org/about/fairness/.

Elliott, S. N. (2015). Measuring opportunity to learn and achievement growth: Key research issues with implications for the effective education of all students. *Remedial and Special Education, 36*(1), 58–64.

Fulcher, G. (1999). Assessment in English for academic purposes: Putting content validity in its place. *Applied Linguistics, 20*(2), 221–236.

Gipps, C., & Stobart, G. (2009). Fairness in assessment. In C. Wyatt-Smith & J. J. Cumming (Eds.), *Educational assessment in the 21st century: Connecting theory and practice* (pp. 105–118). New York, NY: Springer.

Hobson v. Hansen, 269 F. Supp. 401 (D.D.C. 1967).

Karami, H. (2013). The quest for fairness in language testing. *Educational Research and Evaluation, 19*(2–3), 158–169.

Kurz, A., Talapatra, D, & Roach, A. T. (2012). Meeting the curricular challenges of inclusive assessment: The role of alignment, opportunity to learn, and student engagement. *International Journal of Disability, Development, and Education, 59*(1), 37–52.

Liu, J., & Dorans, N. J. (2016). Fairness in score interpretations. In N. J. Dorans & L. L. Cook (Eds.), *Fairness in educational assessment and measurement* (pp. 77–96). New York, NY: Routledge.

McNamara, T., & Ryan, K. (2011). Fairness versus justice in language testing: The place of English literacy in the Australian citizenship test. *Language Assessment Quarterly, 8*, 161–178.

Messick, S. (1989). Validity. In R. L. Linn (Ed.), *Educational measurement* (3rd ed., pp. 13–103). New York, NY: Macmillan.

Rasooli, A., Zandi, H., & DeLuca, C. (2018). Re-conceptualizing classroom assessment fairness: A systematic meta-ethnography of assessment literature and beyond. *Studies in Educational Evaluation, 56*, 164–181.

Salend, S. J. (2008). Determining appropriate testing accommodations: Complying with NCLB and IDEA. *Teaching Exceptional Children, 40*(4), 14–22.

Scott, S., Webber, C. F., Lupart, J. L., Aitken, N., & Scott, D. E. (2014). Fair and equitable assessment practices for all students. *Assessment in Education: Principles, Policy & Practice, 21*(1), 52–70.

Tierney, R. (2014). Fairness as a multifaceted quality in classroom assessment. *Studies in Educational Evaluation, 43*, 55–69.

Warne, R. T., Yoon, M., & Price, C. J. (2014). Exploring the various interpretations of "test bias." *Cultural Diversity and Ethnic Minority Psychology, 20*(4), 570–582.

Xi, X. (2010). How do we go about investigating test fairness? *Language Testing, 27*(2), 147–170.

Zenisky, A. L., & Hambleton, R. K. (2012). Developing test score reports that work: The process and best practices for effective communication. *Educational Measurement: Issues and Practice, 31*(2), 21–26.

Chapter 9

Technology in Classroom Assessment

Ask yourself these questions about an assessment process you have used or observed in school. Did the teacher draw on a computer to determine what kind of tasks would measure standards? Was the task itself provided through an electronic repository? Did students need to interact with technology while performing the task? Did students record their answers using digital technology? Did a computer score the students' work? Did a computer give students or the teacher feedback about the response? If you answered "yes" to any of those questions, you were thinking about an assessment that involved technology.

Computers are, of course, not the only technology available in classrooms. Paper and chalkboards are very old and effective technologies for assessment. And computer-based classroom assessment is not as new to the field of education as you might think. Technology-based systems for students to report responses or message teachers have been used in educational assessment since the late 1960s (Judson & Sawada, 2002), with a strong upswing in their use in the 1990s, particularly for large lecture classes in the sciences (Kay & LeSage, 2009). But the increasing availability of computing devices in K–12 classrooms has opened up a whole new world for classroom assessment.

In this chapter, we will discuss recent trends in the use of computer technology for classroom assessment. We will use the four stages of the CA:SRL framework to present a wide but not exhaustive array of options to incorporate technology in CA, with suggestions about how technology can be leveraged to support SRL. Be aware that although we will use specific applications and computer-based systems as examples, we are not recommending any particular product. We will highlight some features of technology-based assessment that teachers and students can control to ensure it is useful for a learning purpose. A snapshot of prominent features and their advantages is shown in Figure 9.1.

We will also suggest you think about technology in CA in terms of components of assessment design that professional test developers consider when they create technology-based large-scale systems. For technology-based assessment, experts have recommended attention to many components of design that apply well to the situation of the classroom teacher who is considering whether to use technology in assessment (Dragow, Luecht, & Bennett, 2006). These components of assessment design will help us guide you to think about the questions that you will need to resolve when making decisions about the technology for your own CA practices. Finally, we will raise some ideas and questions about assessment in the future, as computing becomes ever more ubiquitous in classrooms.

Three Generations of Technology in Educational Assessment

The development of the use of technology in assessment can be categorized in terms of three generations (Bennett, 2015). The first generation, which is largely complete, was the creation

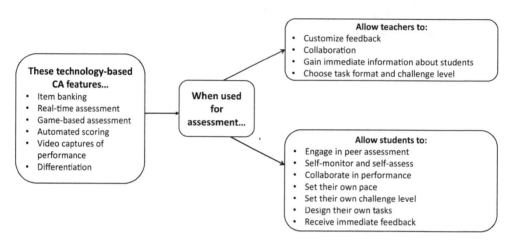

Figure 9.1 Technology Features for Teacher and Student Use

of an infrastructure for administration of technology-based assessments. It involved considerable financial investment on the part of states and schools in computers, networking capability, and human capacity in the form of training teachers of technology and district tech-support to use and maintain the new medium. The actual tests delivered in the first generation of technological assessment differed little from traditional paper-and-pencil tests. They were "drop-from-the-sky" assessments (i.e., high-stakes and external) over which teachers and schools had little control in design. They used static items rather than tasks with which a student could interact. Their main advantages had to do with administration and scoring: they did not require a lengthy process of transferring test responses to data sets for analysis, and they were less prone to cheating or other data manipulation at the local level.

As a distinct feature, some large-scale tests featured what is known as adaptive technology. In computer-adaptive testing, each test-taker receives a form of the test that adapts to their abilities in the content domain, by assessing skill or knowledge with a limited number of items, whose scores, immediately calculated by the computer system, inform the difficulty of the next set of items the test-taker was presented. This allows faster testing and also diminishes the possibility of cheating because not all test-takers see the same items. At this time, only a limited number of educational assessments are offered in the computer-adaptive format, including some tests that are used as interim or benchmark assessment to predict performance on state tests. Some schools still struggle with the infrastructural requirements to offer even traditional assessments online. The schools may own the needed software and meet the networking requirements, but their computers are ill-maintained because of high staff turnover and lack of human capacity. This is particularly true in schools in high-poverty areas, affecting fairness (see Chapter 8).

According to Bennett (2015), most of the U.S. is now in the second generation of technology-based assessment. A variety of new item formats have begun to appear in tests administered via computer, particularly items that allow some interaction between student and prompt. These are called technology-enhanced items, as opposed to technology-delivered items, which are traditional and non-interactive tasks administered via a computer and which Bennett refers to as first-generation. For instance, on a technology-enhanced item to assess conceptual understanding of the relationship between dependent and independent variables, students may be able to "experiment" with different levels of the independent variable (e.g., soil type) to test its effects on a dependent variability (e.g., permeability). They manipulate animations in ways that mimic experimentation, in order to make a recommendation about where to place a play area with grass and trees (Nation's Report Card, 2018). Few state tests are yet using truly interactive or highly enhanced computer tasks, but the NAEP (see Chapter 5) began to administer such tasks nationally in 2009.

Another way that second-generation technology affects assessment is automated essay scoring. Automated essay scoring is used most frequently with online practice tests, but it is also used in place of a second human rater in some high-stakes assessments, such as the GMAT and the GRE (see ets.org). Finally, computers have afforded a whole wave of assistive technology for students with special needs, including voice-recognition software, E-magnifiers, screen readers, text-to-Braille software for the visually impaired, text-based telecommunications devices for the hearing-impaired, and text-to-speech software. Some of these were also discussed in Chapter 8.

The U.S. (and other nations) may be on the cusp of third-generation, technology-based assessment. Such assessment tasks and practices, when and if they happen, will be characterized by several elements. According to Bennett (2015), third-generation technology-based assessments will allow the blending of learning (Stage 2) and reporting (Stage 4) purposes in assessment. They will offer in-the-moment information about performance and feedback to teachers and students. These kinds of assessments will be designed around learning progressions that are not derived from the professional expertise of individual teachers (as described in Chapter 2 and our case studies, Chapters 10–12), but which are grounded in learning theory. They will be rich in opportunities for students—even multiple students at a time—to engage interactively with performance-based prompts. They will no longer "drop from the sky," but will be available for use at almost any time, with short or long samples of tasks in classrooms. Finally, automated scoring will be used not only as a backup for essays, but also for a wide array of open-ended responses and performances.

Technology, CA, and the Four-Stage CA:SRL Framework

Stage 1: Pre-assessment With Technology

Many of you will have used "clicker" technology or automated student response systems at some point in your formal education. Clickers are a well-established technology that allow a teacher to present an objectively scored item (like multiple-choice questions) to a large group. Students respond by "clicking" the response option they prefer on a hand-held device. Electronic systems have evolved from old-fashioned, purpose-specific clickers to the use of cell phones for responding. Popular online services include PollEverywhere and Socrative. For students at early grade levels, teachers can use scannable cards that children hold up at their desks with letters, which act like QR codes. Teachers then use a smartphone to quickly scan the room and capture student response preferences.

With automated classroom response systems, you can immediately check to see whether students have recognized the correct concept or use of skill, and which distractors are preferred. You can use this information to provide immediate feedback or instructional adjustment. For questions students find difficult, you may project aggregated results on a bar chart for the class to see, discuss (e.g., "I see many of you chose answer 'B'—let's talk about that choice"), and then do a quick reassessment to see if understanding has shifted.

This kind of technology is useful in Stage 1 because it does not take up classroom time, can be totally anonymous, and provides you with easily interpretable information that may reveal student misconceptions or learning gaps. You can use exactly the same services or technology to conduct classroom surveys about student interest in, prior exposure to, or beliefs in the value of upcoming content. Once you have created the items (which you can design yourself or input from another source), the results are automatically scored. Automated classroom response systems are excellent methods for short, informal assessments of learning at both Stages 1 and 2, and provide a much better glance at the knowledge or skill of all students in a classroom than whole-class questioning.

Automated classroom response systems also support SRL. When students can perform anonymously, and see one another's responses on a graphic display or through whole-class feedback that does not identify them personally, they may be more accurate in gauging their self-efficacy. You can urge students to use the results they see to set short-term goals based on tangible evidence about their misconceptions or incomplete knowledge.

Stage 2: Assessment Iterations for Learning With Technology

When you begin your instruction and frequent informal assessment, there are numerous online sites that give students real-time opportunities to try out short tasks and get immediate feedback. Quizlet is a resource that allows teachers to create quizzes, flashcards, and other assessment tools for students to use to assess themselves. It was created by a high school sophomore in 2005. Teachers can input study sets, and students can also create their own quizzes, allowing them to self-monitor their needs, get immediate verification feedback as to whether their answer is right or wrong (see Chapter 3), and set targets for more practice based on their performance results. Quizlet Live allows game-based quizzing where students form teams that essentially engage in peer assessment. Similar online learning platforms include Kahoot!, which enables either teachers or students to create items for quizzing and allows team play. Teachers can give "challenge" assessments that students can respond to on mobile devices. Kahoot! was developed by a team of Norwegian entrepreneurs and a professor of Game Technology at the Department of Computer and Information Science at the Norwegian University of Science and Technology.

Quizlet, Kahoot!, and similar technologies have useful characteristics in common. They provide real-time feedback to students, although the feedback is limited. Presentation of tasks can be varied, and content is designed by teachers or students. With the purchase of upgrades, teachers and schools can collaborate and gain access to pre-loaded tasks designed across a wide variety of content domains.

These technologies support SRL because they help students self-monitor during performance. Students or teams of students can earn scores and receive written messages that let them know how well they are doing. Students can practice self-control by designing or selecting their own tasks, format, or pace. You and your students can perform multiple iterations of assessment with instruction simply by going back to tasks and repeating, changing formats, setting new challenge levels, or setting new goals for mastery or completion rates. Some of these technologies include read-aloud options to accommodate the needs of students with visual impairments or disabilities that affect reading, and to build speaking and pronunciation skills.

We also put automated essay scoring under technologies that are useful in Stage 2. We do not recommend automated essay scoring for formal assessment (Stage 3), nor do we recommend that the scores derived from this type of technology be included in grades or reports to parents. However, automated essay scoring can be a useful way for students to work individually or with peers on writing in a process of developing skill and style.

Before we discuss automated essay scoring in CA any further, we note that use of computer—rather than human—scoring for essays is a subject of some debate. Many critics claim that automated scoring systems rate written essays on superficial characteristics; that they are not sensitive to creativity, accuracy of content knowledge, or depth of analysis; and that scoring can be gamed by crafty test-takers who use "sophisticated" vocabulary and lots of subordinate clauses (Hearst, 2000; Yang, Buckendahl, Juszkiewicz, & Bhola, 2002). These critiques have been directed particularly at automated essay scoring and less often applied to automated scoring of constructed-response items in other domains, such as science. Testing companies that use automated scoring point out that computer-based scores are well-correlated with human scores and that they improve efficiency and costs, making it more feasible to assess complex performances, such as writing on a large scale. Fortunately, we have no need to enter this debate. We focus on automated essay scoring in CA at Stage 2, as a way to gain and feedback to students' information about writing performance that can further their skills.

For our discussion, we will focus on one automated essay scoring system used in many schools, PEG Writing, a product of Measurement, Incorporated. There are many other systems (see Dikli, 2006, for an overview). PEG, originally Project Essay Grader, has been around for a long time (Page, 1966) and has a substantial body of research related to it. One thing to note about PEG is that it explicitly is not intended to assess the content of students' written responses, only general writing skill.

When the PEG system is used in schools, the teacher can supply an essay prompt, and students can type in their essay. Before they write, they can pre-write, using various organizers that are provided by the system, such as Venn diagrams and writing maps. If a teacher requires or recommends pre-writing, PEG may be considered to provide an opportunity for students to engage in SRL forethought. When students finish a draft, they submit it for automated scoring, and receive instant feedback of various kinds: a score on each of six traits of writing (see Chapter 6), tips for improvement as a narrative aligned with each trait, and corrections and suggestions in comment bubbles next to their work. Used very simply, students can take this automated feedback and re-write. PEG will also suggest references to short video tutorials that are focused on different writing skills. As stated above, the content of student work is not computer-scored. There is an option in the system for the teacher to provide a content score and feedback on content.

There are numerous ways for a teacher to use the PEG system more interactively. First, teachers can customize the feedback students receive. They can restrict feedback to focus on one or a few traits deemed central to their own specific learning objectives for their students. They can, of course, also add their own feedback at any stage of the writing process. Students (or teachers) can initiate real-time or delayed back-and-forth written conversations via the system. For instance, a student might submit the statement "I don't understand why there was a problem when I wrote . . ."; the teacher then would reply with further feedback that provides elaboration (see Chapter 4).

There are many other capabilities. Teachers can differentiate by assigning specific prompts to specific students or by allowing some prompts to be optional. This can be useful when students clearly need extra practice, and it also supports privacy if some students are getting prompts at different levels of difficulty. Teachers can set up either student-selected or teacher-selected peer review options, in which case the scored essay is accessible to the peer who provides additional feedback. Finally, in this system, students can create multiple drafts and monitor their own performance over several iterations with relative ease.

Does it help students learn when you use an automated essay-scoring system in your classroom? Learning theories on SRL presented elsewhere in this text strongly suggest that when teachers "collaborate" (even with an electronic system) to provide feedback and promote student self- and peer assessment, higher student learning and greater SRL will result. As yet, however, very little empirical research has been done on classroom teacher use of automated essay scoring (Stevenson & Phakiti, 2014). One study reported that students with disabilities were able to improve writing and attain comparable scores to their peers without disabilities over several drafts when their classrooms used PEG, despite starting with lower-quality first drafts. However, no evidence was collected about the amount of feedback teachers provided to students in addition to the data given by the PEG system (Wilson, 2017). In another study, students who practiced and were assessed on writing by teachers in tandem with automated scoring were found to show greater persistence in writing (Wilson & Czik, 2016).

Stage 3: Formal Assessment With Technology

Methods that bring technology into formal assessment can support high-quality information about student learning of concepts and skills, if they are used well. Unlike the tools described previously, they will not help students obtain rapid feedback, but that is not typically expected with formal assessment tasks. We describe below the use of item banks for the construction of formal assessment tasks, particularly M-C tasks. Item banks are generally associated with the construction of standards-based, relatively formal classroom tests, sometimes with the specific purpose of preparing students for state testing.

An item bank is a repository of assessment tasks or questions that have been field-tested widely and stored with information about their administration and quality. Most commonly, these items are in the M-C format, but they may be technology-enhanced, with features that prompt students to listen to a speech before answering or watch a demonstration on a video clip based on which they will solve problems. There are several advantages to using assessment items that are stored in an electronic bank. As we said in Chapter 3, developing M-C items can be tricky. There are many rules to keep in mind, and even if you follow all the rules, you may have items that don't provide you with very much information about student learning. Well-crafted items in a bank can therefore be a great resource. Also, a good item bank provides information to help you decide whether and when the item may be useful in your classroom. An item bank, ideally, should include the state or Common Core standard each item is intended to assess, the correct response, the item's difficulty (p) and discrimination (D) values, and information about how the item analysis data were obtained (see Chapter 4).

The NAEP (Chapter 5) has a bank of freely available items. You can download complete tests with pre-selected items linked to national standards. Another option provided by NAEP is to select individual items linked to national standards and customize your own test. We recommend the latter option, because your assessment tasks should be aligned with the SLOs and instruction that particularly characterize your classroom. With a free NAEP account, you can create a customized test at a particular grade level, content area, and skill, publish it online, and give options for students to take it, see their own scores, and retake the assessment task.

One of the good features of the NAEP item bank is that NAEP provides information about the population of students to whom each item was administered and when, so that you can see not only each item's p and D values, but also how those values may differ by region or group. This does not "tell" you whether the item is an appropriate challenge level for your students, but it can help you make decisions about whether the item will be fair—that is, that its content and standards match your instruction.

Several commercial companies such as Pearson Education and Edulastic provide schools and districts with banks of very large numbers of assessment items and tasks, some of which are technology-enhanced, and all of which are linked to state or national standards. Be aware that assessment items in any bank are not necessarily of high quality, even when they have been vetted by a company or governmental institution. The quality of any individual assessment item in isolation from other tasks is nearly impossible to gauge. The interpretation of a student's response to an assessment must be taken in the context of other similar tasks or multiple iterations of the same task. A single item to assess knowledge of probability may provide an accurate estimate of that knowledge as part of a probability assessment task that is 10 items long, but responses to the single item will be nearly impossible to interpret. Further, items on even professionally developed banks may have flaws that substantially impact the scores of your students.

Before you use banked items, carefully read the documentation provided by the banking company or agency about the population for which the item is suitable. Is it intended to be used with English language learners? Are there instructions for differentiation? We think it likely that the greatest value of item banks is that they provide a standards-linked starting place, based upon which you can develop your own customized items to try out with your own students. Also, we note that there is little in item banking technology that supports student SRL.

Stage 4: Reflections of Overall Learning With Technology

When it comes to collecting and analyzing multiple pieces of formal evidence of student work collected over the course of a substantial span of instruction and learning, technology can be a great asset. In Chapter 5, we already wrote about technology for data management, to organize and summarize many scores earned throughout a prolonged period of study, and we briefly touched on portfolio assessment. With regard to portfolio assessment, digital repositories can greatly help you and your students collect and curate evidence their growth and achievements, and give them space to self-reflect.

The use of portfolios for assessment has been a recommended practice in education for many years. We take our definition of a portfolio from Arter and Spandel (1992): "a purposeful collection of student work that tells the story of the student's efforts, progress, or achievement in (a) given area(s). This collection must include student participation in selection of portfolio content; the guidelines for selection; the criteria for judging merit; and evidence of student self-reflection" (p. 36). Proponents of portfolio-based assessment see it as a way to promote student control of and agency in their own learning, metacognition, and motivation; to increase the integration of instruction and assessment; to inspire rich teacher-student conversations over meaningful work; and to allow students and teachers to see learning as a progression over time. Clearly, all these qualities are consistent with the goals of the CA:SRL framework.

Unfortunately, when advocacy for portfolio-based student assessment systems was at its height in the 1990s, teachers and students in ordinary classrooms found it difficult to meet the many challenges of using such a complex system well. Portfolios for assessment require significant management of documents and other evidence of attainment, as well as time. Space must be allocated for storage of students' completed work samples, so they can refer back to them, curate the portfolio, and reflect on their growth. Busy teachers must find time for their students to work on their portfolios and must themselves take time to provide feedback not only on individual tasks, but on an evolving corpus of work.

While it still requires considerable effort to maintain a portfolio assessment system in the digital age, web-based portfolios have considerable and probably obvious advantages over systems that relied on manila folders and plastic tubs. Digital portfolios, stored in the cloud and accessed via platforms like Google Classroom, can be created with structured expectations that the teacher can announce and continuously update via web-based communications. Students can store many work samples in their own electronic folder, drawing from their folder periodically to reflect on samples that they argue best illustrate their strengths or personal growth in the domains that are to be assessed. Maintenance of the portfolio, while still requiring time and effort, should be conducted during classtime if it is a requirement.

Assuming that your school has the infrastructure to support technology-based assessment, a digital medium for portfolio assessment makes student purposeful planning for assessment and self-reflection relatively easy to structure into classroom routines. For instance, you can start one class period each week with "portfolio time," when students check the week's expectations for portfolio development, access their portfolio, select a work sample that they perceive addresses the expectations, and write reflectively on how their sample relates to the learning objectives.

Samples in the portfolio can be rich demonstrations of student thinking and performance. Students can include recorded readings of their own writing to illustrate narrative voice; video clips to show a variety of performances, from hip hop to graphing; and digital images from poster displays. Most digital forms of media have many commenting features that can be used for students to demonstrate SRL processes of monitoring and self-assessment. Students can keep electronic records of their own responses to SRL tasks such as surveys and chart changes in their self-efficacy over time. Portfolio assessment can even promote interdisciplinary learning. For instance, students can use charts and graphs to chart their SRL or academic growth in a writing portfolio, or use writing in a mathematics portfolio to reflect on complex problem-solving processes.

The Implications of Technology-Based Assessment in the Classroom

It will be obvious from the preceding discussion that we see great potential for technology to enhance the quality of teacher practices in CA. Classroom response systems can help you rapidly identify student misconceptions to improve your instructional planning and make in-the-moment adjustments if needed. Real-time assessment systems with quizzing functions allow you to give students simple tasks that can be quickly completed and that generate real-time data for you to respond to, and they often include features that accommodate students with disabilities. Automated essay scoring can reduce the time you spend preparing feedback, because the electronic system works with you to identify student strengths and weaknesses, like an instructional aide. You can use item banks to find M-C items targeted at particular standards and levels of difficulty, which, if they are well aligned with your SLOs and instruction, can become part of your own personal store of assessment methods. Finally, your students can collect and curate their work digitally, so that when it comes time for you to reflect on their performance over a long course of study, you will have a repository of rich evidence to interpret.

Is it likely you will use technology in your assessment practices in all the above ways? Of course not. There are many considerations you will have to take into account when deciding how or whether to incorporate technology in your CA practice. Some of these considerations are shown in the flowchart in Figure 9.2. The figure takes you in a snake-like pattern through the considerations that test developers make in designing technology-based assessments, with relevant questions to ask yourself when making your own choices about your own CA practices involving technology. The questions to ask yourself start, as always, with the need to make decisions about the construct and content to be measured, and end, as with the four-stage

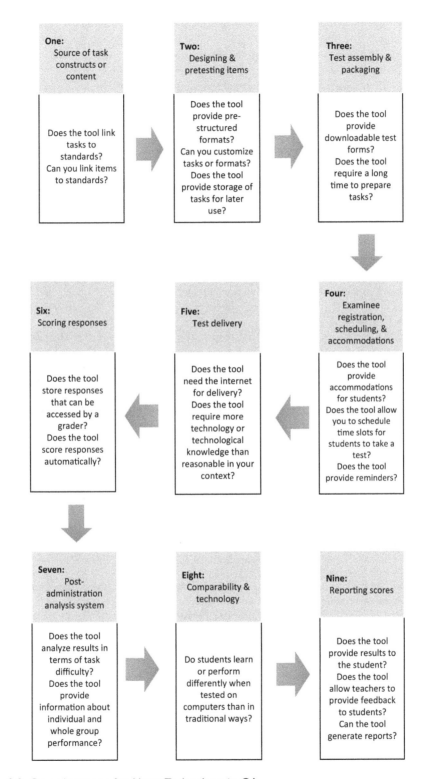

Figure 9.2 Considerations for Using Technology in CA

CA:SRL framework, with reporting. However, in the CA:SRL framework, the end is just a new beginning.

A final word in this section: among all the pushes and pulls that will influence your decisions about technology in the classroom, when it comes to assessment, remember that purpose is paramount. When you assess, you gather evidence about student thinking or behavior that is most relevant to your SLOs, and interpret it to promote student learning. To the extent that you also promote and support student SRL, you increase the potential of the CA process to add to the gains your students make as you teach. If technological tools for assessment help you to help students learn throughout the stages of CA:SRL, by all means avail yourself of them thoughtfully. If they are not available, many other methods, used with equal thought, will serve the same purpose. It is not the tools themselves that are important; what matters is whether you use whatever assessment tools you have at your disposal to make reliable, valid, and fair interpretations of student learning.

References

Arter, J. A., & Spandel, V. (1992). Using portfolios of student work in instruction and assessment. *Educational Measurement: Issues and Practice, 11*(1), 36–44.

Bennett, R. E. (2015). The changing nature of educational assessment. *Review of Research in Education, 39*(1), 370–407.

Dikli, S. (2006). An overview of automated scoring of essays. *The Journal of Technology, Learning and Assessment, 5*(1).

Drasgow, F., Luecht, R. M., & Bennett, R. E. (2006). Technology and testing. In R. L. Brennan (Ed.), *Educational measurement* (4th ed., pp. 471–515). Westport, CT: American Council on Education/Praeger.

Hearst, M. A. (2000). The debate on automated essay grading. *IEEE Intelligent Systems and Their Applications, 15*(5), 22–37.

Judson, E., & Sawada, D. (2002). Learning from past and present: Electronic response systems in college lecture halls. *Journal of Computers in Mathematics and Science Teaching, 21*(2), 167–181.

Kay, R. H., & LeSage, A. (2009). Examining the benefits and challenges of using audience response systems: A review of the literature. *Computers & Education, 53*(3), 819–827.

Nation's Report Card. (2018). U.S. Department of Education, Institute of Educational Sciences, National Center for Education Statistics, National Assessment of Educational Progress (NAEP), *Test yourself on an interactive computer task*. Retrieved from www.nationsreportcard.gov/science_2009/ict_tasks.aspx

Page, E. B. (1966). The imminence of . . . grading essays by computer. *The Phi Delta Kappan, 47*(5), 238–243.

Stevenson, M., & Phakiti, A. (2014). The effects of computer-generated feedback on the quality of writing. *Assessing Writing, 19*, 51–65.

Wilson, J. (2017). Associated effects of automated essay evaluation software on growth in writing quality for students with and without disabilities. *Reading and Writing, 30*(4), 691–718.

Wilson, J., & Czik, A. (2016). Automated essay evaluation software in English language arts classrooms: Effects on teacher feedback, student motivation, and writing quality. *Computers & Education, 100*, 94–109.

Yang, Y., Buckendahl, C. W., Juszkiewicz, P. J., & Bhola, D. S. (2002). A review of strategies for validating computer-automated scoring. *Applied Measurement in Education, 15*(4), 391–412.

Part 3

Section 3 Introduction
Case Studies in the CS:SRL Framework

In this section, you will find three hypothetical case studies of classroom teacher assessment practices in context. These case studies are inspired by the work of real teachers and their students, and highlight how you and your classes can practice assessment in ways that align to the four-stage model. Each case study emphasizes different aspects of the four-stage model, just as in your classroom you will not always address Stages 1–4 with equal emphasis.

The case studies are in the areas of English Language Arts, mathematics, and music. Each case follows roughly the same format. We introduce the subject area, topic or topics to be taught, and information about the context for assessment: details about the school, developmental level, and other characteristics of context for learning. We do this to remind you how important it is that you, as a teacher, are knowledgeable about and aware of the particular context of your classroom and the needs of the students with whom you work. Each case study includes both general information about assessment methods and instruction, and close looks at the work and progression of a few individual learners.

You will see that the teacher in each case study sets a broad general learning goal for his or her students, based on either Common Core standards or professional standards in the discipline. Your instructional goals should also be set in light of the learning needs of your students, the curriculum, and educational importance. We show how the teacher thinks about an informal analysis of the learning progression and success criteria relevant to each goal. By *learning progression* we mean the set of knowledge and skill components that students need to attain in order to achieve the goal (see Chapter 1). The learning progression is the basis for the set of specific learning objectives (SLOs) that shape the teacher's instruction and assessment. While each case roots assessment practice firmly in the context of the community and educational standards, the cases have different emphases related to the four-stage framework.

Chapter 10, the first case, displays the assessment activities of an upper-elementary English Language Arts classroom. This teacher's assessment practice involves extensive work on student self-regulation of learning at Stage 2, with explicit SLOs in SRL. This teacher uses interactive assessment through one-on-one reading conferences and encourages student autonomy at Stage 3 through use of mini-portfolios of student-selected assessment artifacts. This case also illustrates that Stage 4 reporting can take place in evidence-based verbal interactions with parents and colleagues, rather than in the form of grades.

Chapter 11 takes place in a middle school music class. In this case, we particularly note the teacher's strong and consistent alignment of assessment to professional standards and class SLOs. This case illustrates the full progression of assessment, from Stage 1 to 4, and shows how a teacher uses multiple methods, in this case objective tests, performance assessments, and interactive conferencing. This case culminates in a complex formal assessment that synthesizes learning on multiple objectives, following which the teacher explains how he translates his observations of student learning in music into semester grades.

Chapter 12 showcases the four-stage CA:SRL framework in the context of eighth-grade algebra. This case study in mathematics is contextualized within an integrated co-teaching (ICT) classroom, where general and special education teachers work together to lead students with different needs. In this example we emphasize the clear progression from pre-assessment (Stage 1) to instruction and multiple iterations at Stage 2. The co-teachers in this case study offer rich interpretation of student responses to assessment tasks, and relate them to clearly differentiated feedback and instructional responses.

Chapter 10

English Language Arts Case Study

For this case, we give you a glimpse of classroom assessment for learning with integrated opportunities for student SRL and student-teacher co-regulation of learning in an elementary school classroom that is working on English Language Arts. In this hypothetical case study, we focus on high integration of SRL and content learning from Stages 1 through 3.

Mrs. L teaches fifth-grade students. Her school, P.S. 130 elementary school, is an urban public school that serves 708 students in pre-kindergarten through eighth grade. Seventy-four percent of students in the school qualify for free or reduced school lunch; 23% of the student population consists of students identified as having a disability; and 3% are identified as English language learners. Located in a historically Puerto Rican and African American neighborhood, the school's student demographic composition is 62% Hispanic, 27% Black, 6% Asian, 3% White, 1% American Indian, and 1% multiracial. At 94%, the school's attendance rate is well above the city average. The class size in pre-kindergarten through second grade averages 26 students, while class sizes in grades 3–5 average 28 students. In the middle grades of 6–8, class sizes are larger and average 33 students.

P.S. 130 is considered a high-achieving school based on its standardized state assessment scores. Data from the 2016–2017 school year indicate that 59% of students in grades 3–8 were proficient or above on the English Language Arts state test, and 64% were proficient or above on the math state test. The curricula across all grades uses a thematic approach to foster interdisciplinary connections across content areas and skills; in particular, grades 5–8 employ project-based learning approaches to emphasize student-led decision-making. While content specialists provide instruction for subjects such as science, art, social studies, music, technology, and physical education, classrooms are otherwise self-contained in pre-kindergarten through sixth grade and led by one teacher. Students in seventh and eighth grade are divided into home rooms and rotate among classrooms led by content area specialists.

Setting the Scene

Mrs. L values community in her classroom and has set up a physical space that celebrates students' voices through student-created classroom rules, student-run classroom jobs, student-generated genre bins in the classroom library, and student-created table names (this year, students chose to name the tables after gemstones). Student artwork and classwork decorate every empty space that isn't dedicated to a reading anchor chart, math scaffold, or unit project overview. The classroom environment supports students to self-monitor continuously, with questions posted around the classroom prompting students to consider "Is this really 'too hard' or do I need to use a different tool/strategy?" or "Did I 'get it done' or did I 'give my best'?" Bins in the center of each table that are readily available to students are filled with visual instructional plans to facilitate mathematical problem-solving, lists of "juicy" words to replace common language like "happy" or "mad," and blank graphic organizer templates.

In Mrs. L's fifth-grade class of 29, four students are identified as having a disability and three are English language learners who have all tested into the advanced stage of language proficiency. Most students entered her classroom at 10 years old, but three of her students entered at 11 years old due to retention in an earlier elementary grade.

Mrs. L was careful to gather as much information as possible about her incoming fifth-grade class in advance of the first day of school, as part of her pre-assessment and planning. She looked more closely at the data gathered within her school about her students' reading levels. Running record assessments from the previous year indicated that, of her 29 students, nine were entering her fifth-grade class reading at grade level. Twelve students were reading just one or two levels below proficiency, while eight of her students were reading three or more levels below grade level. Six of those students who were reading well below grade level also scored well below proficiency on the English language arts and math state assessments.

Based on this initial information, Mrs. L knew that reading comprehension was likely hindering the reading level growth of her eight most-struggling readers. Her 12 nearly-proficient readers were most likely in need of a mixture of reading comprehension or analysis support. Her highest readers, she predicted, would be able to focus on reading goals around analysis.

A typical instructional day begins with 45 minutes of independent reading time, during which students monitor their reading comprehension while independently reading, and Mrs. L confers with readers. The remainder of the school day allocates 100 minutes to reading and writing instruction, 50 minutes to math instruction, 50 minutes to science or social studies instruction, and 50 minutes to a "specials" period, such as technology or music.

Planning for Assessment and Instruction

Learning Standards

Although she's highly aware that her readers vary in their comprehension and analysis skills, Mrs. L also knows that all readers must be able to support ideas with direct references to the text. Mrs. L's instruction will need to introduce and reinforce explicit reading strategies for making and supporting claims about a text. Relatedly, Mrs. L's readers must be able to make decisions about the significance of identified text details as they synthesize evidence to generate broader ideas or construct interpretations. They must not only support ideas with individual references, but synthesize multiple sources of evidence to define a text's main idea. Mrs. L's instruction will therefore need to support readers not in simply identifying text details but in selecting relevant details that appropriately develop an idea or claim. Because her unit of study will focus on literature, Ms. L. is particularly interested in student understanding of character. Therefore, she has identified the following relevant Common Core standards:

- CCSS.ELA-Literacy.RI.5.1: Quote accurately from a text when explaining what the text says explicitly and when drawing inferences from the text.
- CCSS.ELA-Literacy.RI.5.2: Determine two or more main ideas of a text and explain how they are supported by key details; summarize the text.
- CCSS.ELA-Literacy.RL.5.2: Determine a theme of a story, drama, or poem from details in the text, including how characters in a story or drama respond to challenges or how the

speaker in a poem reflects upon a topic; summarize the text. (National Governors Association Center for Best Practices & Council of Chief State School Officers, 2010)

In addition to understanding to base her instruction on state standards, Mrs. L. wants to address the daily difficulties students may have with the discussion protocols, comprehension questions, and analysis tasks related to the reading curriculum's three anchor texts, through regular activities and assessments. She knows these skills are essential for students to meet long-term performance-based reading assessment requirements and receive full credit for written responses on the fifth-grade English Language Arts standardized state assessment at the end of the school year.

Specific Learning Objectives

The three anchor texts used in Mrs. L's reading curriculum—a realistic fiction novel, a biography, and a historical fiction novel—all feature multiple complex characters who overcome several obstacles. To create connections between students' independent reading texts and the curriculum's anchor texts, Mrs. L delineates a progression of critical steps in learning, which she frames as a sequence of SLOs:

- Students will be able to describe a character's traits by citing evidence from the text.
- Students will be able to draw conclusions about a character's motivation(s) by citing specific evidence related to the character's thoughts, feelings, and actions.
- Students will be able to make inferences about how a character's traits and motivation(s) develop over time by comparing and contrasting evidence related to thoughts, feelings, and actions across the text.

Goals and Objectives for Supporting Self-Regulation

As she thinks about the skills that students need to reach these academic reading goals, Mrs. L also thinks about the metacognitive skills they can build to support their learning, Mrs. L knows her students will first need to strengthen their metacognitive awareness of explicit reading strategies. She realizes that if she encourages them to think about their understanding of the reading, and to communicate with her about their thinking, they will be better able to help themselves, and she will be better able to help them. Students will also need to use self-monitoring skills in order to assess the effectiveness of applied reading strategies. She notes down questions, which we present in Figure 10.1.

With the questions from Figure 10.1 in mind, Mrs. L sets a broad goal for SRL: a student who is able to use accurate and relevant text evidence to support a comprehension-based or inferential claim about the text should be able to make strategic reading plans, self-monitor their understanding, and reflect on their strategy use. She constructs SLOs for these objectives:

1. Students will identify explicit reading strategies that support comprehension or analysis.
2. Students will explain their selection and application (or lack thereof) of a reading strategy.
3. Students will describe their decision-making process as they attempt to comprehend or analyze the text.
4. Students will explain whether or not an applied strategy supported comprehension or analysis.
5. Students will state next steps while reading based on the strategy's effectiveness.

1. What are students thinking about while reading? • What information are students keeping track of, and why? • What information are students disregarding, and why?
2. How do students ensure they understand what they are reading? • When and why do students "stop and think" about what they are reading?
3. When misunderstanding arises, what strategies do students use to problem-solve? • Which reading strategy(ies) are students able to identify? • Which reading strategy(ies) do students report using? • Which reading strategy(ies) do students identify but choose not to use, and why? • Which reading strategy(ies) are readers unaware of?
4. How do students decide if the strategy(ies) used helped or hindered understanding? • What makes a student decide a strategy has "worked"? • What makes a student decide a strategy hasn't "worked"?
5. How do students make decisions about the next course of action while reading? • Whether a strategy "worked" or "didn't work," what else informs what a reader chooses to do next?

Figure 10.1 Thinking About Student Metacognition in Reading

Call-Outs on the CA:SRL Framework in Mrs. L's Stage 1, Planning the "What" of Assessment
☞ Mrs. L's planning is tied to standards.
☞ Mrs. L's planning of a sequence of SLOs shows thinking of learning as a progression.
☞ The SLOs are stated in terms of the three components of *condition, audience*, and *performance*, as presented in Chapter 2.
☞ Mrs. L has explicit SLOs on student self-regulation, corresponding to the following phases: Forethought (1, 2), Performance (3), and Reflection (4, 5).

Pre-assessment

In order to tailor her instruction during independent reading time, Mrs. L develops a three-part pre-assessment (see Figure 10.2). The first part consists of a set of questions to assess students' general reading habits and understandings of what makes a "good" reader. The second part consists of questions to assess students' metacognitive awareness of explicit reading strategies and the self-monitoring and self-assessment habits they use during independent reading. The third part of the pre-assessment uses a short biographical passage used in previous state assessments and released by the state to assess students' understanding of character traits, character motivation, and character development.

Mrs. L administers the pre-assessment during one 45-minute independent reading block at the beginning of the school week. She creates a Reading Binder in which to organize evidence from her student's work throughout the term and her interpretations of it. In her review of the student responses to the short biographical passage, she sees that the character analysis revealed

English Language Arts Case Study   161

Part One

Directions: First, think about yourself as a reader. Then, finish each of the four sentences below. You may use a separate piece of paper to answer questions.
1. A good reader is someone who . . .
2. Three words I would use to describe myself as a reader are:
3. Something I am working on as a reader is . . .
4. One way I'm trying to work on this is . . .

Part Two

Directions: First think about the things you do while you read. Then, finish each of the six sentences below.
1. Some strategies I use to understand what I am reading are:
2. A strategy I use that always works is . . .
3. A strategy I use that only works sometimes is . . .
4. A strategy that does not help me is . . .
5. When I don't understand what I'm reading, the first thing I do is . . .
6. When I'm deciding what to do next to make sure I understand what I'm reading, I think about . . .

Part Three

Directions: First, read the passage. Then, answer the three questions.

[READING PASSAGE]

1. What words best describe _____ and why?
2. In the passage, what is ____ main motivation? How do you know?
3. How does _____ change from the beginning of the passage to the end?

Figure 10.2 Independent Reading Pre-assessment

varying levels of skills among the students. Several students identified vague character traits such as "nice" or "good" instead of using specific words related to characters' actions or dialogue. While most students agreed that the subject of the biography changed over the course of the passage, over half of the class were unable to identify specific examples from the text to demonstrate the described change and instead used a piece of evidence from the beginning *or* end. Students exhibited the most difficulty in explaining the biography subject's motivation, describing instead what the (female) character liked rather than why she spoke, made decisions, or acted in a particular way.

Mrs. L photocopies and stores the students' completed pre-assessments under a separate tab for each student. After reading and analyzing each student's pre-assessment, Mrs. L drafts initial "glows" (explicit and positive noticings) and "grows" (actionable feedback) to discuss with students. Preparing her noticings ahead of time ensures that Mrs. L is able to have a thorough initial conference with each student, during which she can cite specific examples to help him or her create a clear goal. She follows up the pre-assessment with 10-minute conferences with each student during independent reading periods throughout the first school week. During the conference, Mrs. L uses a different colored writing utensil to note when students elaborate upon or deviate from written answers; additionally, if students left any portions of the pre-assessment blank, Mrs. L uses the conference to provide additional prompts related to the question and records students' verbal responses.

Call-Outs on the CA:SRL Framework in Mrs. L's Stage 1, Pre-assessment
☞ Mrs. L pre-assesses for self-awareness, use of learning strategies, and content misconceptions.
☞ Mrs. L uses multiple methods for pre-assessment.
☞ Mrs. L individually responds to results of pre-assessment to make clarifications about her interpretations.

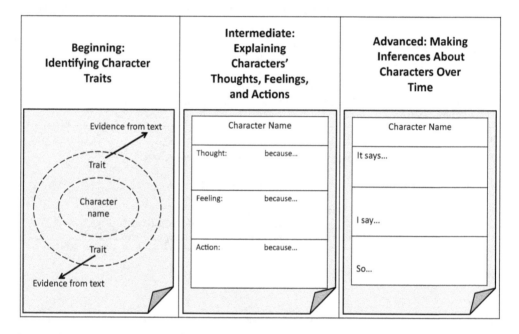

Figure 10.3 Explicit Reading Strategies for Character Analysis

Instruction

Mrs. L develops three different explicit reading strategies to support students' character analysis. The strategies are designed to move students along a continuum from basic comprehension of characters to inferential interpretation, scaffolding through each approach students' use of text evidence to support ideas. The three strategies and the way students can graphically use them for character analysis are shown in Figure 10.3.

Mrs. L uses 15 minutes of the independent reading block to model the application of the Post-it Strategy 1: *Identifying and Supporting Character Traits*, which was designed to fit on a single Post-it note. She models stopping while reading, thinking about words to describe the main character, and referring back to the text to help her identify the most descriptive word. She places the character's name in the center of the circles, uses the outer circle to list a character trait, and includes a detail from the text outside of the circle. Following her model, students apply the strategy during the remainder of the independent reading block and submit the completed Post-it to Mrs. L for review.

The next school day, Mrs. L again uses 15 minutes of the independent reading block to model the Post-it character analysis Strategy 2: the *Thoughts, Feelings, and Actions (T/F/A) because* Post-it. She models stopping and thinking about a character's action and explains why the character had engaged in the action, citing relevant text evidence to support her interpretation. Mrs. L also explains in her own words what the character was thinking and feeling, referring back to the text to include relevant details on her Post-it. Following her model, students again apply the strategy during the remainder of the independent reading block and submit the completed Post-it to Mrs. L for review.

Finally, Mrs. L models the Post-it character analysis Strategy 3: *It Says/I Say/So*, a modification of a strategy first developed by Beers (2003). Mrs. L models first identifying a specific detail in the text (It Says) and connecting the detail to her prior knowledge (I Say) in order make an inference about the character's motivation and/or change over time (So). For the final time that week, students apply the strategy during the remainder of the independent reading block and submit the completed Post-it to Mrs. L for review.

During each model, Mrs. L creates anchor charts with examples of the completed strategy that are then hung for reference in the classroom library. The completed examples are also copied and placed in the middle of each table bin for student reference during independent reading time. Students are given Post-it notes to use while independently reading. Mrs. L develops a reading conference log to keep notes related to students' reading goals and strategy use as they discuss the student's independent reading text during 10-minute, one-on-one conferences.

At the conclusion of the last independent reading block of the school week, Mrs. L explains that each modeled Post-it strategy is an important part of analyzing characters and that selecting which strategy to use depends on each reader's goals and preferences. Making choices about how to use each Post-it, she stresses, is part of learning to make decisions while we read. While completing Post-it notes is required, being able to explain whether or not the strategy worked for the moment in the text, the genre, the reader's reading goal, or even the reader's way of thinking are equally important.

Stage 2 Assessment Methods

One-on-One Reading Conferences

The week after directly modeling the three character analysis strategies, Mrs. L confers with each student about their completed Post-it notes to learn about each reader's strengths and weaknesses using the different strategies they have chosen. Because Mrs. L has students reading at various levels of proficiency, conferring with each reader ensures students are setting appropriate and meaningful reading goals and applying the character analysis strategies in purposeful ways. During each 10-minute reading conference, Mrs. L draws on questioning similar to parts one and two of the pre-assessment to determine the relevance of the reader's goal(s) and support the reader's self-monitoring of the applied Post-it strategies. Through discussion with the students, Mrs. L assesses their ability to cite relevant textual evidence to support the claims or inferences featured in the completed Post-it notes. With the text and the Post-it notes as artifacts, Mrs. L and the student are able to refer back to the text, think aloud about the explicit reading strategy the student applied, and decide whether the strategy was applied accurately and clearly. Based on their discussion, Mrs. L is able to suggest refinements, model revisions, or even re-teach the strategy entirely. She adjusts any formatting concerns, reteaches to students who did not include evidence, and helps each reader review their pre-assessment in order to set a relevant Post-it goal.

In subsequent conferences that she schedules throughout the character analysis unit, completed Post-it notes serve as an artifact that Mrs. L and the student can discuss. She adjusts her conference schedule depending on students' reading goals and data from the other formative assessments (below) administered during the main reading and writing instructional block. She confers with readers on a weekly, biweekly, or triweekly basis and evaluates her conference schedule once a month. In this way she is able to differentiate her assessment work to address the needs of individuals.

As Mrs. L and the student review the Post-it notes, Mrs. L fosters the reader's metacognition by questioning the relevance of the applied strategy. She also supports the brainstorming of other strategies that could have been used, or helps students look back to determine aspects of the text that they did not explore. Mrs. L concludes each conference by discussing the reader's next steps, offering suggestions, or asking questions to further the student's self-assessment.

Frequent Assessment Embedded in Instructional Routines

The week after she modeled the three character analysis Post-it strategies, Mrs. L introduces students to the weekly Post-it log and reflection (Figure 10.4). At the end of each independent reading block, students review the Post-it notes created during reading and select one they feel best showcases their thinking as a reader. This process requires students to self-assess their Post-it notes as they relate to their reading goal(s) and make decisions about the accuracy, clarity, and impact of the Post-it. Students place the selected Post-it on the weekly log under the appropriate weekday. The practice is repeated each school day throughout the week, resulting in five student-selected Post-it notes.

At the conclusion of the independent reading block on the last school day of the week, students engage in self-reflection about the created Post-it notes. First, students select from the five Post-it notes they have made over the week the one that they feel is their "strongest" Post-it. The Post-it that a student selects helps Mrs. L understand the behaviors and strategies that each reader uniquely values, providing her with invaluable data about the student's metacognitive monitoring and self-assessment skills; depending on the reader, a "strong" Post-it may demonstrate a particular strategy assigned by the teacher, or the student may understand "strong" to mean accurate, complete, or creative.

After selecting their "strongest" Post-it, students explain in writing what the selected Post-it shows about them as a reader. This space for strategy-related reflection helps Mrs. L gauge students' self-monitoring skills; in particular, Mrs. L examines students' responses to this question over time to see whether students' strategy selection changes and why. Next, students reflect about how the Post-it helps them as a reader, activating their use of reading strategies and the ways in which readers differentiate between the purpose, significance, or applicability of a given strategy. Lastly, students self-assess through the identification of next steps; some students focus on next steps for a particular Post-it, while others think more broadly about reading goals, a distinction Mrs. L uses to inform her reading conferences with students.

Students submit their weekly Post-it logs and reflection at the end of the school week. Mrs. L reviews students' weekly logs and reflection over the weekend.

Name: _____   **Date:** _____

Book: _____

Weekly Post-it Log and Reflection

Directions: After independent reading time each day this week, select one Post-it you think best shows your thinking as a reader. At the end of the week, you should have a total of five Post-it notes total.

Monday

Tuesday

Wednesday

Thursday

Friday

Figure 10.4 Task and Reflection on Reading Strategy

Name: _____ **Date:** _____

Book: _____

Which Post-it from your reading this week is your strongest?

_____

_____

What does this Post-it show about you as a reader?

_____

_____

How does this Post-it help you as a reader?

_____

_____

What are your next steps?

_____

_____

*********Teacher Feedback: DO NOT WRITE IN THIS SECTION*********

Glow:

Grow:

Student Response:

_____

_____

_____

Figure 10.4 Continued

English Language Arts Case Study · 167

Call-Outs on the CA:SRL Framework in Mrs. L's Stage 2, Instruction and Assessment Iterations
☞ Mrs. L uses both interactive and non-interactive assessment methods.
☞ Using Post-its, Mrs. L seamlessly integrates reading activities with instruction.
☞ Mrs. L's methods provide her opportunities to co-regulate with students on strategy use, part of SRL.
☞ Mrs. L non-interactive methods provide opportunities for SRL such as self-monitoring, self-assessment

Iterations: From Interpretation to Feedback to Further Instruction

Mrs. L typically gives feedback to each student with a written "glow" highlighting any particularly clear, thorough, or well-supported Post-it notes. She also provides each student with a "grow," or piece of actionable feedback. With Common Core State Standards 5.1 and 5.2 in mind, this "grow" most often reflects students' use of textual evidence, unless a glaring misunderstanding related to the reading strategies is observed.

Students receive the reviewed weekly Post-it log and reflection on Mondays, at the beginning of the independent reading block. Students process Mrs. L's written "glow" and "grow" and respond to her feedback in writing in the "student response" section. Students' responses are submitted at the conclusion of Monday morning's independent reading time, giving Mrs. L time to review them during Monday's preparation period or lunch period so that she can use students' feedback to inform her reading conference goals for the week.

Below, you can see the work of three of Mrs. L's students, attempting three different reading strategies: *identifying and supporting character traits, T/F/A because,* and *It Says/I Say/So.* Examples of student work show what Mrs. L is referring to when she makes her interpretations, and what she and the students reflect on when she conferences with them.

Interpreting Student Work on Identifying and Supporting Character Traits Strategy

JOREL

Jorel, one of Mrs. L's readers who is reading three levels below grade-level proficiency, produced the Post-it shown in Figure 10.5.

He identifies the main character as Irena and ascribes the trait "brave." To support his idea, Jorel restates a moment in the text in his own words: "She knows she can get caught helping other Jews but she never stops." While Jorel does identify a character trait and provides textual evidence, Mrs. L wants to support Jorel in applying more descriptive language when analyzing characters. She also wants him to cite specific evidence from the text related to the character's bravery; rather than generalizing about an action the character has done at different points in the text, Mrs. L wants Jorel to refer directly to the moment within the specific chapter that supports the identified trait.

During reading conferences, Mrs. L discusses with Jorel moments from previous chapters that the character acted bravely. Together, they closely read Jorel's current chapter and identify a specific character action—lying to a police officer—that illustrates the character's bravery. They collaboratively review a list of descriptive character traits, and Jorel selects "cunning" after reflecting upon the character's quick thinking in a stressful moment. Using the specific example from the text and new descriptive word, Jorel creates a new Post-it that he will use as a model during reading for the remainder of the week.

Figure 10.5 Jorel's Post-it for Strategy 1

Figure 10.6 Damien's Post-it for Strategy 1

DAMIEN

Damien is one of Mrs. L's proficient readers who entered the school year reading on grade level. In his Post-it, Damien lists two character traits related to one of the main characters and provides specific examples related to each trait (see Figure 10.6).

He first notes that the character is "mad" because "Lavender Brown was dating Ron [who] Hermione likes." He also notes that the character is "frustrated" because "she is always on the top of Harry but Harry is better known." Though Damien lists two relevant and specific moments in the text to support the two descriptive words, Mrs. L notices that Damien has captured two of the character's feelings rather than words that would describe her personality.

During their reading conference, Mrs. L and Damien discuss how the character's anger and frustration are related emotions connected to her desire to be the best. Damien revises his thinking, expressing that the character is "competitive" and that these two pieces of text evidence both support that trait. Damien revises the Post-it to reflect his new thinking. Mrs. L commends him for identifying two of the character's feelings and reminds him of the *T/F/A because* Post-it, re-teaching him how to use it to track his noticings around characters' thoughts, feelings, and actions. In addition to the character traits Post-it, Mrs. L asks Damien to try completing one *T/F/A because* Post-it during reading the following day.

NATALIE

Natalie is one of Mrs. L's most-proficient readers and reads two grade levels above the grade-level average. Unlike Jorel and Damien, Natalie demonstrated proficiency with the character traits Post-it and was eager to expand on the strategy. Mrs. L provided a differentiated assessment opportunity; rather than a *T/F/A because* Post-it, Natalie, on her own, created a Venn diagram to compare two characters' traits and provided text evidence for each (see Figure 10.7).

During their reading conference, Mrs. L commends Natalie for modifying the strategy to meet her reading needs. They discuss the common characteristic shared by the characters: "They both like each other." From this noticing, Mrs. L and Natalie discuss how a third character affects the relationship between the two on the Post-it, and Natalie considers how Percy "feels jealous" because of Luke, whereas Annabeth "feels confused" by Percy's jealousy. They agree that her thinking could have been better organized into two *T/F/A because* Post-it notes due to Natalie's focus on their feelings at that specific moment in the text. To revise the character trait Post-it, Natalie identifies "protective" as the trait related to Percy's need to be near Annabeth. Relatedly, she revises Annabeth's trait to "friendly" because she treats everyone with kindness. Mrs. L suggests that Natalie try to complete separate character trait Post-it notes unless she is contrasting opposing traits in a set of characters. Natalie decides to try creating *T/F/A because* Post-it notes for the two characters during reading the following day.

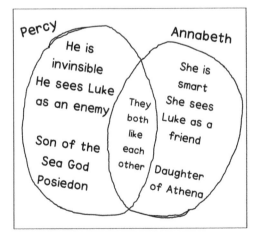

Figure 10.7 Natalie's Post-it for Strategy 1

170 Section 3 Chapter 10

Interpreting Student Work on T/F/A Because Strategy

DAMIEN

In his initial *T/F/A because* Post-it, Damien identified three feelings and provided evidence for each; he did not, however, distinguish between the character's thoughts, actions, and feelings, nor did Damien consistently identify specific examples from the text to support his thinking (see Figure 10.8). In the feelings section, for example, he supports "upset" with "how the kids treated him at school" rather than the specific actions committed by the kids at school.

During their reading conference, Mrs. L and Damien return to the text to reread two pages before the created Post-it. They identify one key action committed by the character—that he stomped out of the classroom—that Damien thinks is connected to being verbally teased by other kids. Next, he shows Mrs. L a moment when the character is thinking about running home during lunch and wonders aloud if those thoughts were because he was embarrassed that he was being bullied. Finally, Damien defends the identification of the "upset" feeling but supports it by noting the specific name-calling the character experienced.

As she and Damien talk, Mrs. L creates a new *T/F/A because* Post-it that captures his interpretations. Together they review the Post-it, ensuring Damien better understands how to organize his ideas on the Post-it as he reads in the future. Damien uses the new, clearer model Post-it to guide his reading moving forward.

NATALIE

Natalie's first *T/F/A because* Post-it demonstrates a clear and well-supported character action (see Figure 10.9). Mrs. L notices that Natalie provides specific evidence to support the ideas in the other two sections, but Natalie cited feelings in the thoughts section. First, Mrs. L commends Natalie on her clearly identified action with evidence. Next, she provides Natalie with the sentence starter "The character is thinking about . . ." to help Natalie frame her interpretation of the character's thoughts. Natalie uses the sentence starter to revise the thoughts section to read "Percy was thinking about Annabeth's health." Mrs. L suggests that Natalie use

Figure 10.8 Damien's Post-it for Strategy 2

T Percy was worried and wanted to see Annabeth	b/c She was wounded in the battle
F Sad, Worried, Guilty	b/c Annabeth took a knife for him
A Went to see Annabeth	b/c To see how she is feeling

Figure 10.9 Natalie's Post-it for Strategy 2

the sentence starter for future *T/F/A because* Post-it notes to help her create clear distinctions between her interpretations of characters' feelings and thoughts.

Interpreting Student Work on It Says/I Say/So Strategy

JOREL

During their most recent previous conference, Jorel expressed interest in the *It Says/I Say/So* Post-it. Though Mrs. L worried that the strategy would be too advanced for Jorel given his generalization of text evidence, she supports him in his attempt and agrees to confer with him the following week to review what he produces.

Indeed, on the next weekly Post-it log, Jorel selects an *It Says/I Say/So* Post-it (see Figure 10.10). On the It Says portion of his Post-it, Jorel identifies a general noticing from his text: "A lot can get caught by helping Jews." This observation, while valid, does not illustrate a specific moment from the text. In the I Say portion of his Post-it, Jorel notes that "Irena didn't get caught yet"; while also correct, Jorel does not draw from his prior knowledge and instead notes a trend in the storyline of the text. Finally, Jorel's So section of the Post-it demonstrates and general interpretation of the text's plot. From his Post-it, Mrs. L determines that Jorel is not ready to remediate this strategy given the same lack of specific detail that he demonstrated in his character trait Post-it.

Jorel cites the inaccurate *It Says/I Say/So* Post-it as his "strongest" on his weekly Post-it log and reflection. Mrs. L infers from her previous conference that Jorel's excitement about applying the strategy informed his selection of it as his "strongest"; rather than engaging in more objective self-assessment, Jorel's selection is connected more to emotions of hope and eagerness to please and achieve. Mrs. L does not want to discourage Jorel, but she is concerned that this Post-it illustrates a lack of pre-requisite ability to accurately cite relevant text evidence to support character traits.

She uses the "teacher feedback" section on the log to provide Jorel with a specific "glow" (positive comment) and an actionable "grow" (a process feedback) that she phrases as a

Figure 10.10 Jorel's Post-it for Strategy 3

question in order to invite Jorel to reconsider how he can respond to his Post-it. Mrs. L gives Jorel her written feedback on the Monday morning after his Friday afternoon submission and provides time during the independent reading block for Jorel to review and respond to her comments. Jorel writes his response to her comments and re-submits the reflection at the end of the period.

She follows up with him on this feedback during his weekly reading conference. They return to the text together to expand on the noticing about Irena from Jorel's *It Says/I Say/So* Post-it. Jorel points Mrs. L to a specific instance in the text in which Irena attempts to provide sustenance for a character in need; with Mrs. L's guidance, Jorel summarizes the evidence on a Post-it: "Irena tried to get a starving child food, but a few hours later the child would be covered by snow in the street because she died while Irena was stealing the bread."

Mrs. L asks Jorel why the specific moment in the text seemed significant to him, using the prompt "What are you inferring about what kind of person Irena is or what is motivating her?" Jorel replies that "stealing is dangerous and you can get in trouble or be punished by the police." Mrs. L commends Jorel by replying "I notice that you're using what you already know about stealing—your prior knowledge—to think about what Irena is doing here. Based on her action and what you already know, so. . .?" Jorel finishes Mrs. L's sentence: "So Irena is a selfless person because she is thinking about others instead of what could happen to her." As Jorel talks, Mrs. L organizes Jorel's text evidence and inference about Irena into a blank *It Says/I Say/So* Post-it. Together, they agree that Jorel will work during the coming school week on making sure the It Says portion of the Post-it clearly cites a specific moment from the text, which he will then add to with relevant prior knowledge before attempting to make the full inference.

Throughout these one-on-one reading conferences, Mrs. L records her qualitative observations concerning students' Post-it notes on her laptop; as she and the student converse, Mrs. L notes the suggestions she makes to the student regarding refinement or quickly summarizes her reteaching approach. She also notes the page number the student is on at the point of their conference and the next step either the student or she identifies based on their discussion. Mrs. L uses a table to organize her notes and recommendations in a document, which is in a school-approved, protected Drive she can access from home to update and reflect upon.

Call-Outs on the CA:SRL Framework in Mrs. L's Stage 2, Feedback and Iterations Into Further Instruction

☞ Mrs. L's non-interactive assessments lead to her initial interpretations and to interactive conferences with individualized instruction.

☞ Mrs. L's initial interpretations inform her interactive conferences over assessment results.

☞ Mrs. L scaffolds the interactive conferences and give students further opportunities to self-regulate and for her to co-regulate with them.

☞ Mrs. L uses multiple iterations of assessment and instruction to differentiate instruction for struggling students.

☞ Although Mrs. L's assessments in Stage 2 are informal, she keeps regular and orderly observational notes.

A Culminating and Formal Assessment

When an independent reading text is completed, each student is required to self-assess and self-reflect using the Top 3 or Top 5 Post-It Reflection Log (Figure 10.11). The organizer provides space for each student to review their weekly Post-it logs and select three or five Post-it notes (the number depends on the students' reading goal(s) and needs) that the student feels best capture their thinking as a reader. For each Post-it, the student uses metacognitive awareness to identify the reading skill connected to the explicit reading strategy evident in the Post-it. Next, the student self-assesses the completed Post-it, articulating how it illustrates a reading strength or a reading need; in this way, students are pushed to constructively critique their reading progress through either an example or non-example of their reading goal(s). Lastly, the student self-reflects on the purpose of the Post-it and its role in supporting his/her reading goal(s).

As students self-reflect and self-assess, Mrs. L is able to assess students' use of accurate and relevant textual evidence to support the claims and inferences captured on their Post-it notes. She is also able to see if students' Post-it selections represent a range of points in the text or represent more student thinking at the beginning, middle, or end; in this way, Mrs. L is better able to gauge the impact of reading conferences against the timeline represented in students' Post-it selections.

Mrs. L feeds back her interpretations of students' formal assessments in much the same way as she has communicated with students before: through individual conferences and written "glows" and "grows." For her own record-keeping, Mrs. L sorts completed reflections into four groups at the end of each month:

1. **Proficient strategy application**: These students are able to independently apply the Post-it strategies and are also able to explain why certain strategies are applicable to specific reading goals or genres in their reflections.
2. **Near-proficient strategy application**: These students are able to independently apply the Post-it strategies, but they do not consistently or clearly explain why certain strategies are applicable to specific reading goals or genres in their reflections.
3. **Approaching strategy application**: These students do not consistently apply the Post-it strategies with independence, but they are able to explain why certain strategies are applicable to specific reading goals or genres in their reflections.

Name: _____   **Date:** _____

Book: _____

My Top 3: Post-it Notes Reflection Log

Directions: Review the Post-it notes that you completed during the reading of your latest text. Choose 3 Post-it notes from anywhere in the text that you feel best show the thinking you did as you read. Once you select the Post-it notes, be sure to respond to the reflection questions provided for each Post-it.

Post-it I

(place the Post-it in the space below)

What skill were you working on mastering when you made this Post-it?

_____

Why did you select this Post-it? What does it show about you as a reader, either your challenges or strengths?

_____

_____

_____

How did this Post-it help you think about/keep track of what you were reading?

_____

_____

Figure 10.11 Culminating Character Analysis Task With Reflection

Post-it 2

(place the Post-it in the space below)

What skill were you working on mastering when you made this Post-it?

Why did you select this Post-it? What does it show about you as a reader, either your challenges or strengths?

How did this Post-it help you think about/keep track of what you were reading?

Figure 10.11 Continued

Post-it 3

(place the Post-it in the space below)

What skill were you working on mastering when you made this Post-it?

Why did you select this Post-it? What does it show about you as a reader, either your challenges or strengths?

How did this Post-it help you think about/keep track of what you were reading?

Figure 10.11 Continued

4. **Near-approaching strategy application**: These students do not consistently apply Post-it strategies with independence, and they do not consistently or clearly explain why certain strategies are applicable to specific reading goals or genres in their reflections.

Mrs. L keeps track of student progress from level to level over time to help her to see large trends throughout the class, in addition to her rich understanding of each individual. Her notes on class trends make it easier for her to customize small group reading instruction targeted at specific SLOs for each group in the upcoming month. Finally, Mrs. L is able to triangulate students' individually created independent reading goals against her own reading conference notes, to ensure that Mrs. L's conclusions about student learning are based on multiple sources of evidence.

Call-Outs on the CA:SRL Framework in Mrs. L's Stage 3, Formal Assessment
☞ Mrs. L's formal assessment gives students an opportunity to integrate their learning.
☞ Mrs. L's formal assessments build from Stage 2, but are a culmination, not a repetition.
☞ Because students self-select artifacts for their formal assessment, student self-assessment is a key part of Stage 3.
☞ Mrs. L takes steps to validate the results of her assessments through triangulation of various sources of evidence.

Communicating Results

At the conclusion of each marking period, students meet with Mrs. L and their parent(s) during the thrice-a-year Parent Teacher Conference night. Rather than listing students' reading strengths and needs, Mrs. L facilitates students' ability to lead this portion of the conference through self-assessment using the Independent Reading Rubric (see Figure 10.12). The week before Parent Teacher Conferences, Mrs. L designates one independent reading block for student self-assessment. Students receive their completed weekly Post-it log and reflections and their completed Top 3 or Top 5 Post-it Log reflections.

On their own, students self-assess and complete the rubric, which Mrs. L uses as an artifact for students to refer to during Parent Teacher Conferences. With their parent(s) and Mrs. L, the student discusses his/her understanding of reading strategies, his/her ability to speak to themselves as readers in terms of habits, strengths, and needs, and his/her progress toward reading goal(s) and next steps to improve. The parent(s) and Mrs. L provide the student with "glows" and "grows," and the parent shares at-home noticings related to independent reading goals that Mrs. L notes for future reading conferences. Mrs. L provides the parent(s) with feedback related to the student's use of textual evidence, sharing tips and strategies for at-home support to strengthen the student's application both in school and at home.

In particular, the more summative Top 3 or Top 5 Reflection Logs and students' completed Independent Reading Rubrics support Mrs. L's contributions to her fifth-grade teacher team. During common planning time, Mrs. L shares with her fellow fifth-grade teachers her noticings from students' completed logs, using understandings about students' use of textual evidence to support claims and inferences to support curriculum map refinement. Together, the

	I'm Not There Yet	I'm Approaching	I'm There!
Reading Strategies	I know some reading strategies, but I'm not sure when I should use them or why one is better to use than another.	I can tell you about some reading strategies and when and why you might use them to help you with your reading.	I can tell you about some reading strategies, the reading skills they help me improve, and the best time to use them depending on what you're reading.
Metacognitive Self-reflection	I'm not sure how to describe myself as a reader how to describe my reading habits.	I can somewhat describe myself as a reader and tell you about some of my reading habits and strengths.	I can describe myself as a reader and tell you about some of my reading strengths as well as some of the reading skills I want to improve.
Metacognitive Self-assessment	I'm not sure I can talk clearly about my reading goal(s) and how I am trying to achieve them.	I can tell you about my reading goal(s) and some of the strategies I'm using to improve.	I can tell you about my reading goal(s) and some of the strategies I'm using to improve. I can also tell you about some of the areas I'm struggling with and my plan to keep improving.

Figure 10.12 Independent Reading Rubric

teacher team highlights patterns in students' reading strategy application and students' ability to accurately apply relevant textual evidence across reading skills. Their collaborative noticings guide instructional revisions to daily teaching points, small group reading instruction goals, and long-term performance assessment project requirements.

Call-Outs on the CA:SRL Framework in Mrs. L's Stage 4, Reporting

☞ Mrs. L's Stage 4 culminating analysis involves reporting to multiple groups outside the classroom (parents, other teachers).

☞ Mrs. L's rubric for student self-evaluation highlights self-reflection as well as content, continuing to put self-regulation up front.

☞ Mrs. L's students take the lead in reflecting on their performance during Parent Night.

☞ Mrs. L's reports about her students to her teaching team put her results into use for the purpose of advancing learning across her whole school.

References

Beers, K. (2003). *When kids can't read: What teachers can do.* Portsmouth, NH: Heinemann.
National Governors Association Center for Best Practices & Council of Chief State School Officers. (2010). *Common core state standards for English language arts: CCSS.ELA-Literacy. RI.5.1.* Retrieved form www.corestandards.org/ELA-Literacy/RI/5/#CCSS.ELA-Literacy.RI.5.1

Chapter 11

Music Case Study

Hayes Middle School (HMS) serves students in grades 6–8 in a pre-dominantly Afro-Caribbean neighborhood in the Washington, D.C., area. HMS is one of two schools located in their building, the other being a K–5 elementary school that most HMS students have graduated from. There are 158 students enrolled in HMS, two classes per grade, plus a grade 6–8 special education class. According to the 2016–2017 School Quality report, 80% of the student body identify as Black, 16% identify as Hispanic, 2% as Asian. Seven percent of the student population are considered English language learners, and 34% are identified as having special needs. Attendance at HMS is 91%, below the city average of 94%. Students at HMS perform below average on English and Math state tests, with an average of 30% and 14% meeting state standards respectively.

Students at HMS have to select one arts elective per semester. They can choose from dance, art, or classroom piano. Mr. E teaches sixth-grade piano. He has 25 students in the class, 19 boys and 6 girls. In the classroom, there are musical terms on posters covering most of the wall, and records are displayed decoratively, hanging from the ceiling. Classroom desks are pushed together with electric keyboards on top of them. There are 14 keyboards in the room so students share, two to an instrument. The class period lasts 45 minutes.

The Unit of Instruction

Music literacy is the foundation of being able to perform music. Music students can only get so far if they do not know how to read notes and rhythms. When students learn these building blocks, they can take the skills and teach themselves simple songs. Ultimately, learning these skills will give students autonomy and musical independence. Because of the importance of musical literacy for fostering further learning in the field, Mr. E's big goal for the semester is that students will be able to perform a simple piece of piano music correctly using sight-reading. This goal relates to the following National Core Music Standards (National Association for Music Education, 2018):

National Standards

MU:Pr4.2.7b When analyzing selected music, read and identify by name or function standard symbols for rhythm, pitch articulation, dynamics, tempo, and form.
MU:Pr6.1.6a Perform the music with technical accuracy to convey the creator's intent.

Mr. E also sets a goal for performance, as he views music as a practice that is intended not only to be learned and appreciated by an individual but to be shared. This goal is aligned with the following standard:

MU:Pr6.1.6b Demonstrate performance decorum (such as stage presence, attire, and behavior) and audience etiquette appropriate for venue and purpose.

In thinking about skills that will help students advance to the big goals, Mr. E starts with broad questions: What should students be able to do by the end of this course? Play beginner piano. What skills do students need to have in order to achieve this? He considers that they need to know rhythms and pitched notes on the staff, and know the names of the keys on the keyboard.

In music, there are multiple orders in which students can achieve these subskills while developing toward the big goal. Rhythm and Pitch are independent concepts that don't have to be taught in a particular order. Likewise, piano can be taught by rote without ever learning to read music. Mr. E opts to sequence his instruction by leading with rhythm, because rhythms are typically easier to learn and he wants students to start out with a quick win. They will move from understanding rhythms as patterns they hear and create, to rhythms they follow from simple notation, to reading notes of different length, time signatures and measures. He will then proceed to learning the treble staff and the vocabulary associated with it. Once they know the treble staff, students will be in a position to try out playing actual songs in the C position on the piano, and will incorporate the names of the notes as they practice.

Based on the learning progression he has laid out, plus Standard MU:Pr6.1.6b on performance etiquette, Mr. E articulates the following specific learning objectives (SLOs). Note some of Mr. E's SLOs include outcome criteria (e.g., 100% accuracy or making fewer than three mistakes). This is because students need to be able to read rhythms and pitched notes with perfect understanding in order to play a piece of music from sight.

SLOs

SLO 1: Given a piece of sheet music, students will correctly identify the names of the notes on the treble staff with 100% accuracy.

SLO 2: Given a piece of sheet music, students will correctly identify the names of the rhythms with 100% accuracy.

SLO 3: Given a keyboard and the sheet music for "Ode to Joy," students will accurately play the notes of the piece, making fewer than three mistakes.

SLO 4: Given a keyboard and the sheet music for "Ode to Joy," students will accurately connect the directions of the keyboard (left to right) with direction on the staff (up and down) as both pertain to pitch.

SLO 5: Given a Code of Conduct outlining performance expectations, each student will perform "Ode to Joy" in front of an audience of their classroom peers while demonstrating proper performance decorum (dress, posture, etc.).

SLO 6: Given sheet music, a conductor, 14 electric keyboards, and one month of practice, students will perform "Ode to Joy" as an ensemble in front of a school audience, starting and ending together and not getting ahead or behind in the middle of the piece.

At the beginning of the semester, Mr. E pre-assesses his students in several ways to find out their prior experience learning music and to gauge their interest in the subject. He leads whole class discussions about musical styles and preferences. He gives students some open opportunity to play on the keyboards, circulating around the room until he has a rough idea of each student's fine motor coordination. Also, he gives a written pre-assessment, shown in Figure 11.1.

The pre-assessment results show Mr. E that experience reading music is very limited among students. Seventeen out of 25 students are unable to answer a single part of questions 6–8

These are questions to answer BEFORE we start learning, so I can know what *you* need to learn. Don't worry if you can't answer them all – this is not a "test". ☺

1) Do you like to listen to music?
2) Do you listen to music at home?
3) Do you know anyone who plays a musical instrument?
4) Have you ever gone to a music concert?
5) Have you ever taken music lessons?
6) If you know the names of any of these musical symbols, please write it on the line under the symbol.

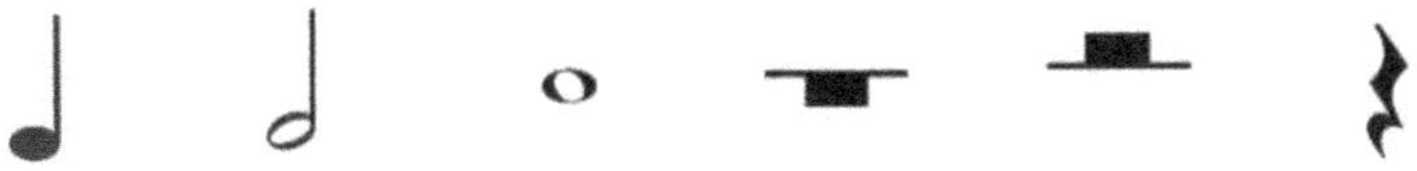

7) Do you know what the group of 5 lines below is called in music? _____

   a. If you can, please label the names of the lines and the spaces.

8) This is a picture of part of a piano keyboard. If you can name any of the white keys, please write them on the keys.

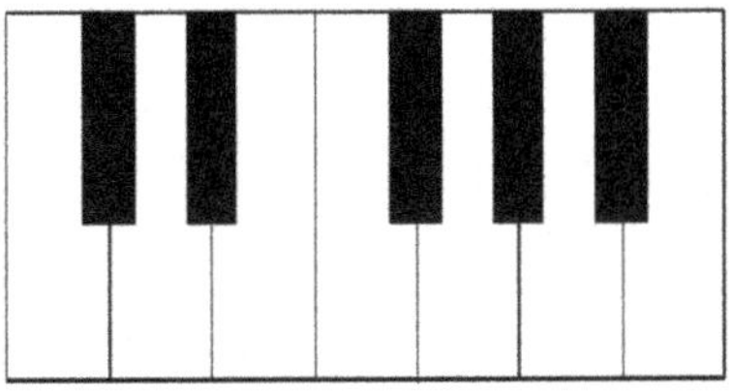

Figure 11.1 Pre-assessment

correctly, although 13 students of these students are able to answer "note" under the first two symbols on question 6. Of other eight students, six demonstrate knowledge of rhythmic literacy and two students are knowledgeable of both rhythmic and pitch-based notes. According to their answers to the pre-assessment items 1–5, both of these students have taken music lessons previously. All students in the class show good starting points for engagement, which Mr. E knows he will be able to draw on as they progress: they all like to listen to music and listen at home, and almost all of them have either been to a concert, know someone who played an instrument, or both.

Stage 2 Instruction and Assessment in Music Class

The semester begins with Mr. E teaching the most basic concepts. Much of the class is spent working in pairs, and Mr. E pairs students heterogeneously. Those students who have demonstrated some knowledge of music literacy work side-by-side with students who have less experience. Students in their pairs take turns being the "student" and the "teacher": "student" plays the song and "teacher" gives feedback. The heterogeneous groups work well in Mr. E's class because none of the students have such high background knowledge that they will be out of one another's "zone." The keyboard is used daily to reinforce the lessons being taught and support motivation. Students like to play. As students learn about rhythm, they play the rhythms on the keyboard. As students play notes, they name them aloud, and connect them to the pitches they are reading on the staff.

In a typical class, Mr. E then teaches a mini-lesson using a keyboard at the front of the room to demonstrate. So that students can all see his demonstration, Mr. E uses Facetime on his smartphone to stream his hands on the keyboard, and then uses Apple TV to project what is streaming on the phone onto the monitor. According to the classroom routine, the mini-lesson is followed by independent and peer-to-peer activities that last the bulk of the period. If there is written work, that is usually completed alone, while playing activities are paired. While students are practicing, Mr. E circulates, informally assessing learning by observing, and answering questions and giving feedback to students. Peer practice is followed by a brief whole-class review. Then students write in their daily journals about their key learning gains and their goals for next class.

At the end of class, students have the opportunity to perform what they have been working on during class, but are not required to do so. For students who have "stage fright," Mr. E takes pains to ask them to play privately or within their peer pair, and builds relationships by telling them about his own experience with music performance anxiety.

For this unit on the treble staff, the class begins with a short review on reading rhythms, which they had already covered in previous lessons. Mr. E then goes into the new material, providing the names of the lines and spaces of the treble staff and the mnemonic devices for remembering them. After the lesson, students receive a worksheet with music written on the treble staff. Students independently identify and label the notes on the staff, then compare their answers with their partner. If there are no discrepancies between the two, students begin playing the sheet music on the keyboard with their partners, each taking turns as the teacher and student. If there are discrepancies between the partners, the pairs first work together to problem-solve, and they can ask Mr. E for hints. According to the class norms, students are supposed to use each other as resources before seeking help from their teacher. The class comes back together to review their answers, and the students take a few minutes to write in their journals. Finally, student volunteers perform in front of the class.

Music Case Study 183

Call-Outs on the Four-Stage CA:SRL Framework in Mr. E's Stage 1, Planning and Pre-assessment
☞ Planning is tied to standards.
☞ Planning of a sequence of SLOs shows thinking of learning as a progression.
☞ SLOs are stated in terms of the three components of *condition, audience,* and *performance,* as presented in Chapter 2. Mr. E also includes a *criterion* to indicate how well students should perform on SLOs 1, 2, and 3 in this unit. The rationale is that he wants to ensure the foundational knowledge and skills stated in SLO 1, 2, and 3 are fully met before students proceed to more complex SLOs.
☞ Pre-assessment gives Mr. E information about prior exposure while prompting students to make connections to music outside of school and practice forethought.
☞ Student pairs engage in daily informal peer assessment by role-taking "student" and "teacher."
☞ Students use journals for daily reflection.
☞ Assessment is targeted at the Depth of Knowledge level appropriate for the step in the learning progression.

Stage 2 Task 1: Non-interactive Supply-Type Task With Reflection

Mr. E creates an assessment task to match what he taught in the lesson, aligned to SLO 1: "Given a piece of sheet music, students will correctly identify the names of the notes on the treble staff with 100% accuracy." This assessment task is geared toward the general goal of sight-playing music on the treble staff; it gives Mr. E a quick look at each individual's learning toward this goal at an early checkpoint in instruction. The learning assessed is at a very basic level in the Depth of Knowledge framework. At this point in instruction, Mr. E is looking more for accuracy at reading than at the synthesis of reading with planning.

The task includes two supply-type items where students can use the mnemonic devices they were taught to help with the answers, and then several items (also supply-type) on note recognition. Students have access to the worksheet, writing materials, a keyboard that is labeled with the key names, and visual aids around the room that have the treble staff. Additionally, students have their class journals where they are able to take notes and reflect on their performance. The task is shown, with students' responses included, in Figures 11.2 and 11.3.

The very first day after instruction in note-reading, Mr. E hands out this assessment task. After students complete the assessment, Mr. E. collects their work, and then students are given blank copies of the task again, and time to play the musical lines that appear on item 3 of the task on their keyboards. This activity is not assessed—it is intended to reinforce learning and make the concepts less abstract. At the end, the class comes together and their ungraded work is handed back. The students are told to put away their pencils and not change their answers. The whole class reviews the problems and discusses which answers were the correct ones. Then the students are given the following questions to answer in their class journals.

1. How many answers did I get right?
2. How many answers did I get wrong?
3. How can I improve next time?

As always, the class ends with one or two student volunteers performing the music for the class.

Mr. E Interprets Individual Student Work: Cyrus

Cyrus is an 11-year-old boy whose parents are immigrants from Jamaica. His older brother is in seventh grade and took the class himself the previous year. Cyrus typically gets grades of Cs and Bs in his classes. On the pre-assessment, Cyrus is one of the students who left the questions about note and rhythm recognition mostly blank. He was quick to pick up rhythms during the previous unit and was excited to learn about reading pitched notes. Cyrus' work is shown and Mr. E's corrective feedback are shown in Figure 11.2.

Cyrus's work was nearly completely incorrect. This surprises Mr. E, given how well he had done with the previous unit. Upon inspection, the reason becomes clear to Mr. E. The first two questions on the worksheet asked that students write the names of the spaces and the lines using the mnemonic devices they had been taught. Cyrus confused the two, accidentally using Every Good Boy Does Fine for the spaces and FACE for the lines, instead of vice versa. When he answered the remaining questions, he referred back to his original mistake, which led to consistent errors throughout.

Figure 11.2 Cyrus's Work Sample

Mr. E's interpretation is confirmed when he consults Cyrus's journal where his answers are as follows:

1. How many answers did you get right? *None*
2. How many answers did you get wrong? *All*
3. How can you improve next time? *Not mix up FACE and every good boy does good.*

From Cyrus's journal, it is clear that he learned from that error. However, additional errors in his thinking start to become apparent from close inspection of his work and his journal. First, Cyrus seems to think that the mnemonic device to remember the names of the lines was Every Good Boy Does Good instead of Every Good Boy Does Fine. Also, when Mr. E reviews the work he notices that F is repeatedly mislabeled as E, in line 1 stanzas 2 and 3, and line 2 stanzas 1 and 2. Cyrus's trouble reading the treble staff is not just attributable to the flawed mnemonic.

Feedback to Cyrus and Individualized Next Steps for Learning

Mr. E's feedback is given to students during the next class. For Cyrus, he gives corrective feedback on the front of the worksheet, and more detailed feedback on the back. The more detailed feedback is provided below.

- *Good effort! Remember, F-A-C-E helps to remember the names of the spaces (Face rhymes with space!) and we can remember the names of the lines by remembering Every Good Boy Does Fine. Another way to remember it is Every Good Boy Deserves Fudge!*
- *I'd like you to go back and try again, this time remembering to use FACE for spaces and EGBDF for the lines.*
- *Think: How is your first try different from your second try? When you put the lines and spaces together, what does the musical alphabet look like on your first try compared to your second try? Which one makes more sense? When you play each version on the piano, which sounds better to you?"*

Mr. E. provides Cyrus with the prompt to look at the whole musical alphabet because it provides a way to check whether notes are correctly named. When you label the lines and spaces on the staff correctly, they form an alphabet from A to G, starting with E. When you label the lines and spaces the way Cyrus did initially, the alphabet skips around: F-E-A-G-C and so on. The students haven't yet been explicitly taught this convention of notation, but Mr. E's prompt may help Cyrus if he is confused by the mnemonic another time.

In his class notes, Mr. E records that Cyrus did not meet the criterion for SLO 1: "Given a piece of sheet music, students will correctly identify the names of the notes on the treble staff with 100% accuracy." For Cyrus, the next step is to repeat the original assignment, correcting the initial errors. If he is successfully able to do that, his next steps will be to wean himself off the visual aid, memorizing the names of the lines and spaces of the treble staff.

Mr. E Interprets Individual Student Work: Odessa

Odessa is an 11-year-old girl who was born in Jamaica, but has lived in the U.S. since the first grade. She is a serious student who typically receives high grades. Odessa takes diligent notes, writing down even mundane details. As a result, her classroom journal is several pages

186 Section 3 Chapter 11

fuller than her classmates. Odessa was one of the last students to finish the assessment task (see Figure 11.3). Once completed, her work was flawless. She seemed to understand the concepts that were taught and was able to apply them to her work. Her journal entry is as follows:

1. How many answers did you get right? *I got every answer right.*
2. How many answers did you get wrong? *I didn't get any answers wrong.*
3. How can you improve next time? *There is nothing I could do to improve.*

Feedback to Odessa and Individualized Next Steps for Learning

Mr. E's feedback highlights what Odessa did correctly, and then prods her to get her thinking about the next steps she should be taking. Mr. E is a little concerned that Odessa does not

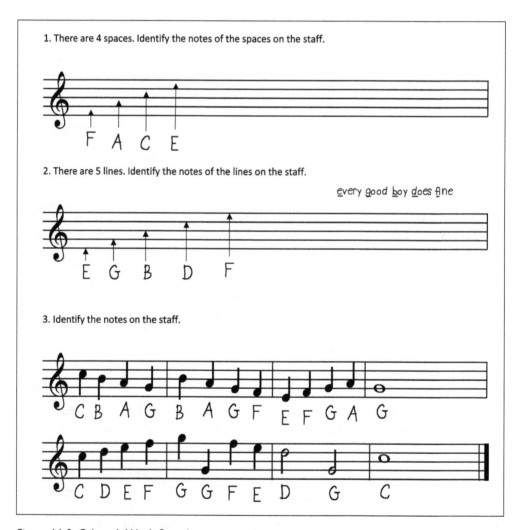

Figure 11.3 Odessa's Work Sample

recognize that there is always room for more learning. He wonders if the reason she took so much time with the task was high reliance on referring back to the memory device or other resources.

- *Great work! You remembered the memory trick for the lines and spaces and that really helped when you were answering the rest of the questions. You labeled all of the notes correctly. Next steps: Try labeling the notes on the staff <u>without</u> the memory trick written out in front of you. Can you do it?*

In his class notes, Mr. E records that Odessa met the criterion for the SLO. The next step for her is to continue practicing identifying the notes on the treble staff, but without the visual aid of the mnemonic devices in front of her, memorizing the note names instead. At the same time, she should be playing the notes on the keyboard and making connections between what is on the page and the keyboard, and the sound of what she plays. Her learning gaps seem to be lack of internalized understanding of the notes on the treble staff, and an understanding of the relationship between what is written and what is played. These next steps will help these concepts to become less abstract and more tangible.

Instructional Responses Based on This Assessment

After Mr. E reviews each individual's work, he reflects on the whole class, and he finds that his students generally performed well on the task. Of the 25 students, 12 scored 100%, indicating that they met the expectations for the SLO. Of the remaining 15 students, seven made fewer than three mistakes, two did not finish the assignment and four made mistakes related to the mnemonic devices they were taught. Three students used the correct memory trick, but started from the top of the staff instead of the bottom, and the fourth confused the two, using the one for spaces on the lines and vice versa.

Overall, Mr. E thinks the class is on the right path. Nearly half of the students met the criterion for SLO 1, accurately naming the notes on the treble staff. The remaining students made one initial error based on the first two questions, which then lead to additional errors. Once this original error is corrected, they should be able to move on to the next steps. Mr. E's notes, such as those he recorded for Cyrus and Odessa, will help him monitor their individual progress as his instruction progresses, and re-administer tasks when students have needed more practice, as he plans to do in the case of Cyrus.

Call-Outs on the Four-Stage CA:SRL Framework in Mr. E's First Iteration of Stage 2 Assessment
☞ Mr. E's assessment task matches what he taught in the lesson.
☞ The assessment has multiple items, which improves reliability.
☞ Students are allowed to use resources as they perform the assessment, supporting self-control.
☞ Mr. E blends interactive and non-interactive assessment methods to get a deep understanding of student learning.
☞ Mr. E relies on more than one source for interpreting learning (assessment task and journal).

188 Section 3 Chapter 11

| ☞ Feedback is elaborated for students who need different strategies. |
| ☞ Students have multiple opportunities to be re-assessed. |

Stage 2 Task 2: PA With Interactive Feedback

After several days of additional instruction and practice with an emphasis on putting notes together with rhythm to play songs, Mr. E administers a second assessment. At this point in instruction, Mr. E is ready to assess not only identifying isolated notes, but making the connection to play. His assessment is targeted at the following SLOs:

SLO 3: Given a keyboard and the sheet music for "Ode to Joy," students will accurately play the notes of the piece, making fewer than three mistakes.

SLO 4: Given a keyboard and the sheet music for "Ode to Joy," students will accurately connect the directions of the keyboard (left to right) with direction on the staff (up and down) as both pertain to pitch.

To perform this task, students have access to a keyboard with the letter names written on the keys and the sheet music for "Ode to Joy." The sheet music is something students have seen before, as it has been part of practice throughout the semester. They were first introduced to "Ode to Joy" during the rhythm unit, where they clapped and played the rhythms on Middle C of their keyboards.

This assessment takes place over two class periods. While the rest of the class works on other activities, students are called individually to the teacher's keyboard where they sight-read the music for "Ode to Joy." They are not required to play the correct rhythms or use the correct fingerings. There are no time limits and Mr. E tracks the music with his finger so students won't lose their place. Following the assessment, Mr. E has a short conference with each student regarding the student's performance.

Cyrus's Conference

Cyrus is one of the last students to be assessed at Mr. E's keyboard. He completed the activity faster than most of his peers. He speeds through the sections with stepwise motion, but struggles a bit when the music jumps from one note to another. The first jump, from E to C, he initially plays incorrectly, but hears his error and correct his mistake. The second jump is to the same interval, and he has no problem with it. He has no additional errors, but he does slow down for the jumps after that. Cyrus performed so well on the assessment that Mr. E has no doubt that he has learned to the level of expectations.

Following his assessment, Cyrus and Mr. E have the following conversation:

Mr. E: How do you think you did?
Cyrus: Pretty good.
Mr. E: What parts were hard for you?
Cyrus: [Points at the first jump] This here.
Mr. E: I noticed you made a mistake there, but then you corrected it right away.
Cyrus: Yeah.
Mr. E: How did you know to correct it?

Music Case Study 189

Cyrus:	I heard this song before and it didn't sound right.
Mr. E:	So, it sounded wrong to you, and that is how you knew you made a mistake?
Cyrus:	Yeah.
Mr. E:	What if you had never heard this song before? How would you know if you had made a mistake then?
Cyrus:	Um . . . [Shrugs]
Mr. E:	What if instead of using your ears to know what to play, you used your eyes and read the music?
Cyrus:	Yeah, alright.
Mr. E:	So, what can you do to improve next time?
Cyrus:	Um, practice?
Mr. E:	Sure, practicing is really helpful. And keep working on our worksheets so you can get really, really good at reading the notes! Ok?
Cyrus:	Ok.

Odessa's Conference

Odessa participated in the assessment at the end of the first day of administration. As with the first assessment, Odessa approached this exercise slowly and methodically. As she played each note, her hands shook, and she hesitated several times. She took nearly twice the time to get through the song as the rest of the students, but she only had two mistakes, when she played a note with the correct pitch, C, but played the upper octave instead of the lower octave that was written, which happened twice. After completing the exercise, Odessa and Mr. E had the following conversation.

Mr. E:	How did you feel about that?
Odessa:	That was really hard!
Mr. E:	But you did really well! What made it seem so hard?
Odessa:	I was scared I was going to mess up. Also, between notes, I would lose my place on the keyboard and I'd have to find it again.
Mr. E:	Yeah, that happens sometimes. It is easier when you are using all of your fingers and stay in one place rather than just use your pointer finger. We're going to talk more about that later though. You know what though? Every time you thought you were going to play the wrong note, you still played the right one! You just have to trust yourself more.
Odessa:	[nodding]
Mr. E:	How did it sound to you?
Odessa:	It sounded good.
Mr. E:	Did you know this song before today?
Odessa:	It sorta sounds familiar. I heard it in church maybe?
Mr. E:	Maybe. Do you see this note here [pointing to middle C on the sheet music] What note is this?
Odessa:	That's C.
Mr. E:	That's right. Can you find C for me on the piano?
Odessa:	[Plays middle C]
Mr. E:	Can you find any other C on the piano?
Odessa:	[Plays C above middle C followed by C an octave higher]

190 Section 3 Chapter 11

Mr. E: Very good! What do you notice about those notes. Do they all sound the same?

Odessa: No, this one is really high but this other one [plays middle C again] is kind of low.

Mr. E: That's right! How about if we look at the treble staff. Where are the Cs here?

Odessa: [points to middle C and the space for C above middle C]

Mr. E: Yup, that's right! So, we have two Cs. Do you think they sound exactly the same or do you think they sound different?

Odessa: I think this C [pointing to C above middle C] is higher.

Mr. E: That's right! Why do you think that?

Odessa: Because this C is higher on the staff.

Mr. E: Exactly. So, when notes go up on the staff they get higher, and when notes get higher on the piano they're going . . .

Odessa: [pointing toward the right] That way.

Mr. E: You got it! So, what's your take-away? What are you going to do to improve next time?

Odessa: I'm, um, I'm going to trust myself?

Mr. E: That's right. Trust your gut. You know what you're doing.

Instructional Responses and Interpretations in Reference to SLOs

Mr. E takes notes about the performance and conference results and how they affect his instructional plans. He writes that Cyrus has an excellent ear, and can quickly learn a new song without relying on reading the music. Mr. E knows this can be both an advantage and a disadvantage. Students like this often go under the radar when learning to read music, as they can easily fake it. However, once the music becomes more difficult, they find themselves behind their peers and are unable to catch up. To prevent this, Mr. E will ask Cyrus to continue writing the names of the notes on his sheet music before he has a chance to sit down and play a song on the piano. Secondly, it will be important for him to be assigned music he is unfamiliar with, so his instinct won't be to rely on his ear to learn the music.

In regard to the SLOs, Cyrus appears to have met the accuracy criteria, despite relying on his ear rather than reading the sheet music. He was able to play the song and only made one mistake, performing better than the SLO 3 required – he would have still met the criterion if he had made as many as three errors. Likewise, on SLO 4, Cyrus played all of the notes in the correct octaves, indicating he understands the directional aspects of piano and pitch. However, it is unclear as to whether he understands the directional relationship the staff has with pitch, as he was not relying on reading the music. In light of the evidence, Mr. E marks down that Cyrus has met both objectives, but to remember to keep an eye on Cyrus's sight-reading.

Mr. E notes that Odessa performed technically well on this assessment, although she played cautiously. Her only mistakes were when she played the correct note, but in the wrong octave. She made fewer than three mistakes, so she met the specific criterion for SLO 3. Regarding the second SLO, Odessa initially did not appear to have met the objective, as demonstrated by playing notes in the wrong octave. However, in the student-teacher conference that followed, Odessa was able to piece together the directional relationship between the piano (notes to the right are higher than notes to the left) and the staff (notes that are higher on the staff are higher in pitch as well). Like Cyrus, Odessa is ready to move on to the next stage of instruction, which incorporates playing correct rhythms and pitches at the same time. Mr. E marks down that Odessa has met the objectives, and writes himself a reminder to help her develop self-efficacy in performance.

Call-Outs on the Four-Stage CA:SRL Framework in Mr. E's Second Iteration of Stage 2 Assessment
☞ Performance assessment shows learning by doing an authentic task.
☞ Assessment, feedback, and learning are integrated in the PA-conference episode.
☞ Feedback is differentiated according to evidence from the assessment and conference probes.
☞ Assessment results are recorded and used for further planning.

Formal Assessment and Self-Assessment: Stage 3

By the end of the semester, students have met and mastered the SLOs on all their previous assessments and have primarily been focusing on applying their acquired skills toward playing the piano. After developing a repertoire of songs, students prepare for a performance at a school assembly, which will be their culminating, most formal assessment in the course. In the weeks leading up to the performance, the class practices performing as a group. Up to this point, the main focus has been individual performance, so this takes some practice. The lessons focus on starting and stopping together and staying together during the songs, as well as what to do if you became out of sync with the rest of the group. Additionally, a lesson is devoted to performance etiquette, and expectations are established regarding behavior and dress code.

Prior to actual performance, students receive an evaluation form and discuss it as a class. It will be due at the beginning of the class following the performance. They receive and review it in advance to help them engage in forethought about expectations. The evaluation form consists of 12 questions, six focusing on personal performance, including etiquette, and six focusing on the performance of the class. These questions all consist of Likert-type items written on a scale of 1–5 (see Figure 11.4). After the performance, students will use it to assess themselves and their peers on their performance quality and etiquette skills.

The performance takes place in the auditorium during the last period of the day, and the entire sixth grade is in attendance. As a whole, the class perform well. They are able to start and stop together, although there are some wrong notes here and there. However, the class had been instructed to wear black bottoms with a white button down or polo shirt; only half of the class actually show up dressed appropriately. Furthermore, many students in the class whisper to each other between songs and wave to their friends in the audience.

Students bring in their completed evaluation forms the class period after their performance. In the classroom, Mr. E writes each question from the form on a separate sheet of poster paper, and posts the questions around the room. He instructs the students to put a tally mark next to the number they have personally selected for each question. Once this is complete, the class as a whole discusses each question.

On the self-assessment part of the evaluation form, the majority of students rate themselves very highly across all questions. However, scores are much lower when students rate their peers. It is apparent that even though this is not a graded assignment, there is some score self-inflation. Notably, the big exception to this relates to dress code. Students are apparently quite self-aware and aware of one another's behavior in terms of dress.

Please circle the number that best represents **YOUR** performance.

Did what you wore meet the dress code requirements?

Not at all   Perfectly

1   2   3   4   5

How often were your eyes on the conductor?

Not at all   At all times

1   2   3   4   5

How quiet were you when not performing?

Silent   Talked constantly

1   2   3   4   5

How was your performance posture while you were on stage?

Slouched   Perfect

1   2   3   4   5

How accurately did you play the songs?

Lots of mistakes   No Mistakes

1   2   3   4   5

How well did you follow the conductor's cues?

Missed many cues   No missed cues

1   2   3   4   5

Please circle the number that best represents **THE CLASS'S** performance.

Did what students wore meet the dress code requirements?

Not at all   Perfectly

1   2   3   4   5

How often were the eyes of the whole class on the conductor?

Not at all   At all times

1   2   3   4   5

How quiet was the class when not performing?

Silent   Talked constantly

1   2   3   4   5

How was the performance posture of your classmates while you were on stage?

Slouched   Perfect

1   2   3   4   5

How accurately did the class play the songs?

Lots of mistakes   No Mistakes

1   2   3   4   5

How well did the class follow the conductor's cues?

Missed many cues   No missed cues

1   2   3   4   5

Figure 11.4 Self-Assessment

Cyrus Reflects on His Performance

As students are entering the classroom on the day after the performance, Cyrus apologizes to Mr. E for not dressing properly for the performance. He had worn black shoes, dark blue jeans and a white t-shirt. He says that he doesn't own black pants or white shirts, aside from a t-shirt. He rated himself a 3 out of 5 possible points when asked about the dress code.

Cyrus rated himself as a 5 on watching the conductor and a 4 on following cues and posture. This is aligned with what was observed of him during his performance. On accuracy, Cyrus rated himself as a 3, and although he had originally given himself a 4 on staying quiet during the performance, he crossed that out and gave himself a 2. This is likely due to this question being reverse-coded from the rest or the questions, which may have caused some confusion.

When it came to rating his classmates, Cyrus was a bit more critical. Aside from the reverse-coded question, which he gave a 4, the highest rating he gave was a 3. For dress code, he rated his peers as a 2 out of 5 (see Figure 11.5).

Odessa Reflects on Her Performance

Odessa rated herself a 5 out of 5 on dress code (see Figure 11.6). She had arrived at the performance wearing black shoes and pants along with a white polo shirt, meeting the expectations outlined before the performance, so this was not an inflated score.

Overall, Odessa gave herself high ratings. In addition to dress code, she rated herself as a 5 on following cues and accuracy. She gave herself a 4 out of 5 on posture and watching the conductor, and a 1 on staying quiet, indicating that she was silent when she was not performing.

Odessa was far less critical of her class's performance than many of her peers. She gave high marks for posture, accuracy, and following cues. For watching the conductor, she gave a neutral score of 3 out of 5. However, she did indicate that her peers talked nearly constantly, and only rated student dress code requirements as a 2.

Mr. E's Interpretations

Mr. E sees from the students' self-assessment that they are, by and large, self-aware and accurate. Although some of the students seemed to inflate their ratings, Cyrus and Odessa were both fairly accurate in their self-assessments. For instance, during performance, Cyrus was observed watching the conductor closely. At one point, Mr. E indicated students should sit up tall and Cyrus straightened his posture and stayed this way throughout the rest of the performance. In his self-evaluation, he did indicate that he struggled with accuracy. This was not surprising. Although Cyrus thrived at the beginning of the semester, he struggled with the hand coordination required for playing piano, particularly with his non-dominant left hand.

During the performance, Odessa was also observed watching the conductor. She was seen keeping time by nodding along to the beat. She was initially slouched, but fixed her posture at the same time as Cyrus. She gave herself a perfect rating on accuracy. This is consistent with her performance leading up to the assembly. Although it took her more time than some of her peers to learn the repertoire, she practiced diligently and seemed to master each song. The high marks Odessa gave herself were warranted.

In evaluating their peers, Cyrus and Odessa were fairly aligned in their assessments. Although they did not give the exact same ratings, they were consistently within one point of each other.

Please circle the number that best represents **YOUR** performance.

1. Did what you wore meet the dress code requirements?

Not at all   Perfectly

1   2   ③   4   5

2. How often were your eyes on the conductor?

Not at all   At all times

1   2   3   4   ⑤

3. How quiet were you when not performing?

Silent Talked   constantly

1   ②   3   4   5

4. How was your performance posture while you were on stage?

Slouched   Perfect

1   2   3   ④   5

5. How accurately did you play the songs?

Lots of mistakes   No Mistakes

1   2   ③   4   5

6. How well did you follow the conductor's cues?

Missed many cues   No missed cues

1   2   3   ④   5

Please circle the number that best represents **THE CLASS'S** performance.

7. Did what students wore meet the dress code requirements?

Not at all   Perfectly

1   ②   3   4   5

8. How often were the eyes of the whole class on the conductor?

Not at all   At all times

1   2   ③   4   5

9. How quiet was the class when not performing?

Silent Talked   constantly

1   2   3   ④   5

10. How was the performance posture of your classmates while you were on stage?

Slouched   Perfect

1   2   ③   4   5

11. How accurately did the class play the songs?

Lots of mistakes   No Mistakes

1   2   ③   4   5

12. How well did the class follow the conductor's cues?

Missed many cues   No missed cues

1   2   ③   4   5

Figure 11.5 Cyrus's Self-Assessment

Please circle the number that best represents **YOUR** performance.

1. Did what you wore meet the dress code requirements?

Not at all   Perfectly

1   2   3   4   (5)

2. How often were your eyes on the conductor?

Not at all   At all times

1   2   3   (4)   5

3. How quiet were you when not performing?

Silent   Talked constantly

(1)   2   3   4   5

4. How was your performance posture while you were on stage?

Slouched   Perfect

1   2   3   (4)   5

5. How accurately did you play the songs?

Lots of mistakes   No Mistakes

1   2   3   4   (5)

6. How well did you follow the conductor's cues?

Missed many cues   No missed cues

1   2   3   4   (5)

Please circle the number that best represents **THE CLASS'S** performance.

7. Did what students wore meet the dress code requirements?

Not at all   Perfectly

1   (2)   3   4   5

8. How often were the eyes of the whole class on the conductor?

Not at all   At all times

1   2   (3)   4   5

9. How quiet was the class when not performing?

Silent   Talked constantly

1   2   3   (4)   5

10. How was the performance posture of your classmates while you were on stage?

Slouched   Perfect

1   2   3   (4)   5

11. How accurately did the class play the songs?

Lots of mistakes   No Mistakes

1   2   3   (4)   5

12. How well did the class follow the conductor's cues?

Missed many cues   No missed cues

1   2   3   (4)   5

Figure 11.6 Odessa's Self-Assessment

Some of their ratings were more critical than Mr. E would have given the class. For instance, Cyrus rated the class's accuracy as a 3 out of 5. Mr. E considered this was a harsh judgment. Although there were a few mistakes, by and large, the class played correct notes and rhythms. Also, both Cyrus and Odessa gave the class a rating of 3 on watching the conductor, and a 3 on following cues. However, very few students in the class were actually looking away, and almost all attended when the conductor gave a cue. These were behaviors emphasized in classes leading up to the performance, and in Mr. E's estimation, they stuck. It occurs to Mr. E that the students may not have had a good opportunity to observe one another's attention to the conductor, so lacked the information to assess that item accurately. If students are expected to keep their eyes on the conductor, it would be difficult for them to observe if their peers are doing the same. Likewise, if students are focusing on their own performance, they may not be paying attention to how well their classmates are following the conductor's cues.

In hindsight, Mr. E reflects on possible flaws in the questions on his student self-assessment. First, he considers that in the future, he will leave out the questions about eyes on the conductor and following cues, in the whole-class part of the survey. Second, he realizes he should have worded the item about talking differently, so that the negative behavior (talking constantly) was on the right, as it was in all the other items.

Feedback on the Final Performance Assessment

Most feedback is directed to the class as a whole. Mr. E leads a discussion about what went well, specifically staying together and following the conductor. The class also talks about areas for improvement, specifically stage decorum and talking while on stage. They also talk about the problem of inconsistent dress, which clearly did not show that the class as a whole met the standard of decorum and proper attire. However, in light of Cyrus's private comment that he didn't own the correct clothes, Mr. E asks (without naming Cyrus) whether any students could not find the right clothing. Several nod, and the class discuss a possible new dress expectation for future performances—one that is dignified and consistent for the class, but doesn't place a burden on anyone.

Toward the end of the class, students break off into small groups to discuss what they would do to improve next time. During this time, Mr. E is able to circulate around the room to provide individual feedback to students. When he comes to Cyrus, they discuss his performance as well as his evaluation form. Mr. E tells him that he is pleased with his performance overall. Mr. E says he particularly noticed how closely he was paying attention to the conductor. Being self-reflective, Cyrus says that to improve next time, he will practice the songs more to memorize them. Mr. E replies that memorizing is always good, but that he hopes Cyrus appreciates the importance of balancing when looking at the conductor and reading the music. To motivate Cyrus to continue to develop his sight-reading skills, Mr. E emphasizes that sight-reading would help Cyrus learn songs on his own.

When Mr. E talks to Odessa, he tells her that he thinks she did very well during her performance. Mr. E is particularly pleased with her stage presence. She followed the dress code, she kept quiet when she wasn't playing and she kept her eyes on the conductor, following cues. When Mr. E asks what she wants to do to improve next time, she says she could sit up straighter and Mr. E agrees that would be a good thing to focus on. At this point, Mr. E also probes Odessa about the kinds of songs she would like to learn to play. As with Cyrus, he wants to build Odessa's intrinsic motivation, in this case by helping her build an appreciation for music. Mr. E's personal impression, which would never be reflected in his performance feedback to Odessa, is that she did well in Piano not so much because she likes music as because she is a naturally diligent student. The habit of diligence can make a good technical musician, but Mr. E hopes to ignite a love of music as well.

Call-Outs on the Four-Stage CA:SRL Framework in Mr. E's Second Iteration of Stage 2 Assessment
☞ Self-assessment is signaled ahead of time to raise awareness of success criteria.
☞ Assessment of whole-class performance is a whole-class activity—the class as a community engages in group/self-reflection.
☞ Mr. E reflects on the quality of his assessment tasks.
☞ Mr. E takes into consideration whether his success criteria were fair to all students.

Summary Perceptions and Reporting

Mr. E reviews his notes and the accumulated evidence of student learning over the course of the semester. Mr. E has good evidence to show that over the course of the semester, Cyrus and Odessa went from knowing very little about music to being able to read rhythms and notes on the treble staff and play them on the keyboard. Especially at first, Cyrus excelled and mastered reading and playing rhythms ahead of the rest of his peers. As the class progressed through the semester, however, Cyrus's progress began to slow. He struggled with reading pitched notes and the hand coordination of playing the piano. He did eventually master reading notes on the treble staff, but had problems with hand coordination that impeded his ability to play throughout the semester.

Odessa had a more even learning experience. Although rhythm and pitch did not come as naturally to her as Cyrus, Odessa had excellent study skills coming into the class and this translated well into practicing. Like Cyrus, Odessa finished the semester having mastered reading rhythms, notes on the treble staff. She had a solid foundation for applying these skills to playing the piano. She had no problems with hand coordination.

The final performance is rated using a very simple checklist (Figure 11.7). After he realizes that many students simply did not have the mandatory clothing, Mr. E drops the second criterion from grading. Both Cyrus and Odessa receive full credit for the final performance.

After this final performance assessment, the semester comes to an end, and Mr. E reports the students' grades. To report his overall or summary interpretations of student learning, Mr. E scores for assessments like the non-interactive supply-type task on the number of correct

Criteria:	Yes (1 point)/No (0)
1. Did the student play in the performance?	
2. Did the student dress appropriately for the performance?	
3. Did the student use the evaluation form to reflect on the performance?	

Figure 11.7 Basic Checklist for Performance Assessment

responses and allows students (like Cyrus) as many do-overs as they need to show mastery. The objective is truly about meeting the criterion. Performances such as the one described as Iteration 2 are graded on a pass/fail basis, also with multiple opportunities to try again. Mr. E never administers surprise quizzes or unannounced performance assessments. Music performance puts students in an exposed and vulnerable state, compared to a math class, for instance, where any errors they make are mostly on paper and largely between the student and the teacher. Willingness to perform involves taking risks, and Mr. E thinks that with frequent grading and stringent requirements, students will not take the risk of performing. The downside of Mr. E's grading practice is that there is potential for individual students to fall behind, and Mr. E does occasionally have to tell a student it is time to move on.

For computing an overall course grade, in-class assessments like the non-interactive Task 1 are weighted 45%, and short performances like Task 2 is also weighted 45% of the grade. Because there were no opportunities for re-dos, and because for most students, a performance in the auditorium was intimidating enough without having to worry about a grade, the final performance counts only 10% toward the grade.

Call-Outs on the Four-Stage CA:SRL Framework in Mr. E's Stage 4, Assessment
☞ Mr. E bases grades on many sources of evidence and multiple iterations of assessment and instruction.
☞ Grades are about meeting the criterion, not about meeting it by a deadline.
☞ High-risk performances are low stakes in grading.
☞ Mr. E shows fairness by adjusting his standards (e.g., the dress requirement) when evidence suggests the assessment may contain hidden biases.

Reference

National Association for Music Education. (2018). *Core music standards (PreK-8)*. Retrieved from https://nafme.org/wp-content/files/2014/06/1-Core-Music-Standards-PreK-81.pdf

Chapter 12

Mathematics Case Study

This hypothetical case study shows the CA:SRL framework in action in the content area of eighth-grade mathematics, during a unit on systems of linear equations. In this case we have not one teacher, but two: Ms. N and Mr. M. For simplicity, henceforth we will refer to them as N and M. This is an integrated co-teaching class (ICT); Ms. N is a general education teacher certified in mathematics, and Mr. M is a special education teacher. In their math class, N and M engage students in iterative processes of multiple assessments while developing student self-regulated learning and using teacher-student co-regulation. They use assessment results to make instructional adjustments, and provide feedback to move students' understanding of algebraic concepts and practices forward, ultimately to narrow learning gaps among learners of diverse math skills. While the four-stage framework is comprehensive and encompasses every aspect of classroom assessment, in this case we focus on use of assessment for learning, with a particular emphasis on feedback.

N and M work at a small middle school in a city in the southwestern U.S. serving about 250 students in grades 6–8. This public middle school shares a set of interconnected buildings with an elementary school. Its students are 70% Hispanic, 27% Black, 1% Asian, and 1% White. English language learners make up about 10% of the student population. About 30% of students need special services and receive an Individualized Education Program (IEP). Class sizes range from 21 to 29 students, and there is one self-contained special education class per grade, with no more than 12 students. The school is considered to be well-performing. Almost 90% of the school's former eighth graders are on track for on-time high school graduation at the end of the first year of high school, in a region with an overall high school graduation rate around 75%.

N and M have an eighth-grade math class of 26 students, ages 13–15, 18 of whom are Hispanic and 8 of whom are Black, with 5 English language learners and 8 students with IEPs. The students with special needs have disabilities such as Specific Learning Disability, Emotional and Behavior Disorder, and Other Health Impairment. The English language learners are all native Spanish speakers. The two teachers use various co-teaching methods, such as turn teaching, with one teaching at a time and the other assisting; and station teaching, where students work as a small group at a station, with a specific task. There are laptops and iPads that students can use during the station teaching time. There are eight mathematics class periods per week of 50-minutes each, with double-periods on three days. With a wide range of student ability, both teachers provide students with multiple entry points and as much individualized instruction as possible.

The Instructional Unit and Learning Standards

N and M will be spending 24 instructional periods for a unit on systems of simultaneous linear equations, with at least one class period per week using iReady (an internet-based program designed to improve student math skills). The school mandates the use of iReady, as well as a specific curriculum. N and M adapt the curriculum and use additional resources and materials from other sources to supplement the unit of instruction and assessment.

N and M's main goal for this unit is that all learners will be able to use a system of simultaneous linear equations to solve real-world problems. The aligned Common Core State Standards (CCSS) focus on algebraic expression and equations (EE), particularly on analyzing and solving pairs of simultaneous linear equations:

> **8.EE.8.A**: Understand that solutions to a system of two linear equations in two variables correspond to points of intersection of their graphs, because points of intersection satisfy both equations simultaneously.
>
> **8.EE.8.B:** Solve systems of two linear equations in two variables algebraically, and estimate solutions by graphing the equations. Solve simple cases by inspection. *For example, 3x + 2y = 5 and 3x + 2y = 6 have no solution because 3x + 2y cannot simultaneously be 5 and 6.*
>
> **8.EE.8.C:** Solve real-world and mathematical problems leading to two linear equations in two variables. *For example, given coordinates for two pairs of points, determine whether the line through the first pair of points intersects the line through the second pair.* (National Governors Association Center for Best Practices & Council of Chief State School Officers, 2010).

N and M include the 8.EE.8.C standard in this unit because they see its educational importance for their students: how math is in our daily lives and useful to know. N and M want to convey the understanding that mathematics is used in real-world situations and want math knowledge to be meaningful to her class.

N and M have noted in the past that their students need to build up their knowledge in small increments, acquiring bits of content knowledge and taking time to mentally link concepts, before they are ready to solve complex problems such as applying equations to real-world situations. To help their students achieve the "big" goal, N and M delineate what they consider to be the critical steps in acquisition of math content knowledge and practices. In this case, N and M take CCSS 8.EE.8(A-C) and break each standard into smaller specific learning objectives (SLOs). When all the SLOs are mastered in increments, they think students should be able to achieve the broader standards.

N and M plan for teaching by organizing the SLOs under each standard to show how their students will meet the standard if they are able to exhibit the learning outcomes in the SLOs. For the sake of brevity, we omit SLOs that will not be assessed as part of this case study, and show only those SLOs when their assessment is showcased here. N and M's overall plan represents the standards comprehensively, but the particular sequences of Stage 1 and 2 depicted here are more limited in focus. This is as it should be, given their understanding that their special needs and English language learner students learn best when they have very specific targets.

Specific Learning Objectives to Be Assessed in This Unit

1. Given a system of linear equations, the student will be able to identify the solution as a coordinate pair. (Standard 8.EE.8.A)
2. After identifying the solution to a system of linear equations, the student will be able to justify that the solution simultaneously satisfies both linear equations of the system. (Standard 8.EE.8.A)
3. Given a real-world mathematical problem, the student will be able to graph a system of linear equations. (Standard 8.EE.8.C)

4. Given a real-world mathematical problem, the student will be able to represent each real-world scenario as a linear equation. (Standard 8.EE.8.C)
5. Using the solution of a system of linear equations in a real-world world, the student will be able to interpret the solution by explaining the meaning of the ordered pair in context. (Standard 8.EE.8.C)
6. Given a system of linear equations, the student will be able to solve the system and justify the answer using multiple pieces of evidence from different mathematical methods. (Standard 8.EE.8.C)
7. Given a real-world mathematical problem, the student will be able to use different methods to solve the system, based on the context of the problem. (Standard 8.EE.8.C)
8. Given a real-world mathematical problem with multiple representations (graph, description, and table), the student will be able to compare the rate of change. (Standard 8.EE.8.C)

Call-Outs on the Four-Stage CA:SRL Framework in N and M's Stage 1, Planning the "What" of Assessment
☞ N and M include a standard about real-world applications in their assessment planning, which is consistent with a classroom culture that develops motivation and meaningful goal orientation about learning, not only achievement.
☞ The SLOs are stated in terms of the three components of *condition*, *audience*, and *performance*, as presented in Chapter 2.
☞ When N and M break standards down into learning chunks or critical steps, they delineate a learning progression.
☞ N and M's selection of which SLOs are to be covered in this, the first iteration through the four stages in CA related to these standards, is guided by their knowledge of their students' needs (finely-grained steps) and their orientation toward real-world applications.

Pre-assessment

N and M's prior teaching of middle-school algebra alerts them to watch out for a couple of misconceptions and instances of incomplete knowledge that are often demonstrated by students. Students with limited prior knowledge may be familiar with using x or y to represent an unknown, but need assistance to solve an equation with an unknown. Also, some students may have had exposure to solving equations with one unknown, but not to graphing equations, or vice versa. Their pre-assessment questions are at different degrees of difficulty to identify where students' prior knowledge. They decide to focus pre-assessment on the SLOs under Standard 8.EE.8.A. Their rationale is that this standard is the building block to meet the other standards on systems of linear equations.

N and M design a pre-assessment task with 12 constructed-response supply-type items. Because this is an ICT class, the pre-assessment is conducted in "stations"—this allows students with IEPs to verbally explain their reasoning to Mr. M. Figure 12.1 shows two pre-assessment items. Task 1 is intended to see whether students have prior knowledge about obtaining ordered pairs for equations, without solving the system of equations. Task 2 is intended to see whether students can graph equations and find the ordered pair by ascertaining the interaction point between the two lines.

Task 1

Directions: Complete each table using the given equations. Circle the ordered pair that satisfies both equations.

Table 1: $y = 2x + 10$	
x	y
1	
2	
3	
4	
5	
6	
7	

Table 2: $y = 5x - 11$	
x	y
1	
2	
3	
4	
5	
6	
7	

What have you noticed about the values of y in Table 1 and Table 2? Explain your observation.

Task 2

Directions: Graph both equations on the coordinate plane and find the point of intersection.

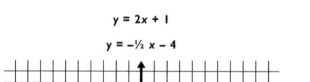

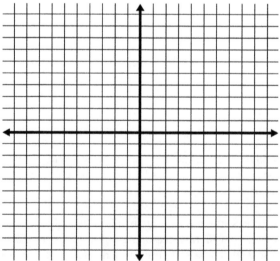

Figure 12.1 Pre-assessment Tasks

N and M note two things in their analysis of the pre-assessment results. First, a common error is that many students provide a solution for only one equation. They apparently do not hold the concept of two equations as a system, which requires them to work simultaneously on the equations to find the solution; they stop working after they find a solution that satisfies one equation and do not check that their solution works for the other equation. A related and common misconception they observe during the pre-assessment is that some students think the answer is only one number, rather than a coordinate pair (x, y) that satisfies both equations simultaneously.

To address these conceptual gaps, N and M first modify their unit plan to incorporate the use of substitution to check solutions with both equations more frequently than they had originally planned. They hope that by frequently self-monitoring and self-assessing, students will learn to recognize their own errors. To address the second misconception, they also add an SLO on graphing single lines, so that students who have not completely understood coordinate pairs in equations can visualize that only equations with two variables make a line. From there they can proceed to graphing two lines on the same grid, and then showing their point of intersection. Graphs enable students to visualize a simultaneous solution to two equations as a point where two lines intersect.

Call-Outs on the CA:SRL Framework in N and M's Stage 1, Pre-assessment
☞ N and M were selective in their pre-assessment design in terms of the SLOs they covered. They pre-assessed SLOs under the first standard only, because these SLOs represented the first steps along the learning progression.
☞ N and M chose their pre-assessment method because they were more interested in misconceptions than attitude.
☞ N and M differentiated their pre-assessment method to give special needs students an option for verbal explanation.
☞ N and M made changes to their instructional plans, adding a foundational SLO in response to pre-assessment results.
☞ One of N and M's changes to instructional planning involved student self-monitoring of performance (checking by substitution).

Stage 2: Instruction and Performance

Based on the pre-assessment results, N and M decide to narrow down the original list of SLOs to those they consider particularly important to teach and assess under standards 8.EE.8.A and 8.EE.8.C, as we have listed above. They decide to save Standard 8.EE.8.B entirely for a later unit of instruction, which will let them cycle back and refresh students on the material covered in this unit.

At the beginning of instruction in this unit, students work in homogeneous pairs to practice writing and solving equations, and graphing lines to find the ordered pairs. The teachers circulate to informally check with pairs of students about their understanding of the concepts and graphing skills. After two class periods of structured instruction and practice, N and M administer an assessment task. They construct two similar assessment tasks for this first iteration of assessment with instruction. Each task is intended to measure the same standard, 8.EE.8.C, but with different levels of scaffolding and difficulty. Given the wide spread of performance levels in the class, the teachers want to ensure that all students have an appropriate entry point to demonstrate their learning of this content. Students with special needs have a differentiated version that gives more scaffolding to write the pair of equations to be solved. A number of the English language learner students also receive the less difficult version of the task, which has slightly less reading. Students who have shown on the pre-assessment and during the teachers' table questioning that they are ready for greater challenge receive a more difficult task. Also, two students with learning disabilities have the questions read aloud to them and receive extended time to complete the tasks.

Once students finish the task, they complete a self-assessment survey (see Figure 12.2, adapted from Heritage, 2013). The self-assessment survey engages them in reflecting on their performance and progress, and allows teachers to monitor students' understanding. Students will refer back to this self-assessment throughout the unit, and use it to monitor their own progress, with additional SLOs as they are introduced by the teachers.

Learning Objective	Stu 1	Stu 2	Stu 3	Stu 4	Mean	Class Mean
1. I can identify the solution as a coordinate pair, which is the point of intersection on a graph.	5	5	4	5	4.75	4.16
2. I can prove that the solution satisfies both equations by checking my work.	4	5	3	4	4	3.68
3. I can accurately graph a system of linear equations to find the solution.	5	5	3	5	4.5	4.04
4. I can write a linear equation in slope-intercept form to represent a real-world problem.	4	5	4	5	4.5	3.68
5. I can explain the meaning of the solution in the context of the real-world problem the solution to a system of linear equations.	3	5	3	4	3.75	3.52
6. I can justify my solution using multiple piece of evidence.	5	5	4	4	4.5	3.78
7. I can solve the system of equation using different methods.	4	5	4	4	4.25	3.96
8. I can compare the rate of change of a system of linear equations.	4	5	5	4	4.5	3.96
Mean	4.25	5	3.75	4.38	4.34	3.85

Figure 12.2 Self-Assessment Data for Round 1

Mathematics Case Study 205

More Call-Outs on the CA:SRL Framework in N and M's Stage 2
☞ Assessments are integrated with peer-group learning.
☞ Assessments involve interactions with peers (task work) and interaction with teachers (questioning).
☞ Teachers aggregate student self-ratings to look for patterns in students' perceptions.

After students render their self-assessment, the class convenes for a whole-group discussion. Students volunteer to explain to the entire class how they solved the task they were given. N and M then collect all the students' task work and self-assessments. They analyze the results together, first by comparing the individual responses on the mathematics tasks to the keyed (correct) responses, and making informal, qualitative interpretations of student explanations. They enter the self-assessment ratings on a spreadsheet so they can quantify the results easily.

In a series of figures, you can see examples of the work of four students, each one followed by the teachers' interpretations of the work sample and their feedback to the student. N and M's feedback questions are mostly stated in ways that are not simply corrective, but elaborative, to encourage a student to probe more deeply into their own thinking, with recap, scaffold, and exemplify prompts (see Chapter 4). Furthermore, N and M provide an overall summary to indicate which learning outcomes each student is close to or far from meeting. In their regular teaching practice, N and M provide this level of extensive feedback to each student in the class selectively, not every single day, not on each and every assessment, and not always to every student. But every student is given detailed feedback at least weekly.

Aimee

Aimee is a student with a specific learning disability and has shown misconceptions and learning gaps in the pre-assessment results and the assessment obtained by their teachers in prior units. Figure 12.3 shows Aimee's work on the high-scaffolded task of comparing rates between two taxi companies, along with teacher feedback; we will discuss her work and teacher feedback separately, below.

N and M's Interpretations of Aimee's Work

Aimee accurately wrote linear equations to represent the information presented in the table. In addition, for both equations in the task (A), she graphed the *y*-intercept correctly. She found the point of intersection and wrote it as a coordinate pair. However, she wrote the coordinate pair as (1, 10). This is incorrect, as the *x*-axis scale is increasing by units of two. The solution should have been (2, 10). There is an inconsistency in Aimee's answers: she graphed the correct solution, but labeled it incorrectly. Her teachers aren't sure whether she graphed the slope of each equation correctly or graphed it correctly by chance. Aimee did not explain the solution in relation to the context of the problem; she only stated in writing that the two lines intersect at (1, 10). This explanation does not provide any interpretation of the meaning of the solution. Her solution would mean that after one mile, both taxi companies charge $10, but her teachers can't tell if that's the interpretation she intends. Although Aimee has an IEP, she did not provide verbal explanations to Mr. M. Without any further explanation, N and M

Task (Lower Level Students):

Directions: Find the solution for each system of linear equations using the graph. Check your work to make sure that the solution simultaneously satisfies both equations.

The table shows the cost of two taxi companies

	Initial Fee	Cost per mile
Taxi Company A	$2	$4
Taxi Company B	$6	$2

Part A: Represent the number of miles in x and the total fee in y.

Write a linear equation to represent Taxi Company A: ____$y = 4x + 2$____

Write a linear equation to represent Taxi Company B: ____$y = 2x + 6$____

Part B: Graphing both linear equations and find the solution or point of intersection.

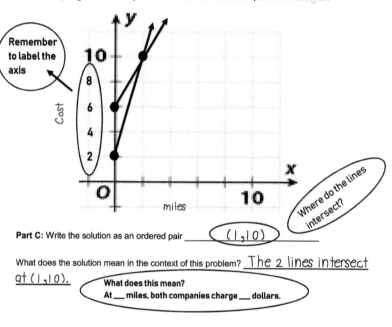

Part C: Write the solution as an ordered pair ____(1, 10)____

What does the solution mean in the context of this problem? ____The 2 lines intersect at (1, 10).____

What does this mean?
At __ miles, both companies charge __ dollars.

Figure 12.3 Aimee's Work on a Highly Scaffolded Task, With Feedback

could not interpret the extent to which Aimee had the conceptual understanding to coordinate points in relation to two variables. This is an area where Mr. N needs to have a conversation with Aimee, and he makes a note of it.

N and M's Feedback to Aimee

Ms. N gives feedback directly on Aimee's worksheet, as well as a summary of strengths and weaknesses. Ms. N. is very explicit and uses different prompts in her feedback to Aimee. For example, she uses a recap prompt by writing, "remember to label the axis." As scaffolding, Ms. N shows the correct units on both the *x*- and *y*-axis by putting in 2 and 4, but leaves out

6 and 8 to see whether Aimee will be able to figure out correct missing increments. She asks in writing in the margins, "What should the numbers be in those two blanks on the *y*-axis? What numbers should go into these four blanks on the *x*-axis?" Since Aimee works with Mr. M one-on-one, Mr. M. asks Aimee to provide oral explanations of her thinking. For example, Mr. M asks probing questions on Aimee's solution to Part C of the task, "Where do the lines intersect?" Aimee responds, "The two lines intersect at (1,10)." Mr. M follows up with a probing question of "What does this (1, 10) mean? Can you explain (1, 10) in terms of Taxi Company A and Taxi Company B?"

Roddy

Roddy is a general education student in N and M's class who was given the high-scaffolded task based on his pre-assessment work and the observations of N and M as the students worked in pairs. Roddy's work is shown in Figure 12.4; the problem to be solved is the same as that presented in Figure 12.3.

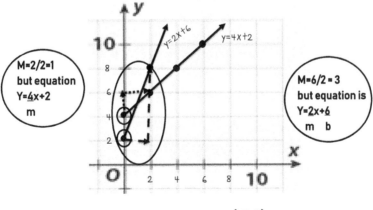

Figure 12.4 Roddy's Work on a Highly Scaffolded Task, With Feedback

N and M's Interpretations of Roddy's Work

Roddy showed he was able to write linear equations to represent a problem from information given in a table. However, when he graphed his equations, he drew the lines incorrectly. N and M infer from his work that he probably took the value that should be the slope in the first equation ($y = 4x + 2$, slope = 4) and graphed 4 as the y-intercept instead. Roddy made the same mistake in graphing the equation $y = 2x + 6$. N and M interpreted this to mean that Roddy did not understand the relationship between miles and total cost in the "Taxi Company" question.

They also inferred from the evidence in Part C that Roddy recognized that the y-axis was increasing by two at each tick mark, but did not recognize or forgot that he had also labeled the x-axis to increase by two at each tick mark. Thus, it looked like Roddy was attempting to graphing a slope of 6 (based on misunderstanding the y-intercept for the slope), but made the additional error of incorrectly identifying the units, and graphed a slope of 3 (6 units/2 units = 3). Roddy made the same mistake graphing his second equation, again on topic of his confusion between the intercept and the slope. Finally, Roddy identified the solution as $(0.5, 5)$. This was correct according to Roddy's last step, since as the two lines intersect at that point, but ultimately the wrong solution to the problem, because the graph was incorrectly depicted. However, based on the work and according to the graph, the solution is a reasonable one and N and M infer that Roddy understands the concept of the solution as a point of intersection.

N and M's Feedback to Roddy

N and M provide individual feedback to Roddy by circling (error-flagging) the mistakes that he made on the units of y-axis. In addition, N and M provide examples of how slope can be calculated based on the graph, and how the slope can be identified from the equation. Although the directions of this task Part C did not ask students to verify their solutions using another method, N and M ask Roddy to do so, to help him think of another way to solve the question and to be self-reflective when doing math problems.

Maura

Maura is a general education student who takes the less-scaffolded task, comparing rates among three "Cell Phone Plans" (see Figure 12.5). She is generally higher-performing in mathematics, based on their pre-assessment results and prior math performance in N and M's class.

N and M's Interpretations of Maura's Work

N and M observe that Maura accurately wrote a system of linear equations to represent the data in the problem. She correctly labeled the axes, scaled the units, and identified the slope and the y-intercept for both equations. However, her graph of the equations was inaccurate. N and M discuss this and decide that the student had mixed up the two equations, $y = 40x + 100$ and $y = 30x + 150$. On the equation, $y = 40x + 100$, Maura correctly placed the y-intercept at 100, but graphed the linear equation with a slope of 30, which is the slope of the other line. On the equation $y = 30x + 150$, she placed the y-intercept correctly, but graphed the slope of the other line, 40. Therefore, the lines on her graph did not have a point of intersection. Because the lines did not intersect, the student determined that there was no solution to the system.

Despite the incorrect solution by graphing, Maura was able to answer part B of the task correctly by using substitution to compare the two cell phone plans. However, the task required Maura to justify her answer using two pieces of evidence, and her two pieces of evidence were contradictory. N and M note that Maura did not refer to the graph at all when providing her justification; instead, she only used one piece of evidence. When asked to compare the two plans to the third plan (part C of the question), Maura accurately wrote a linear equation from a table and used this equation to compare the rate of change (slope) of all three linear equations.

Task: Higher Level to Extend Thinking

Use the graph and the space provided below to answer all parts of the question.

You are deciding on a new cell phone plan. Company 1 charges $100 for a phone and $40 per month. Company 2 charges $150 for a phone and $30 per month.

Part A:

In how many months will the total cost of both options be the same? no solution
What will be the cost? no solution

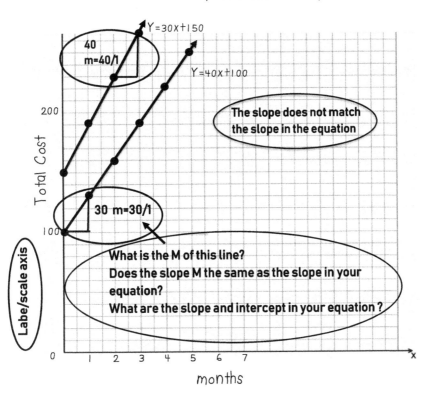

Figure 12.5 Maura's Work on a Less-Scaffolded Task, With Feedback

210 Section 3 Chapter 12

Part B: You plan on canceling your cell phone service after **7 months** because you are moving. Which is the cheaper cell phone option? Explain and justify your answer using at least two pieces of evidence.

Company 2 would be cheaper for 7 months. It would cost $360. Company 1 would cost $380 which is more expensive than $360.

Use evidence from the graph to justify your answer.

Company 1
$y=40(7)+100$
$y=280+100$
$y=380$

Company 2
$y=30(7)+150$
$y=210+150$
$y=360$
cheaper

Part C: You recently heard about a new company, Company 3. The rates of Company 3 are shown in the table below.

Month	Cost
4	280
7	340

$340-280/7-4 = 60/3 = 20$
$y=20x+b$
$280=20(4)+b$ $y=20x+200$
$280=80+b$
$200=b$

Of all 3 companies, which company has the greatest rate of change? Why? *Company 1 has the greatest rate of change. Company 1 has a slope of 40. Company 2 has a slope of 30 and Company 3 has a slope of 20.*

Can you clarify what you mean are greatest rate of change? 40 vs. 30 vs. 20 means of slope?

Figure 12.5 Continued

N and M's Feedback to Maura

N and M provide feedback to Maura by error-flagging and circling errors on the *y*-axis. N and M also drew lines to show how the "rise" and "run" of both slopes would not equal the slope in the student's equations. They used scaffolding questions by asking Maura, "Based on the graph, what is M of this line? Does the slope M have the same value as the slope in your equation? What are the slopes and intercepts in your two equations?" For this student, N and M did not provide answers as feedback; instead, they provided questions so that Maura could move forward and narrow the learning gap.

Juan

Juan is an English language learner student who takes the more difficult, less-scaffolded task. Juan's work is shown in Figure 12.6; the problem to be solved is the same as in Figure 12.5.

N and M's Interpretations of Juan's Work

Juan wrote the two equations correctly to reflect the data provided in the problem. He was able to graph the two equations correctly to show an intersection between the two lines. For part B of the question, he referred to the linear equation ($y = 40x + 100$), rather than the name of the company that the linear equation represents (Company 1), and explained that one company was cheaper because the line was lower than the other one in the graph. While this is correct, N and M don't consider that this response shows full mastery of the SLOs. Juan did not clarify where the line was "lower" on the graph and what the line being "lower" meant. In addition, Juan did not use two pieces of evidence to justify he answer, as the task required. There was no evidence of substitution or use of another method to complete that part of the task. For part C of the question, Juan found the rate of change for Company 3, then compared the three cell phone companies by citing the rate of change for the three companies.

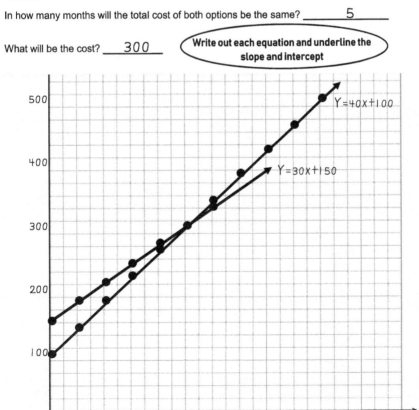

Figure 12.6 Juan's Work on a Less-Scaffolded Task, With Feedback

212 Section 3 Chapter 12

Part B: You plan on canceling your cell phone service after **7 months** because you are moving. Which is the cheaper cell phone option? Explain and justify your answer using at least two pieces of evidence.

$y=30x+150$ would be cheaper for 7 months because the line is (lower) then $y=40x+100$ on the graph. ?

> How many pieces of evidence do you need to justify your answer

> Do you remember another method we talked about earlier this week?

Part C: You recently heard about a new company, Company 3. The rates of Company 3 are shown in the table below.

Month	Cost
4	280
7	340

$280-340/4-7 = -60/-3 = 20$

Of all 3 companies, which company has the greatest rate of change? Why? Company 1 because 40 is higher than 30 and 20.

> What does 20, 30, and 40 represent?

Figure 12.6 Continued

N and M's Feedback to Juan

Based on the evidence of Juan's work, N and M interpret his grasp of understanding of the concepts in this unit. N and M are very explicit with their feedback and use recap prompts in their feedback to Juan. For example, N and M write, "Write out each equation and circle the slope and intercept" N and M also use recap questions to cue Juan, "So you remember another method we talked about earlier this week to solve a similar question?" and "Read the directions again. How many pieces of evidence do you need to justify your answer?" N and M also use example prompts to cue Juan, "Why don't you first say what 20, 30, and 40 represent before you say what the answer is?"

N and M's Interpretations of Whole-Class Trends in Performance

N and M also aggregate their observations into a summary of evidence for the whole class. They find five trends in class performance: there seems to be overall confusion between slope and y-intercept when graphing. This gap was particularly apparent with most of the lower-performing students; when graphing the equations, four students (out of 10) flipped the numerals of slope and y-intercept. A second problem was graphing with scale. Nine of the 10 lower-performing students incorrectly graphed the system of linear equations because they miscounted the units on the axes which were not pre-labeled on the graph. Third, as a class, students did not check their solution through the substitution method. N and M estimate that only about one-third of the class checked whether their solution was correct by using substitution. Fourth, both lower- and higher-performing students had difficulty explaining the solution. Only two of the 10 lower-performing students could explain the solution to the system of linear equations in relation to the context of the problem. Most students identified that the solution was the point of intersection. While this was true, it did not answer the question. Although higher-performing students could explain their solutions and provide their reasoning, it was difficult for the class to understand the "why" of their reasons. Many students did not or could not correctly interpret the coordinate points in relation to the problem scenario. Fifth, many of those students who took the more difficult task did not use multiple sources of evidence to justify their solution, although they were asked to do so. It seemed that students struggled to see that the two different mathematical methods were related and could be used together to support and strengthen their explanations.

From this assessment, N and M learn that providing explanations to a solution is the most difficult task for the students in this class. Further, it is clear that students are having difficulty with the concepts of slope and intercept. When slope and intercept were represented two different forms (graphic and equation), students did not fluidly move between forms.

N and M also analyze the data from the self-assessment that they had recorded on their spreadsheet (refer back to Figure 12.2), and looked at the general tendency in confidence among the class. Based on the mean (arithmetic average) value, the teachers note that as a class, students felt least confident about the learning outcome "I can explain the meaning of the solution in the context of the real-word problem and the solution to a system of linear equations," as compared to the other outcomes listed on the self-assessment. They also calculate a total "confidence" score, where they note that confidence, or lack thereof, was distributed widely throughout the class and was not particularly associated with performance level, special needs, or language status.

Call-Outs on the CA:SRL Framework in N and M's Stage 2 Feedback

☞ The feedback to students included elements of error-flagging, elaborating, and providing examples, strategies, and questions prompts to guide students about their next course of actions (Shute, 2008).

☞ N and M differentiate feedback for the two lower-performing students according their needs and level of understanding.

Second Iteration of Assessment for Learning

From these results, N and M decide to target the five gaps in the next iteration of instruction and assessment. With this iteration, N and M decide that all the students should solve the same task to measure four of the same SLOs listed in the first iteration of assessment and added two SLOs for the second iteration. For students with special needs, the questions and the directions are read to them, and Mr. M interacts with students to assist them in completing the task. In addition, for a couple of students with special needs, the teachers work with them again on graphing, before the students attempt to solve the system of equations algebraically. Also, students are given back a new page of the same self-assessment surveys they completed on the first iteration of assessment, with some new SLOs, to complete afresh. Then the teachers return to the students their prior ratings of confidence, so students can compare and see changes as they have had more opportunity to learn. N and M clip together all the confidence surveys completed throughout the unit, so there is a long-term record of student self-perceptions.

Victor

Victor is a student with special needs and a lower performance in the class. Mr. M reads the questions to Victor to make sure he understands the questions; in addition, Victor has extended time to work on his math assessments. The problem and Victor's work are shown in Figure 12.7.

N and M's Interpretations of Victor's Work

As students typically do in this unit on equations, Victor wrote a system of linear equations to represent the real-world mathematical problem he was given. He wrote equations ($y = 100 +$

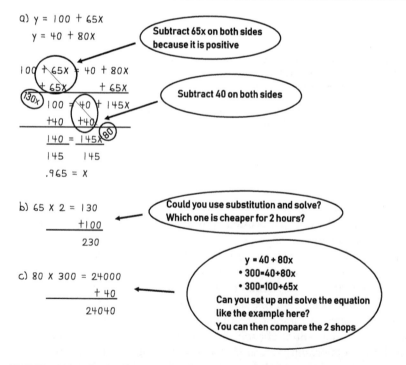

Figure 12.7 Targeting Gaps in Victor's Work

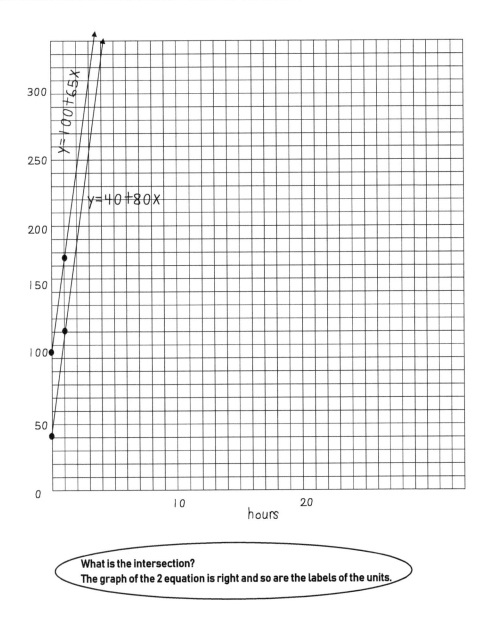

Figure 12.7 Continued

65x and y = 40 + 80x), both of which are mathematically correct based on the problem and correctly set up the problem to solve algebraically (100 + 65x = 40 + 80x). Then he attempted to apply the additive inverse to move the variable terms to one side, adding 65x to both sides of the equation. However, because 65x is positive in the original equation, the student should have subtracted 65x on both sides. As a result of this error, the student simplified the equation to 100 = 40 + 145x. Next, Victor tried to apply the additive inverse to move the terms to one side of the equation. Again, Victor incorrectly applied the additive inverse, adding 40 on both sides of the equation. Like 65x, 40 is also positive. To correctly apply the additive inverse, the student should have subtracted by 40 on both sides of the equation.

Based on the work Victor showed, N and M infer that he simplified the equation to $140 = 145x$ and solved for the variable by dividing by the coefficient (145) on both sides. He found that $x = .965$. In terms of Part A of the task, Victor stopped at this point. He did not go on to solve for the value of y or identify the solution of the system of linear equations as a coordinate pair.

In Part B, Victor found the correct answer by multiplying 65 and 2 and then adding 100. While he didn't show the substitution written as an equation, his work was correct. In Part C, Victor used the information from the other equation to multiply 80 and 300, and then he added 40. Victor failed to recognize that he was supposed to substitute for the dependent variable.

N and M's Feedback to Victor

N and M notice that Victor was able to write a system of linear questions, and to set both equations equal (balance) to each other to solve algebraically. On Victor's work, N and M provide example prompts: "You set the equations up correctly; then you subtract $65x$ instead of adding $65x$." The teacher modeled to the student by error-flagging and showing the step of the procedure by indicating "Subtract 40 on both sides" and providing a recap prompt: "Remember to use substitution to solve Part B so you can know which repair shop is cheaper."

Based on the evidence of Part C, the student attempted to set up an equation to solve x but was unsuccessful at that time. N and M then modeled for the student by setting up and solving the equation, and provided scaffolding prompts, by stating "Can you set up and solve the other equation like the example here? Then you can compare which shop is cheaper." Much of the feedback for Victor was also verbally delivered by Mr. M.

Several students, including Victor, were still having difficulty with graphing. Thus, the teachers had some individual students do an immediate follow-up assessment by asking them to graph the equations in this task. In this way, assessment was differentiated. Victor's case illustrates both differentiated assessment and differentiated feedback. Mr. M asked Victor to first label the units on the x- and y-axis before graphing the two equations by finding coordinate points.

Victor was able to correctly label the axis and units, as well as the graph. Although Victor graphed the equations correctly, however, it was difficult to visually identify the intersection between the two lines to locate the solution as a coordinate pair. N and M wrote on Victor's graph, "Where is the intersection?" N and M also provided verification feedback to let Victor know that the graph and unit labels were correct. He indicated to the teachers that the intersection was hard to discern from the graph, and he needed to go back and solve the equations algebraically. The teachers noted that on Victor's self-assessment survey, Victor rated his confidence low on the self-assessment item 4 "I can explain the meaning of the solution in the context of the real-world problem," and he was less confident about this skill than about any other.

Bettany

Bettany provides a second example. She is a student in general education with a high level of math performance. Her work is presented in Figure 12.8.

N and M's Interpretations of Bettany's Work

Bettany's work in Part A shows she can write a system of linear questions, set up both equations equal (balance) to each other, apply the additive inverse, and solve the question algebraically. In Part B, she found the correct answer by multiplying 65 and 2 and then adding 100 to find the solution for one equation. Similarly, she was able to find the solution by multiplying

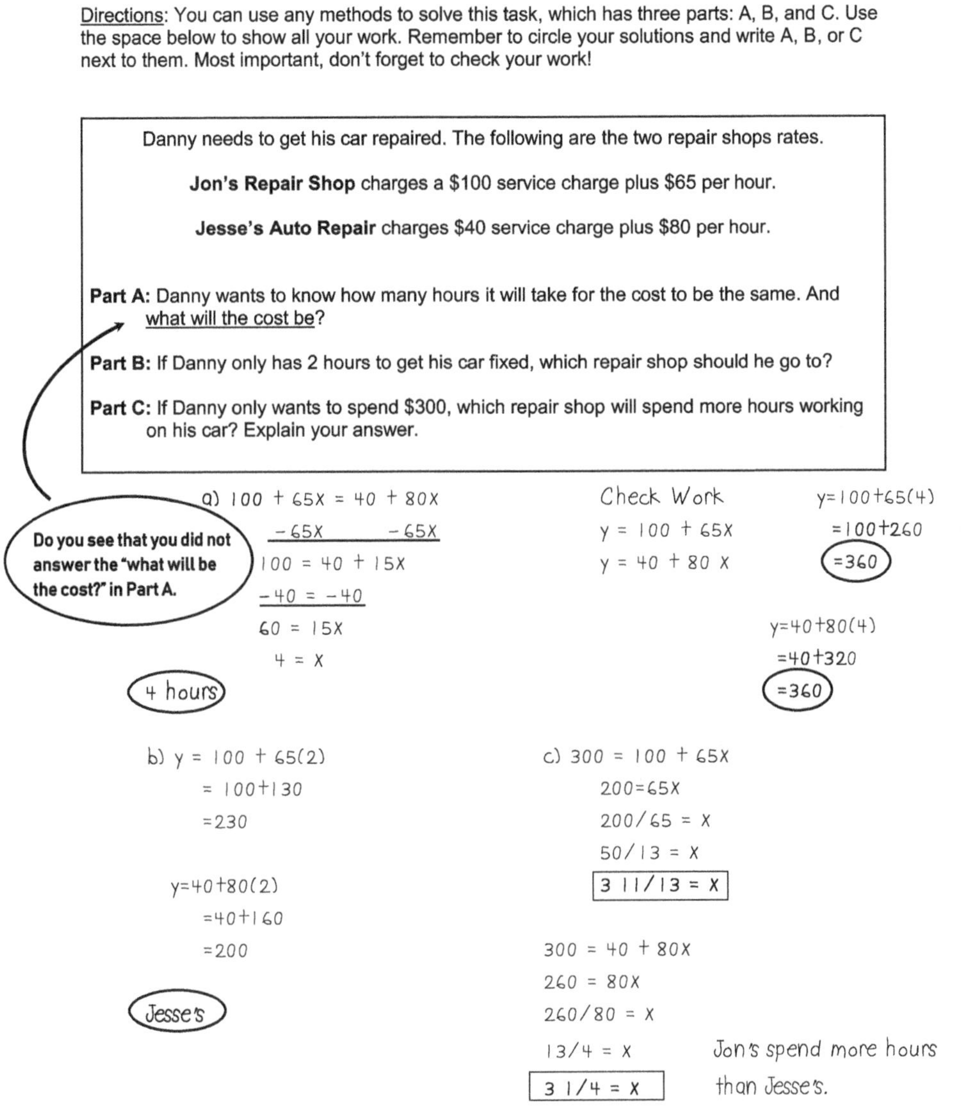

Directions: You can use any methods to solve this task, which has three parts: A, B, and C. Use the space below to show all your work. Remember to circle your solutions and write A, B, or C next to them. Most important, don't forget to check your work!

Danny needs to get his car repaired. The following are the two repair shops rates.

Jon's Repair Shop charges a $100 service charge plus $65 per hour.

Jesse's Auto Repair charges $40 service charge plus $80 per hour.

Part A: Danny wants to know how many hours it will take for the cost to be the same. And what will the cost be?

Part B: If Danny only has 2 hours to get his car fixed, which repair shop should he go to?

Part C: If Danny only wants to spend $300, which repair shop will spend more hours working on his car? Explain your answer.

Do you see that you did not answer the "what will be the cost?" in Part A.

a) $100 + 65x = 40 + 80x$
$\quad\quad -65x \quad\quad\quad -65x$
$100 = 40 + 15x$
$\quad -40 = -40$
$\quad 60 = 15x$
$\quad\quad 4 = x$

(4 hours)

Check Work
$y = 100 + 65x$
$y = 40 + 80x$

$y = 100 + 65(4)$
$= 100 + 260$
($= 360$)

$y = 40 + 80(4)$
$= 40 + 320$
($= 360$)

b) $y = 100 + 65(2)$
$\quad = 100 + 130$
$\quad = 230$

$y = 40 + 80(2)$
$\quad = 40 + 160$
$\quad = 200$

(Jesse's)

c) $300 = 100 + 65x$
$\quad 200 = 65x$
$\quad 200/65 = x$
$\quad 50/13 = x$
$\boxed{3\ 11/13 = x}$

$300 = 40 + 80x$
$260 = 80x$
$260/80 = x$
$13/4 = x$
$\boxed{3\ 1/4 = x}$

Jon's spend more hours than Jesse's.

Figure 12.8 Targeting Gaps in Bettany's Work

---

80 and 2 and then adding 40 for the other equation. In Part C, Bettany was able to solve for x (hours) for each equation before making a comparison. She checked her work by substituting 4 in both equations to arrive at the same answer of 360. However, Bettany did not write on the paper to show that 360 was the solution to Part A of the question, "What will be the cost?"

N and M's Feedback to Bettany

In their feedback to Bettany, N and M noted that she was able to write linear equations, and accurately set up and solve a system of linear equations. N and M also indicated that she checked her work, but they posted a reminder prompt: "Did you forget to answer 'what will be the cost?' in Part A?"

For this mathematics task, the teachers decided beforehand that they would also conduct mini-conferences with a few particular students to gather in-depth information about their understanding. They prepare conference questions ahead of time as a reference point for speaking with individual students. The teachers particularly want to know how students explain and justify their solutions. Bettany is one of the students pre-selected for individual conferencing on this iteration. Ms. N holds a conference with Bettany to review her work. Because Bettany seemed to be approaching proficiency, Ms. N probes for any remaining learning gaps. The following is a transcript of an excerpt from the conference:

Ms. N: "Looking at your two answers to Part A_____, what is the relationship between the two answers?"

Bettany: "That is the y-value to the intersection, if I would have graphed the two equations." (Pause. Ms. N provides time for Bettany to think)

Bettany: "The co-ordinate pair is (4, 360)."

Ms. N: "Yes. Let's look at Part B. Why did you select Jesse's repair shop?"

Bettany: "Well, for two hours, Jesse's costs 230, and Jon's costs 200 and, Danny only has 2 hours to fix his car, 200 is less than 230. So that's a cheaper deal."

Ms. N: "Thank you. I just wanted to be sure you understand, and you do! Now let's look at Part C. Your answer indicates that Jon's spends more hours than Jesse's, so how do you know your solution is correct? How would you use another method to show that your answer is correct?"

Bettany: "3 and 11/13 hours is more than 3 and 1/4 hours. So that's one reason." (Pause. Ms. N provides time for Bettany to think)

Bettany: "If 300 is what Danny can spend on fixing his car, then he should try to get more hours. It just makes sense."

Noticing that Bettany is not independently arriving at the idea of checking by graphing, Ms. N suggests that she look back at the previous assessment task (the first Stage 2 iteration) for ideas. When Bettany sees her own graphing work, she recognizes that graphing is a way to check the correctness of a solution.

N and M's Interpretations of Whole-Class Trends After the Second Iteration

As before, N and M analyze their individual interpretations to look for whole-class trends. They notice that about 4 of 26 students still struggled to differentiate between the slope and the y-intercept from the way the task was described. Those students are still confused about the slope and the y-intercept. Through conversation with two of the students, N and M learn that in equations $y = 100 + 65x$ and $y = 40 + 80x$, the students thought the slopes were 100 and 40 because those were the first numbers that came first in each equation. The students have a misconception about the nature of a constant.

The same four students in the class were not yet able to set up a system of linear equations to solve algebraically in a way that would allow them to find an accurate solution. Students tried to use substitution to set up and solve the equations. Conversation with these students brings to light that they think they "had to substitute the whole expression." However, when they substituted, the students removed the variable from both equations and rewrote an equation such as $y = 65(40 + 80) + 100$. When asked what happened to variable x in the expression, the students respond that "because they were substituting, they did not need to include variable x." N and M note from these conversations with students that they do not understand why to use substitution.

For solving multistep equations with variables on both sides, about one-third of the class is still struggling. They struggle to identify and combine like terms, as well as apply the additive and multiplicative inverse. As for finding the solution as a coordinate pair, only a few are still struggling to identify a coordinate pair as the solution to the problem. The task did not ask for the "solution" in which the students had to write their answer as a coordinate pair. However, the task did ask for the solution in terms of the context of the real-world problem. In the context of this real-world problem, the students needed to find the coordinate pair solution to answer both parts of the question. Although the students could solve a problem with a system of linear equations when it was presented in the slope-intercept form, they are less able to manipulate the problem into this form algebraically.

About half of the class still need to work on checking by substitution. Many students incorrectly answered Part B and Part C of this task, which required them to take a given value from the question and substitute it for one of the variables (x and y). Using the equation in which they wrote, for example, $y = 100 + 65x$, students struggled to identify whether they should substitute the given value (2 hours in Part B) for x or for y. When asked why they substituted \$300 for the x in rather than for y, it seems evident that some students had memorized the procedure of solving for x and using substitution. Instead, to substitute correctly, they need to think about which variable corresponded to their solution, and whether it was the x or y variable.

As for explaining the meaning of the solution, many students need assistance to provide explanations for the solution in the context of the problem. For example, when Ms. N asks a student what the solution means in regard to Jon's and Jesse's auto shops, he says it is where the two linear equations would meet, and that point on the graph would be the solution. He interprets the solution only by explaining the algebraic result, not its implications in the scenario.

Based on this information, the teachers group students into three clusters: those who still do not understand how to identify the constant vs. the slope; those who cannot yet use algebra to put an equation in the slope-intercept form, and those who understand the basic concepts but cannot yet relate a solution to the real-world scenario. Each teacher works with these small groups in-depth, and provide worksheets for them to practice and check their answers among their peers by substitution. Each group is assessed using a task that includes all three types of problems at the different levels of complexity: explicit identification of the slope term and the intercept, regardless of where in an equation they are presented (e.g., $y = 200 - 2x$), when variables appeared on both sides of the equation (e.g., $150 - 3x = 2x + y$), and when they have to interpret their solution in terms of the real world.

Call-Outs on the Four-Stage CA:SRL Framework, N and M's Pre-assessment (Stage 1) and Instruction and Assessment (Stage 2)

☞ N and M developed a pre-assessment before teaching the unit to their class.

☞ N and M used pre-assessment results were used to revise SLOs.

☞ N and M's ensuing Stage 2 instruction and assessment included multiple iterations.

☞ N and M's assessments were aligned to their SLOs.

☞ N and M's assessments were differentiated for students who needed either low or high entry points, less or more linguistic complexity, and graphical representations.
☞ N and M interpreted student work to identify misconceptions.
☞ N and M's feedback at each iteration was individualized and differentiated.
☞ N and M's practice leads from non-interactive to interactive assessment.
☞ N and M took instructional actions in response to assessment at individual, whole-class level, and small-group levels.
☞ N and M gave opportunities for students to assess and re-assess their confidence in the material, allowing them to see growth.

We have given you a detailed look at a co-teaching classroom where Stage 1 pre-assessment feeds instructional planning, and multiple iterations of instruction and assessment take place at Stage 2. After the period covered in this case study, N and M continued to engage in additional iterations of instruction and assessment. After several iterations, N and M constructed a culminating assessment for students to demonstrate their accumulated learning in the unit. They used a "choice board" with three short performance assessments. There were tasks at different levels of difficulty. N and M prepared a rubric to rate work on each SLO that they could use across the tasks in that row, regardless of level of task difficulty. Students were required to perform a task from each row, but could choose the difficulty level, with guidance from N and M. When students completed this three-part performance assessment, N and M provided feedback using the rubrics and returned students' initial self-assessments to them for them to complete again, reflecting on their own growth. N and M entered the scores from the three-part Stage 3 performance assessment in the gradebook, and allowed students to choose which of the three performance assessments they would like to post as classroom artifacts to display and show their parents on Parent Night.

References

Heritage, M. (2013). *Formative assessment in practice: A process of inquiry and action.* Cambridge, MA: Harvard Education Press.

National Governors Association Center for Best Practices & Council of Chief State School Officers. (2010). *Common Core State Standards for mathematics: CCSS.Math.Content.8.EE.C.8.* Retrieved from www.corestandards.org/Math/Content/8/EE/#CCSS.Math.Content.8.EE.C.8

Shute, V. J. (2008). Focus on formative feedback. *Review of Educational Research, 78,* 153–189.

Index

Note: Page numbers in *italics* indicate figures and in **bold** indicate tables on the corresponding pages.

accommodations *see* special accommodations for testing
accountability tests 92–93
Adequate Yearly Progress (AYP) 142
analytic rubric 65, *67*, 72–73, 90, 107, 116
Andrade, H. 124
Arter, J. A. 151
assessment *for* learning (A*f*L) 2
assessment for learning and self-regulation 7–8
attribution 13, 41, 52
audience in SLOs 25
authenticity 61–62, 104
automated classroom response systems 147–148
automated scoring systems 109, *146*, 147, 149–150

Bandura, A. 30
Beers, K. 163
Bennett, R. E. 146, 147
bias: cultural 132, 141; minimization of, in interpretation and scoring 119–120, *120*; scoring 81, 83, 119–120, *120*
blended purposes of classroom assessment 2
blending methods in iterative assessment 53–54
Bloom's Cognitive Process Dimension 26
Boothroyd, R. A. 125
box-and-whisker plot 126, *126*
Bradbury, R. 114

carryover effect 120, 134
case studies 155–156; English language arts 157–178; mathematics 199–220; music 179–198
checklists 6, 11; pre-assessment *33–34*, 33–35
classroom assessment (CA): assessment informed by theory 7–9, *8*; blended purposes of 2; as contextualized, interactive, and evolving 3; evaluating and reducing error from subjective interpretations in

106–108, 107–109; fairness in (*see* fairness in assessment); formal (*see* formal assessment); as impactful, not just informational 3; objectives in understanding 3–4; reliability in (*see* reliability in assessment); self-regulated learning (SRL) and 1–2; as specialized field of study 2; technology in (*see* technology and technical quality); validity (*see* validity in assessment)
classroom assessment with self-regulated learning (CA:SRL) framework 5–6; case studies in (*see* case studies); as four-stage framework *8*, 8–9; interpretations and inferences from evidence 14–16; organizing principles 16–17; stage 1: SRL forethought and pre-assessment 9–10 (*see also* pre-assessment phase); stage 2: SRL performance within the cycle of learning, doing, and assessing 10–12 (*see also* learning and assessment cycle); stage 3: SRL performance and formal CA 12 (*see also* formal assessment); stage 4: summarizing assessment evidence 12–14 (*see also* summarizing performance); technology in (*see* technology and technical quality)
classroom conduct 83–84
clicker technology 147
cognitive processes, levels of 10–11
College Board 142
Collins, A. 129
Common Core State Standards (CCSS) 17, 22; mathematics 200; validity in assessments and 128–129
complex learning outcomes assessment 29, 57–58, 64
complex task evaluating and reducing error in 104
complex thinking, measurement of 29–30, *30*
composition of grades 88–91, **89–91**
condition in SLOs 25
confidentiality *139*

222 Index

consequences: of using large-scale assessment approaches results 136, *139*, 140; long-term academic 78; self- 11; social (of testing) 140–141, *142*
consistency 97
construct-relevant thinking processes 117–119, *118*
constructs 14, 16–17
continual assessment for improved learning 40–41
continuum of methods in iterative assessment *42*, 42–43
co-regulation 16
correlation coefficient 104
criterion-referenced testing (CRT) 92, 136–137
Cronbach, L. 140
Cronbach's alpha 106, 140
cumulative assessment *see* summarizing performance
curricular alignment 113
cut score 101
cycle of instruction and assessment for learning 12

day-to-day fluctuations as source of random error 98–101, *100–101*
decision-making and interactive feedback 15–16
demon effect 134
Depth of Knowledge (DOK) levels 26–27, *27*; formal assessment and 57–58, *58*, 63, *64*; multiple-choice items and 43, 46–47, *47*; open-ended questions and 28
design of pre-assessments 27–35
Differential Item Functioning (DIF) 134
differentiation 11, 37, 53, 113, 129, *142*, 151
difficulty index *69*
digital portfolios 151–152
direct-question format 28
discrimination index 48, 68–73, *69–70*
distribution *45*, 100–101, 104, 106, 121–122, *122–124*, 126, 137
"drop-from-the-sky" assessments 146
dropping of low scores 84
Du, Y. 124

Edulastic 150
effort, student 82–83
elaborative feedback 205
electronic gradebooks 88
English and multilingual language learners (ELL/MLLs) 40, 44; essay tasks for 64
English language arts case study: assessment methods in 163–172, *165–166, 168–172*; communicating results of 177–178, *178*; culminating and formal assessment 173–177,

174–176; frequent assessment embedded in instructional routines in 164, *165–166*; instruction in 162–163; iterations in 167–172; one-on-one reading conferences in 163–164; planning for assessment and instruction in 158–161, *162*; pre-assessment in 160–161, *161–162*; setting the scene for 157–158
equity: fair assessment for 141, *142*; as meeting of measurement of political philosophy 140
essay tasks 63–64, *64*; item analysis for *72*, 72–73; scoring rubrics for 65, *66–67*
Every Student Succeeds Act (ESSA) 92, 143
external feedback 8

fairness in assessment 131–132; classroom approaches for 137–139, *139*, 143; developing assessments for 132–136, *135*; fair processes and 136–139, *139*; in large-scale assessment 132–134, 136–137; supporting fair outcomes for all learners as goal of 140–143, *142*; technical quality and 134–136, *135*
feedback: defined 38; elaborative 205; external 8; giving students formal 73–76, *75*; interactive 15–16; music performance assessment with interactive 188–190; music performance final 196–197; peer 41; process versus outcome 38–39; self- 1, 8, 15, 74; verification *74*
"feed-forward" feedback 15
fixed mindset 13
forethought phase 9–10, 20; *see also* pre-assessment phase
formal assessment 12; in English language arts case study 173–177, *174–176*; essay tasks 63–64, *64*, 65, *66–67*; evidence from, place in stage 4 grading 82; giving formal feedback to students after 73–76, *75*; item analysis in 68–73; methods for 58–73; in music case study 191–197, *193–195*; performance assessment (PA) 58–63, *60–62*, 65, *66–67*; reasons for 56–57, *57*; scoring rubrics for 65, *66–67*; with technology 150–151; what is assessed in 57–58
formal feedback for students 73–76, *75*
formative assessment 2
Frederiksen, J. R. 129

GMAT 147
goal orientation 10
goals: setting of 9, 22, *34*, 34–35, 79; societal 95
Google Classroom 152
grade reporting 86–88, *87*
grades: composition of 88–91, **89–91**; cumulative test 89, **89**; for group work 81, **89**; homework 89, **89**; participation 59, 83,

85, 151; standards-based 86, 111; weighting of 88–91, **89–91**; zero 90, 138
GRE 147
growth mindset 13
guessing 29, *69*, 103, *110*

Hadwin, A. F. 16
Haertel, E. H. 63
halo effect 120, 134
Hattie, J. 74
help-seeking 41, 138
histograms 121
Hobson v. Hansen 141
holistic rubric 65, *66*

Individualized Education Programs (IEPs) 22, 40, 133; formal assessment and 62
Individualized Family Service Plans (IFSPs) 133
Individuals with Disabilities Education Act (IDEA) 133, 141
inferences 57, 63, *64*, 81, 116–117, *117*, *124*
instruction, assessment aligned with 113–117, *115*, *117*; in English language arts 162–163; in mathematics 203–213, *204–207*, *209–212*; in music 182–190, *184*, *186*
instructional responses 49, 54, *67*, 187–191
intentional learning 9
interactive assessment methods 42, *42*, 42–43, 49–51, *50*
interactive feedback and decision-making 15–16; in music case study 188–190
internal consistency 106
interpretive exercises *45*, 45–46
inter-rater reliability 109
interviews 42, 49–50, 54, 81, 119, 138
intrinsic motivation 83–84
item analysis: for items scored with rubrics *72*, 72–73; with multiple-choice items 68–72, *69–70*
item analysis in formal assessment 68
item bank 128, *146*, 150–152
item and task characteristics as source of random error 101–106, *102*, *105*
iterative assessment 39–41; as bedrock of practice 11; blending methods in 53–54; continuum of methods in *42*, 42–43; in English language arts case study 167–172; how to engage in 42–54; interactive methods in 49–51, *50*; for learning with technology 148–150; in mathematics case study 213–220, *214–215*, *217*; non-interactive selected-response methods in 43–49, *44–45*, *47–49*; self- and peer-assessment in *51–52*, 51–53, *54*

Kahoot! 148
Kane, M. T. 124

Khan Academy 142
KR-21 106
Krathwohl, D. R. 26

large-scale assessment: fairness in 132–134, 136–137, 141–143; inter-rater reliability in 109; reliability in 104–106, *105*; summarizing performance 91–93
learning and assessment cycle 10–12, 37–39, *38*; blending methods in 53–54; continual assessment in 40–41; continuum of methods in *42*, 42–43; evidence from, and stage 4 grading 81–82; how to engage in iterative assessment in 42–54; interactive methods in 49–51, *50*; non-interactive selected-response methods in 43–49, *44–45*, *47–49*; reasons for iterating assessment in 39–41; self- and peer assessment in *51–52*, 51–53, *54*; what to assess in stage 2 41–42
learning progressions 5, 155; fairness in assessment and 138; formal assessment and 62, 73; in mathematics 201, 203; multiple iterations of learning and assessment and 40, 43, 53–54; in music 180, 183; student prior knowledge and 26–27; technology in assessment and 147; validity in assessment and 122
left-skewed distribution 121–122, *122*
leniency, scoring 65
Likert-scale items 191
Limited English Proficient (LEP) Accommodation Plan 133
low-entry assessment methods 29, *29*

Mager, R. F. 25, 114
Martian Chronicles, The 114
mastery 84, 198; scoring reliability and 109; specific learning objectives for 25, 211; technology and 148
mathematics case study: instructional unit and learning standards in 199–201; instruction and performance in 203–213, *204–207*, *209–212*; pre-assessment in 201–203, *202*; second iteration of assessment for learning in 213–220, *214–215*, *217*
McMorris, R. F. 125
mean *44–45*, 104, *122–123*, 126
measurement error 97–98
median *45*, 122–123, 126, *122–123*
Messick, S. 140
metacognition 7
metacognitive control 16
meta-level cognitive processes 10–11
mindset of intelligence 13
minimization of bias in interpretation and scoring 119–120, *120*
monitoring 1, 5, 8, 10, 152; metacognitive 11; self- 159–160, 163–164, 203

224 Index

Moss, P. A. 124
motivational beliefs 9
multilingual language learners (MLLs) 28, 44
multiple baselines 99
multiple-choice (M-C) items 43–49, *44–45*,
  47–49; blending with other methods 54;
  item analysis with 68–72, *69–70*; technology
  and 150
multiple sources, basing assessment
  interpretations on evidence from 120–124,
  122–124
music case study: feedback on final
  performance assessment in 196–197; formal
  assessment and self-assessment in 191–197,
  193–195; instruction and assessment in
  182–190, *184, 186*; non-interactive supply-
  type task with reflection in 183–187, *184,
  186*; performance assessment with interactive
  feedback in 188–190; pre-assessment
  in *181*, 181–182; summary perceptions
  and reporting in *197*, 197–198; unit of
  instruction in 179–182, *181*

Narens, L. 10, 37
National Assessment of Educational Progress
  (NAEP) 92, 147, 150
National Center for Fair and Open Testing
  (FairTest) 141
National Core Music Standards 179–180
"Nation's Report Card" 92–93
Nelson, T. O. 10, 37
New York State Standards 22–23, *23*
No Child Left Behind (NCLB) 142, 143
non-interactive assessment methods 42, *42*,
  42–43; in music case study 183–187, *184,
  186*; selected-response methods 43–49,
  44–45, 47–49
non-reactive measurement 3
norm-referenced testing (NRT) 92, 136–137

objectives, assessment aligned with 113–117,
  115, 117
object-level cognitive processes 10–11
one-on-one reading conferences 163–164
open-ended questions 28–30, *28–30*
operationalizing learning 17, 31
opportunity to learn 54, 61, 72, 74, 143, 214
outcome expectancies 10; fairness and
  140–143, *142*
outcome feedback 38–39
overall performance *see* summarizing
  performance

parallel forms 104–105
participation grades 59, 83, *85*, 151
Pearson Education 150
peer assessment and feedback 41, *51–52*,
  51–53, *54*

PEG Writing 149–150
performance assessment (PA) 58–63, *60–62*;
  evaluating and reducing error in 104; with
  interactive feedback in music case study
  188–190; item analysis for *72*, 72–73;
  scoring rubrics for 65, *66–67*
performance in SLOs 25
performance phase 9, 10–12; formal
  assessment in 12
person x task interaction 102–104, 110
portfolios, digital 151–152
Post-It Reflection Log 173, *174–176*
pre-assessment phase 9–10; checklists in
  33–34, 33–35; design tools for 27–35;
  English language arts case study 160–161,
  161–162; evidence from, in stage 4 grading
  81; external resources for design in 35;
  mathematics case study 201–203, *202*;
  music case study *181*, 181–182; open-
  ended questions in 28–30, *28–30*; rating
  scales 30–32, *32*; reasons for 20–22;
  specific learning objective (SLOs) in 24–27;
  technology in 147–148; what is assessed in
  22–27, *23–24, 26–27*; who and when to
  assess in 20
process feedback 38

question and statement prompts 49–50, *50*
questions, open-ended 28–30, *28–30*
quizlet 148

random error 97–98, *110*, 110–111; day-
  to-day fluctuations as source of 98–101,
  100–101; item and task characteristics as
  source of 101–106, *102, 105*; raters as source
  of *106–108*, 106–109
raters as source of random error *106–108*,
  106–109
rating scales 30–32, *32*
Rehabilitation Act of 1973 133
reliability coefficient 104–105
reliability in assessment 39, 95, *110*, 110–111;
  day-to-day fluctuations and 98–101,
  100–101; defining 97; item and task
  characteristics and 101–106, *102, 105*; large-
  scale testing approaches and 104–106, *105*;
  random error and its sources and 97–98;
  test-retest 100–101, *101*
Response to Intervention (RTI) 99, 141
responsiveness 141
rubrics: analytic 65, *67*, 72–73, 90, 107, 116;
  holistic 65, *66*

SAT 132, 140, 141–142
scatterplot 105, 126, *127*
Scriven, M. 2
Section 504 133, *135*
selected-response items 43–49, *44–45, 47–49*

Index 225

self-assessment *51–52*, 51–53; in music case study 191–197, *193–195*
self-control 10
self-efficacy 9–10, 22, 30, *32*
self-evaluation 13
self-feedback 1, 8, 15, 74
self-monitoring 10–11, 159–160, 163–164, 203
self-reaction 13
self-reflection phase 9; non-interactive supply type task and music 183–187, *184*, *186*; summarizing performance of student learning and 12–14; technology and 151–152
self-regulated learning (SRL) 1–2, 8; forethought and pre-assessment 9–10; goals and objectives in English language arts for 159, *160*; goal setting in 34–35; performance and formal classroom assessment 12; performance within the cycle of learning, doing, and assessing 10–12; *see also* classroom assessment with self-regulated learning (CA:SRL) framework
severity, scoring 65
shared regulation 16
short-answer items 30, *31*
Shute, V. J. 74
social constructivist views of learning 123
socially shared regulation 16
societal goals 95
Spandel, V. 151
special accommodations for testing 133–134; technical quality and 134–136, *135*
special needs students 15, 35, 53, 62, 95; fairness in assessment of 133–134, 140–141; in math 199–204; in music 179; technology in classroom assessment and 147
specific learning objectives (SLOs) 17, 24, *24*, 24–25; analyzing 26–27, *27*; assessment aligned with standards, objectives, and instruction and 114; continual assessment and 40; English language arts 159; formal assessment and 59, *60*, 63, *64*; mathematics 203–204; multiple-choice items and 46–47, *47*; music 180–181; writing 25–26, *26*
split-half reliability 106
standard deviation 100, *101*, 104–105, *126–127*
standard error of measurement (SEM) 100–101
standards: assessment aligned with 113–117, *115, 117*; breaking down 23–25, *24*; English language arts 158–159; looking at state and national 22–23, *23*; mathematics 199–201; music 179–180; specific learning objective (SLOs) and 24–27; *see also* specific learning objectives (SLOs)

standards-based grading 86, 111
Standards for Educational and Psychological Testing 95
state testing 84, 150
Stiggins, R. J. 59
student-teacher conferences 155, 161, 163–164, 167, 169–173, 190
student-teacher relationship 49, 113, 143, 157
sufficient information *58*, *66*
summarizing performance 2, 12–14, 77, 85–86; composition of grades in 88–91, *89–91*; in English language arts case study 173–177, *174–176*; grade reports for 86–88, *87*; large-scale assessment of 91–93; in music case study *197*, 197–198; other factors in 82–85, *85*; place of stage 1 pre-assessment evidence in 81; place of stage 2 evidence in 81–82; place of stage 3 formal evidence in 82; reasons for 77–79, *78*; what students do in stage 4 79–80; what teachers do in stage 4 *80*, 80–82
supply-type, open-ended questions 143, 183–187
survey development 27–30, 121, 148, 213
survey questions *32*
systemic validity 129

task analysis 9
teaching, co-regulation and shared regulation 16
technology and technical quality 95–96; assessment iterations for learning with 148–150; fairness in 134–136, *135*; formal assessment with 150–151; implications of technology-based assessment in the classroom and 152–154, *153*; pre-assessment with 147–148; reflections of overall learning with 151–152; three generations of educational assessment 145–147, *146*
testing, accountability 92–93
test-retest reliability 100–101, *101*
theoretical models 7
theory of attribution 13
"think alouds" 50–51, *118*, 119
time fluctuations 98–101, *100–101*
Timperley, H. 74
Title I funding 92–93
tracking 141

unit of analysis 17
unintended impacts of testing 140
usefulness of tests 124–126, *126–127*

validity in assessment 39, 95, 112–113; assessment aligned with standards, objectives, and instruction for 113–117, *115, 117*; assessment processes eliciting construct-relevant inking processes and 117–119, *118*;

assessment processes having minimal bias in interpretation and scoring for 119–120, *120*; basing assessment interpretations on evidence from multiple sources for 120–124, *122–124*; defined 112; evaluating whether tests are useful for their purpose and 124–126, *126–127*; mini-case study on 128–129; systemic 129
verification feedback *74*

washback 140, *142*
Webb, N. 26
Weiner, B. 13
whole-class questioning 121, 148
Wiliam, D. 8

zero grades 90, 138
Zimmerman, B. 8–10, 12–13, 15–16, 37, 79